Embrace of the Daimon

Healing through the Subtle Energy Body:
Jungian Psychology & the Dark Feminine

SANDRA LEE DENNIS, PH.D.

Foreword by Thomas Moore

WEST COUNTY PRESS

First print edition was published in 2001 by

Nicolas-Hays
P.O. Box 2039
York Beach, ME 039102039

Revised edition

Library of Congress Cataloging-in-Publication Data

Dennis, Sandra Lee.
    Embrace of the Daimon : sensuality and the
integration of forbidden imagery in depth
psychology / Sandra Lee Dennis ; with a
foreword by Thomas Moore,

Includes bibliographical references
ISBN 978-1-939812-03-2

Jungian psychology.   2. Psychoanalysis 3. Jung, C. G. (Carl Gustav), 1875-
1961.I. Title.
BF175.D457 2001
150.19'54—dc21

Revised Cover design by: Joel Friedlander

Cover illustration is: "The Great Red Dragon and the Woman Clothed in the Sun"
by William Blake, 1805, Washington, D. C., National Gallery of Art.

Rumi quote on dedication page is from *Unseen Rain,* John Moyne and Coleman
Barks, translators (Watsonville, CA: Threshold Books, 1986), p. 77. Used by
permission.

To Dennis Lee Kojan

Sometimes afraid of reunion, sometimes
of separation: You and I, so fond of the notion
of a you and an I, should live
as though we'd never heard those pronouns.

—*Rumi*

Also by Sandra Lee Dennis

Love and the Mystery of Betrayal:
Recovering Your Trust and Faith after
Trauma, Deception and Loss of Love

Praise for *Embrace of the Daimon*

Foreword Reviews' 2012 Book of the Year Finalist, Body, Mind, Spirit
USA Best Book Awards 2014 Winner, Philosophy
Next Generation 2015 Indie Book Awards Winner, New Age

"Sandra Dennis has written a courageous, important book. In *Embrace of the Daimon* she moves psychology into a fuller engagement with the uncharted depths of archetypal, imaginal reality embedded in bodily experience. In this pioneering work, she forges a bridge between the worlds of the scholar and the visionary, and in so doing makes a significant contribution to the phenomenology of altered states of consciousness. Her prose is eloquently descriptive, precise, at times compactly poetic. Her first person accounts are moving, often searing in realms that traditionally resist description. Our era needs to hear her call for a descent into the dark recesses of the psyche that can reunite body and soul."

Richard Tarnas, author of *The Passion of the Western Mind: Ideas that have Shaped our Worldview* and *Cosmos and Psyche: Intimations of a New World View.*

"While I served as Dean of the School of Holistic Studies at JFK University several years ago, I came across a copy of *Embrace of the Daimon*, and immediately read it. I was stunned. Not only because I deemed it the most honest work on the psychoid/imaginal realms since Corbin, but also because I never heard anyone speak of it. "How was that possible," I asked? I am very glad that it shall be republished. I was stirred by the head-on engagement with these archetypal invasions, more like Jung in the Red Book than the scholarly Corbin. I shared it with a colleague at JFKU, who also praised it, and we would discuss it after hours."

Peter Rojcewicz, PhD., Vice President, Academic Affairs and Dean of Faculty, Antioch University Seattle

"When I first read the draft for *Embrace of the Daimon* I was thrilled to be reading such an intimate portrayal of profound change embedded in the framework of experiences of other explorers of personal depth like Jung, Sade, and Blake. This book is a rare documentation of a spontaneous eruption of wild stories and monstrous characters from the primeval spaces of the unconscious psyche, characters who, over time, become benevolent carriers of an emotional reunion of soul with body. Moreover, the theoretical framework she builds adds to Jungian theory concerning the role of the body in the body/mind equation. Dennis takes us to the edge of imaginal experience and traces an implicit road map for the millennial tasks of healing the harmful separation between body, soul, and spirit that now afflicts us."

> **Betty DeShong Meador,** Jungian analyst, author of *Uncursing the Dark: Treasures from the Underworld* and *Princess, Priestess, Poet*

"This is a gorgeous book, beautifully conceived and written. Sandy Dennis re-imagines the work of integrating shadow, helping us find beauty and dignity in the Dionysian elements, elevating the direct experience of the body and its sensations, and trusting in the psyche's ability to ultimately render all that happens to us into something of meaning and value"

> **Jeremiah Abrams**, author/editor of *Meeting the Shadow: The Hidden Power of the Dark Side of Human Nature*, and *The Shadow in America: Reclaiming the Soul of a Nation*

"It is rare to find an exploration of the daimonic that is not moralistic, that doesn't try to spare us from encountering its power....This book is different in that it is truly sensitive to the soul....I am especially drawn to it for the many passing insights that are expressed so beautifully and tersely. I will cut them out and make them my appendix, my guidelines for dealings with the Devil. We need courageous, imaginative, and intelligent tracings of the daimon, such as are offered here."

> **Thomas Moore,** author of *Care of the Soul, Dark Nights of the Soul,* and *Dark Eros*

"*Embrace of the Daimon* is a rare and beautifully written book, one of a scant handful of books that addresses a complex and often misunderstood psychic process that frequently accompanies states of spiritual emergence: the dark urges of inner life...Sandra Dennis' own inner confrontations with the instinctual forces of the dark feminine are the driving forces of the book. It is from this rich ore that the healing power at the heart of these experiences is made relevant and meaningful in the context of Jung's alchemical theory of opposites. By gently unfolding and amplifying the inherent intelligence and creativity within the dark forces of the psyche, she shows us how we, too, can lovingly embrace the daimon and thereby unleash our own self-actualizing potential toward wholeness"

Melina Costello, author of *Seeking the God of Ecstasy*

"I find this an extraordinarily well written, original and profound work that extends our understanding of the relation between psyche and soma. Dr. Dennis' integration of personal material and theory makes possible a synthesis of active imagination, the daimonic and the subtle body. Much of the region is still unexplored and any reader will have the excitement of seeing new lands for the first time. I believe the material to be deeply practical for individual integration of psyche and soma"

Alan B. Ruskin, Jungian analyst, San Francisco

"I was deeply moved by the force and effort of these personal revelations that show that in spite of the alarming and painful character of the visions, they may represent something more than the bad effects of childhood, past lives or defective genes. Dr. Dennis suggests that they may represent a cultural movement into the next era of great importance, as they indicate the emergence of a dark, descending spirituality, like the lower worlds of the shaman, which is absolutely necessary to balance the recent emphasis on "light." This world indeed corresponds with the rise of "the feminine" and its values. This book advances our understanding of this ongoing process tremendously."

Donald F. Sandner, author of *The Sacred Heritage: The Influence of Shamanism on Analytical Psychology*

"In this unique, engaging work, Sandra Dennis goes beyond the split that continues to underlie the phrase 'mind-body.' She takes us on a journey to the profound levels of *subtle body* reality in that landscape of the psychoid, also known as the imaginal world. Through her explorations, we learn to recognize and navigate this subtle, imaginal realm and its daimonic denizens, and to heal through its energy. Engaging these often taboo energies, associated with the presence of Sophia, divine feminine wisdom, this book takes us to the leading radical edge of Jungian psychology today."

> **Veronica Goodchild, PhD.**, Core Faculty, Jungian and Imaginal Psychology, Pacifica Graduate Institute, author *Eros and Chaos: The Sacred Mysteries and Dark Shadows of Love*, and *Songlines of the Soul: Pathways to a New Vision for a New Century*.

"*Embrace of the Daimon* invites us through personal revelation and compelling theory to dare to engage the vast expanse of the psyche, including the dark, the chthonic and the erotic. Sandra Dennis explores the imaginal extremes, terrains of ecstasy and terror we are inclined to avoid. She guides us through human dream landscapes beyond the mundane to the numinous. As a phenomenologist of the daimonic realms, she summons the fair witness in all of us, showing the way to deepen into embodied lucidity despite our fears or aversion. Her explorations encourage us at every turn to welcome the life-affirming potential of the full range of our humanity. Recommended reading for all students of the imaginal."

Daniel Deslauriers, Core Faculty, California Institute of Integral Studies, author of *Integral Dreaming: A Holistic Approach to Dream*

Contents

Preface
Why Reprint this Book?

Times have changed since this book was first published more than ten years ago. Back then, the long-standing cultural prejudice toward "the light" rendered even more horrifying the dark imagery that was percolating up from my subconscious. At the time, just mentioning these shameful images of violence and bestiality drenched in erotic overtones felt threatening and marginal, even in the atmosphere of tolerance and scholarly interest I found at The California Institute of Integral Studies. Yet, working with these imaginal visitations I now describe as 'daimons,'—messengers of the gods—I marveled at how they deepened my connection to life. I decided finally to write and, with encouragement from my mentors, publish this book. Despite my squeamishness at making such personal revelations, I wanted to claim public space for the sacred dimension of the dark recesses of our collective psyche they were revealing.

Although the emergence of the archetype of the "Dark Feminine" was the original theoretical focus of this study, I was discouraged, in keeping with the times, from bringing much attention to this perspective on the images. It was a theory that had not yet gathered sufficient force to be publicly tenable. Since then, scores of books have been written on reclaiming the Dark 'Feminine,' Goddess or Mother energies of the psyche: books on pre-historic goddess cultures and rituals, on the Black Madonna, the redeemed Magdalene story, the Black Sun, and more, so that recognition of this phenomenon has now become widespread. A new 'dwarf' planet, Eris (goddess of strife), has even been discovered. In the archetypal psychology world, planetary discoveries are thought to symbolize the emergence of new qualities of consciousness. I have reworked the material here to put more emphasis on the rising of these long-rejected dark, destructive, chthonic, erotic, instinctual energies to conscious awareness. In a similar spirit, encouraged by the archetypal astrological community, I have also stepped beyond another cultural prejudice and added an addendum describing the "cosmic connections"—the correlations of astrological signifiers of higher consciousness—with the timing and the content of images in this study.

Times change quickly in our era. In another indicator of rapid change, graphic representations of the daemonium of violence and unrestrained sexuality confront us on a daily basis that would have been unthinkable even a decade ago. The increase in gratuitous ultra-violence, marked by explicit depictions of brutality in video games, TV, books, and films tells me that dark eruptions from the underworld are becoming more commonplace. No longer is a simple murder the ultimate crime, now we have casually cool violence expressed in sex crimes, torture, and other heinous acts as part of most crime dramas, even on network T.V. Lurid depictions of sexuality are becoming ubiquitous as well. Portrayal of women is increasingly sexualized—"pornified" even—in mainstream media. Pornography has exploded to become the biggest business on the internet, and pornography now, almost by definition, mixes sex with violence. Perpetrators in porn videos are overwhelmingly men, with targets being women, often shown taking pleasure in response to the aggression. Long-hidden sex abuse scandals have become so prevalent that hearing of yet another has become almost a matter of course. These repressed energies of the dark coming to mainstream awareness are still colored by the paradigm of power and control that threatens to destroy us.

Society now finds itself steeped in this dark archetypal imagery, yet how much closer are we to knowing how to bring the power of love, rather than the love of power to these forbidding qualities associated with the Dark? Can we learn to handle these burgeoning influences of destruction and eroticism in a life-enhancing manner? What will it take to begin to honor and respect the sacred power of the dark that has the potential to either nail us to our animal nature or open us to higher realms of fierce heart consciousness?

Now more than ever, we need to learn to revere these rejected parts of inner life that frighten and disgust us lest they turn demon in our psyches and reduce rather than enhance our humanity. As Rainier Rilke said, "Perhaps everything that frightens us is, in its deepest essence something helpless that wants our love." As we come to a deep acceptance of what most disturbs us, we begin to reap unexpected gifts of higher awareness and compassion of heart for the dilemmas of human nature they reveal. But, if we continue to repress and misunderstand these powers, their awakening call will only solidify our fears. Their paradoxical intensity of their numinous darkness will continue to distance and alienate us from each other, rather than deepen and awaken us to the heart of wisdom from which they stir.

Straight from the soul, these dark messengers come as agents of radical change, here to expand our consciousness and connect us with the healing qualities our world is waiting for. I am heartened that a public forum has opened to encompass the daunting taboos surrounding these daimonic energies of Eros, chaos, sensuality, violence, birth and death. And it is my hope that, with its re-release, this book can contribute to a further awakening of our personal and collective responsibility to engage their mysteries with awareness, compassion, and respect for their capacity to either destroy or transform us.

Foreword

by *Thomas Moore*

Nothing is more important than reflection on the daimonic, which is the source of both human creativity and human depravity. It is rare to find an exploration of the daimonic that is not moralistic, that doesn't try to spare us from encountering its power. And so I am writing in support of this thoughtful foray into the world of darkness that tries to shed some light and offer some guidelines while all the while acknowledging the obscurity of the task.

It is not easy to stand in the presence of the daimonic, with the intention of arriving at a creative position at the other end of the encounter, without succumbing to the literalization of the myth of the hero. That myth fades in and out of this book, but for the most part it retains its mythic and therefore poetic nature. Of course, faced with uninvited images and characters that are obscene and disgusting, we want to move somewhere and get something. But the St. George fantasy of slaying the dragon is always a temptation, especially for those of us who try to be smart and subtle. We may not *realize* that our sophisticated language is simply our version of the saint's long, sharp lance. This book comes to the edge of that kind of heroism here and there, but then it recedes back into complexity, and the subject of its attention, the daimonic, continues to live.

I am especially drawn to *Embrace of the Daimon* for the many passing insights that are expressed so beautifully and tersely. I will cut them out and make them my appendix, my guidelines for my dealings with the Devil. For example: "Every union leads to yet another separation, as round and round the cycle goes, bringing the soul into earthly existence." It is refreshing to reach the dynamic whereby we give soul earthly reality instead of psychologizing experience into the bodiless ether of pure reflection.

This book has led me to think about the body in ways I haven't precisely considered before. Here the body is neither literalized nor intellectualized. Again, we remain in the mid-realm of soul where we may not be clear and secure about what we're talking about, but neither do we lose the imagination or our physical existence. Sensation is indeed a form of imagination and is a potent way of encountering the figures of the soul.

We live in a world that moralizes against the daimonic incessantly and then goes on to enact its darkest possibilities. As has often been said, when we repress the daimonic, it metamorphoses—undetected—into the demonic. We need courageous, imaginative, and intelligent tracings of the daimon, such as offered by Sandra Dennis.

I confess I do not agree with everything presented here. But I admire the subtlety of approach and the intelligence brought to very slippery areas—the connection between soul and body, generalizing about stages in the processes of the soul, treating gender poetically, and deliteralizing such things as goals, endings, and success. If the reader is looking for a way to avoid the dark nights and days of the soul, or to squirm out of them when they come along, there are many other books that speak for her literal stance.

This book is different in that it is truly sensitive to the soul. It doesn't offer a clear, direct, one-dimensional path through the swamp of the daimonic, although at times it speaks to and from that wish. Instead, it gives us sufficient fresh imagination of the problem for us to survive and even thrive. The soul demands equal courage and patience on the part of the reader to reveal its mysteries.

I'd recommend reading these pages with, in Emerson's words, the flowers of the mind rather than its powers. Let its labyrinthine nature lead you to deeper imagination, while successfully avoiding conclusions. Allow yourself to be taken down many alleyways, the natural haunt of the daimonic, where light is sparse and the shadows are full of monstrous spirits that bear strange gifts.

—*Thomas Moore*

Embrace of the Daimon

The Daimon as Divine Messenger

IN STANDARD ENGLISH USAGE, we use 'daimon' as the equivalent of demon to represent an evil force, a degeneration of the original numinous connotations of the term. The Greeks called the daimon the intermediary between gods and humans, the guardian spirit assigned at birth, connecting heaven and earth.[1] Messages were delivered in both directions by the daimons, permitting a correspondence between the human and the Divine that otherwise could not have taken place. I have chosen to reintroduce the original use of the term for this study partly for its poetic force. In its literary sense, it still contains elements of the original meaning, suggesting the opposites good and evil, birth and death, creation and destruction, light and darkness that underlie the realm of the archetypes I will be exploring here.

My attention was first riveted on the realm of the daimonic by an eruption of strange and wild, bestial and violent characters from the unconscious that precipitated a period of descent into the dark recesses of my own psyche. The alarming and painful nature of these visions worked as a strange attractor to compel my investigation of this taboo realm at the edges of our daylight world. The initially threatening and horrifying images became, with time and attention, carriers of a union of outcast soul qualities with my conscious personality that increased my sense of wonder and connection with the life force, as well as my sense of belonging in the world, and convinced me of the importance of adding my voice to naming this territory.

Reintroducing the original use of the term daimon for this mapping of inner life seemed necessary to help set off the living images and related processes I will be describing from other forms

INTRODUCTION

of imagery with which they are easily confused, such as active imagination, directed dreaming, creative imagination, visualization, hallucination, and fantasy. These images and processes also must be distinguished from feelings alone that may reach daimonic intensity, but remain unconnected with a spontaneous, self-regulating image that confounds the mind while still carrying meaning. Above all, the daimonic images reflect the ontological reality of the imaginal realm, that subtle body inner world of alchemical connectivity where body meets soul, and transformation begins. Daimonic events come as signposts and agents of change. They purify and irradiate our emotional, mental and physical being through the subtle senses. We could call them "ensouled" or soul images. When they arise, and we welcome rather than fight them, they carry the potential to bring us closer to a wholeness we long for.

It is not surprising that the original term daimon has degenerated to denote a dangerous or evil force. We want nothing to do with the "dark side" to which we assign demons and exiles. They rouse our suspicions. Cast them into the void. Get thee behind me. In our happiness-biased culture, we are at risk of losing our capacity to recognize the beauty in the sinister side of the opposites of darkness and light, especially when it comes to the hidden, outcast corners of our own minds. When we think of a divine messenger these days, we tend to envision an angel of light at the foot of the bed benevolently offering guidance and succor, conveniently forgetting the terror the overarching beauty of a Spirit presence can bring. Rainer Maria Rilke reminds us, "For beauty is nothing but the beginning of terror we can just barely endure, and we admire it so because it calmly disdains to destroy us. Every angel is terrible." [2]

Artists, poets, visionaries, depth psychologists, and religious mystics are a few who have journeyed to that land at the outer reaches of the psyche—the imaginal world, from which the daimons arise—and have begun to map its geography. These pioneers tell us that daimons often strike us with confusion and awe. The old man falling on his knees, head bowed in reverence

INTRODUCTION

before the departing angel in Rembrandt's painting of *The Angel Leaving the Family of Tobias* displays this attitude of trepidation and wonder. When archetypal psychologist James Hillman characterized daimons as guardian spirits, he described them as powers with claims to be recognized religiously.[3] It is through these figures, he says, that the transcendent becomes immanent in the medium of the subtle body. When we are ready, these daimonic energies arise to aid in the expansion of consciousness, facilitating the incarnation of higher vibratory soul qualities into the physical body.

But we are often not ready to recognize the higher purposes of these energies. Divine messengers humble us with their fearsome presence. They shake our confidence in ourselves and unhinge our sense of being in control of our lives. Daimons come to us as *they* please, unbidden, when we least expect them, appearing as shocking external events or uncanny, autonomous phantoms that somehow attract us, yet cause us to question our sanity and pull the covers more tightly over our head. We need to learn to recognize and courageously face their call to a deeper life, both for our own well-being, and for the preservation of our world.

In our time, spiritual forces are pouring into our lives with great intensity asking that we expand the light of awareness into these darkest corners. Some even say we live in apocalyptic times. The creative death/rebirth processes that these intensified spiritual forces unleash initiate us into greater consciousness, but they are inherently chaotic and destructive. A prejudice against acknowledging these ever-present dark forces of dying may be our culture's leading taboo. This cultural prejudice against not only the annihilating qualities of these heavenly energies, but against the mortal body itself stands in the way of embracing their call. After millennia of deification of the sky gods—the mind, light, the 'masculine,' and Apollonian reason and order—we are now asked to embrace this descending spirituality, to reclaim the exiles of the 'Dark Feminine'—the earth, instincts and body, as well as the Dionysian, erotic turmoil of the inner world they bring. We are being called to reclaim these cast-off parts of ourselves that also include sacred sensuality, sexuality, as well as the mysteries of birth, death, and resurrection.

Possessing, as we do, the capacity to destroy our planet and ourselves, we can no longer afford to ignore or repress these wake-up calls to higher consciousness. Our first responsibility, cliché as it may seem, rests with ourselves. We must embrace our night selves, face the undisclosed basement of the mind, those recessed closets where we find the axe murderers, reptiles, cockroaches, torture chamber instruments, and the cat's old dung. The screams and shames of our early life as well as the unlived tendencies of our ancestors all reside here. Here one may also open a well-covered door to the Divine. With the increased intensity of our times, we need to learn to welcome these dark gifts of the hidden psyche, or tighten ever more forcefully into our fears and delusions.

We can start by beginning to recognize daimonic energies, which appear to the subtle senses as an autonomous presence connected to powerful feeling. Usually we experience the emotional/instinctual and mental components of an imaginal presence separately. We *see* a dragon, for instance, in our mind's eye, or we *feel* like a dragon. The daimon aims to unite these disparate ways of experiencing. The invite us to dare to become more whole, to dissolve our limited, one-sided perspective, and to awaken our slumbering capacities as a vessel for Spirit to shine through. For a truly transformative, numinous, awe-inspiring, daimonic event, both aspects of the imaginal experience must come together in an internal "sacred marriage". When we can finally allow ourselves to both see and feel the dragon breathing its hot breath upon us, we have entered fully into daimonic reality. Once we enter, and are willing to stay, getting past our fears and tendencies to reject or repress the disturbing, chaotic energies or their visual counterparts, then soul work proper begins.

INTRODUCTION

We cannot but emerge changed by the encounter with the dissolving forces of darkness brought on by the daimons. Here at the frontier of our inner world, pieces of limited identity get sheared off, we are "annihilated" and new qualities are absorbed. Through our willingness to enter into relationship with what most repels or frightens us, we become explorers of the great frontier of inner life, the unfolding darkness of the unknown. This process goes against both our cultural programming to favor 'the light' and our instinctual proclivities to avoid pain. Daimonic events may take us to both extremes of human experience. They may come as carriers of ecstasy, joy, beauty, and bliss, or of chaos, misery, sadness, and despair. We cannot know which, when or how they will appear. As we grow to trust in the intimidating, often intoxicating, forces, our conscious contact with the daimons' world and theirs with ours draws us into the alchemical creation of new psychic space.

Further, the data collected here shows that once the daimonic image has emerged from the depths and established itself in consciousness, it eventually strives toward a state of union with the body, strongly charged with erotic and sexual overtones. That is why, when I discovered that Jung places the mystical marriage symbol at the heart of his conception of the psyche, I seized on it to elucidate the "bodily conjunction" I explore throughout this book. Though the accounts I include here stake more modest claims, reports of this level of experience, characterized by fervid inner unions and dissolving deaths, can be found in Christian mysticism, especially in the writings of the bridal mystics such as John of the Cross and Teresa of Avila, in shamanic literature, in accounts of the pre-Hellenic mysteries, in reports from LSD sessions, and in the myths of the dalliances of gods and goddesses with mortals. All signal the dignity and beauty of the Dionysian, passionate elements of life associated with darkness and the body that have been long eclipsed in our culture in favor of the more rational, light-drenched Apollonian ideal.

What I hope to contribute is a personal, subjective portrait, supported by other reports, of what I believe is an impersonal, collective phenomenon pressing upon us. This study aims to shed light on some of these imaginal closets of the mind. In their exposure they reveal the unexpected: a gold interior, we might say, at the center of the bleakness they seem at first to present. The data used for this study was gathered over eight years, principally from my own experiences and some from work with clients in body-focused work. I have included examples from clinical literature to help elucidate certain points in the discussion of the material. I wrote this book first for myself, driven to understand the daimonic as it burst into my previously well-ordered life, as a need to bring clarity to the chaos within. I continued to write for anyone who recognizes these psychic fragments of bestiality, violence, and strangeness as their own, for those who wonder whether to flee or to explore this territory, and for those who accuse their defects of character, history or ill-fated stars for bringing forth such monstrosities of the mind. I have revised and am re-releasing this book in order to bring this underworld material to light for a larger audience. I tell a story intertwined with a theory whose time, I believe, has come. I hope this book will satisfy to some degree our need, both logical and irrational, to better come to terms with these possessing forces we have so compulsively banned from our lives, and to recognize the ecstatic promise they bring.

—Sandra Lee Dennis, 2012

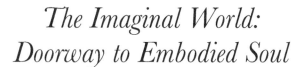

CHAPTER 1

The Imaginal World:
Doorway to Embodied Soul

Reflection arises when perception yields contradictory impressions.[1]

—Plato

IMAGINAL REALITY TOUCHES us at exceptional moments and leaves us with an uncanny sense of having tapped into an alternative world. It may announce its presence during sleep in the transporting dream or nightmare, or stir us when we wake as a muse, guardian angel, or demon. Some call the imaginal the realm of the archetypes, the home of the gods and goddesses, the land of the daimons, or the source of the creative muse. Some simply call it the soul. Here we find a realm of connectivity that at once attracts and frightens us, a realm we little understand in the West, where we tend to reject the cast of imaginal characters as trivial or pathological. We fear their explosive, entrancing energies, their capacity to undermine our solid beliefs about who we are and the world we live in. Yet how fundamental this imaginal layer of consciousness is, how deeply its invisible activities influence us, bubbling up in more and more people as the pressures and opportunities of the 21st century unfold.

Through immersion in the imaginal, we enter the tension of the unseen relationships of opposites that structure inner life. Here we discover the relation of consciousness to the vast unconscious, the attachment of the familiar mind to the hidden recesses of the body, and the fluid play of thought and feeling through our seemingly solid identity. The numinous image plays magician, conjoining disparate parts of ourselves, uniting these realms of body and mind, of consciousness and the unconscious—

if we open to its call. The image also links us to a sphere outside our consensus reality, for it is in the world of images that the spirit meets the senses to inform our particularly human vision of what we may be.

PERSONAL IMAGINAL INVASIONS

My own interest in imaginal realms began with a series of confounding invasions of daimonic imagery into my everyday life. Some months after the birth of my daughter, just prior to my fortieth (40th) birthday, startling episodes of spontaneous non-ordinary states of consciousness began to intrude upon my comfortable orientation to reality. Repulsive, sometimes horrifying images burst into my mind at odd hours of the day and night. Vivid scenes erupted from nowhere complete with dismembered bodies, excrement, and violent sexual assaults by wolf-men and other strange, half-human creatures. In a flash, my inner life would shift from the ordinary landscape of the 'wash the dishes' patter of relived events of the day, the chatting with the dog or planning for tomorrow, to one teeming with images of harrowing mythological creatures, axe murderers, tarantulas, rapists, rats, maggots, and snakes in surreal settings—like a Salvador Dali painting. Was I losing my mind? Had I tapped into a sadomasochistic shadow self? Was a demon force invading me? Was I having flashbacks to childhood, or was this a nightmare hallucination breaking into my daylight world? Needless to say, I was deeply disturbed by the insistent reality of these images over which I seemed to have no control.

When these eruptions came upon me, I had trained intensively for more than a decade in inner work—inquiry and meditative practices in the Gurdjieffian and Buddhist Vipassana traditions. I had routinely observed and deconstructed mental activity and believed inner imagery of any kind to be unreal, nothing more than an amplification of physical sensations, as when the blanket falls off in the middle of the night, and one dreams of trekking through the Antarctic. I understood waking fantasies, as these episodes appeared to be, to be purely "excretion of the mind," something to be observed and let go, with no intrinsic meaning. However, these unprecedented, hellish images continued to resist my feeble efforts at "witnessing" and noting. These were not simple mental "fantasies," but more like hallucinations involving both my emotions and my senses. The living quality of these images knocked more loudly on the door of my awareness than anything I had previously noticed. They erupted into consciousness, like a film clip where I was the lead character in an alternate reality. Drawing me in, they overwhelmed my feeble efforts at witnessing.

These intrusive scenes left me confused and concerned about my sanity,[2] for they upset not only my sense of self, but my existing frames of reference about reality. They disturbed my equilibrium, my concentration, and my sleep. Initially, they seemed to come over me quite unexpectedly, then gradually I began to notice the presence of a foreshadowing state of tension and mental confusion lasting for hours or even days prior to an imaginal visitation. I learned to sit with pen in hand and, in a form of what felt like automatic writing, let the imagery flow into words as the growing tension erupted into form. Once the episode passed, I would feel relieved, as if a catharsis had occurred.

The sensation-laden images that appeared presented a strange paradox. They frightened and repelled me with their monstrous animality, creepy sensuality, and sexual violence, yet they also incomprehensibly attracted me through their erotic intensity and the subtle luminosity of the otherworldly medium in which they took place. The harrowing contents stood in stark contrast to their numinosity of tone and color, resulting in a tumultuous, semiconscious meeting of extreme opposites that captured my interest. The physical tension, anxiety, fear and horror appalled me, yet the supernatural, spontaneous nature of the images—their insistent ethereal *presence*, as well as the distinct kinesthetic component they aroused—compelled my attention. I could sense, hear, and see these beings who seemed so intent on entering my world. I was particularly intrigued by the magical

3

realm in which the scenes took place. It was vivid, but perceptually unreal, imaginary, but ontologically tangible.

A love/hate relationship with the images developed as I confronted an apparently irreducible tension between two poles of experience. If I distracted myself away from the revolting images (a very tempting alternative, which often prevailed when the imaginal scenes were too overwhelming), along with it went the blossoming, life-giving, force—the evocative realm—in which they moved. On the other hand, if I pulled myself together to attend to the offensive story or characters, yet more intolerable episodes drew me into a discomforting intimacy I could barely endure.

For in this daimonic realm, I myself ached as a dismembered child, I took delight in the power of the sadist, and coiled, swayed, and struck as a cobra. I was no more my previous self, but had become a devouring, poisonous, scaly creature, a laughing demon bent on cruelty, a torture queen, or muck and slime, or a grand turd. These images were usually accompanied by intense physical sensations that added to their quality of being "real," including sharp pains, a sense of strangulation, prickling or itching, putrid smells, frozen panic, sensual and sexual arousal, dizziness, or dismembering disorientation. In the framework I held at the time, I thought I had succumbed to complete identification with a mad, horrifying world, and wondered why I could not simply "the work": observe, be present, and release all this mind stuff.

AN ARCHETYPAL PERSPECTIVE EMERGES

Having no other explanation and no one whom I thought would remotely understand what was happening to me, I was agitated and concerned for the next few years while the images continued intermittently to appear. I continued to wonder, was I unearthing unspeakable childhood or "past-life" memories, discovering basic character flaws, or worse, simply losing my mind? In my search for an explanation, finally I read Carl Jung's description of the invasive nature of the unconscious breaking through to consciousness, and it so well captured these incessantly troubling events that it led me more deeply into his work:

> Such invasions have something uncanny about them because they are irrational and incomprehensible to the person concerned. They bring about a momentous alteration of his personality since they immediately constitute a painful personal secret which alienates and isolates him from his surroundings. It is something that we "cannot tell anybody." We are afraid of being accused of mental abnormality—not without reason, for much the same thing happens to lunatics. Even so, it is a far cry from the intuitive perception of such an invasion to being inundated by it pathologically, though the layman does not realize this. [3]

Excerpts like this one were an oases in the desert of my search for some understanding of these experiences. As it turned out, Jungian and post-Jungian archetypal psychology offered a context I could find nowhere else, to help me comprehend these imaginal episodes. Thus, I often use terms and concepts of Jungian thought in this work, finding it an invaluable container for grounding these events. Later, I even entered Jungian therapy, a project that went on for nearly ten years. While I do not subscribe to all of Jung's theories, he was clearly at home in the sphere of the imaginal, and his pioneering in the realms of intuitive perception against the rational spirit of his times opened for all who have come after a door previously jammed shut to these invisible realities.

Gradually, living with these intrusions and studying similar episodes of others radically altered my original layman's conceptions about imaginal events. As I mentioned when the disturbing images first appeared, I unsuccessfully tried to view them as merely clever, albeit distorted, interpretations of sense data from the creative brain. I then learned how my training in spiritual practices tempted me to bypass this intermediate, subtle body layer of the psyche, which in fact I needed to traverse in order to access energies and teachings I could not receive by simple mindful observation.

Later, as my contact with these imaginal spheres increased, the somatic components of the images suggested possible repressed episodes of my past history. Still later, the images began to resonate with ancestral and collective history, as in witch trials, rape as a tactic of war, torture, and other institutionalized abuses. Over the years, however, the multitude of disturbing episodes, all taking place in the same realm, bigger than life, weakened any conviction I had about them being memories of this life or other lives, or indications of fundamental proclivities of my personality, including incipient psychosis.

Finally, I have come to see the images as a reflection of a still larger reality, a world loosely described as archetypal, "an ordered expression of certain primordial essences" or universal constants revealing themselves at all levels of existence.[4] Though I still do not eliminate the possibility that imaginal processes are colored by earlier events of personal life, I sense with growing certainty their connection to forces beyond the personal, and their emergence as part of the natural unfolding of the farther reaches of the psyche.

This archetypal framework for understanding these images gradually formed in my mind. I saw that the numinosity and connectivity of the imaginal realm were its most significant features. This aspect, over time, commanded more interest than the fluctuating images themselves, however disturbing. In addition, too many images emerged that required fantastic metaphoric stretches to be translated as biographical events. Even when the biographical implications of the material were confirmed and worked through, for instance, with some threatening images I came to terms with my terror of my father, the images would subsequently reveal connections to ancestral or collective realms. Images of one ancestral family secret, a grandfather I had never met or even known about, began to appear, later a collective Hitler figure made a number of appearances. All of these emanated from a similar somatic source near the heart and the solar plexus.

THE BODY MIND CONNECTION

Radical encounters with the daimons stimulate taboos, those sacred unknowables that combine fear and loathing with fateful attractiveness.[5] Since these energies require instinctual, bodily, receptivity for their assimilation, they especially activate taboos associated with sensation, feeling, and instinct. The daimons activate the full range of feelings such as aggression, rage, fear, sexuality, repulsion, sensuality, power, and sadness, and bring to awareness what has been previously repressed or denied. In theory, both the mental (verbal and visual) and instinctual (feeling, sensation) aspects of the image should command equal attention as it emerges into awareness, but our longstanding cultural hostility toward the instincts mitigates strongly against acceptance of body energies. Thus, we find innumerable reports of fantastical mythic images in Jungian-related texts especially. But these can leave one longing for the juiciness of their passionate underpinnings.

It is important to note that most early explorers of the imaginal terrain were heavily influenced by the prevailing attitudes that favored the mind and devalued the body. This bias skewed their insights, methods, and conclusions about the imaginal, leaving us with reams of information about the psychic or mental aspect of the image and nearly nothing about its bodily impact. Thus the instinctual ramifications of daimonic images, how they make us *feel*, are little understood. Most importantly, when we block acceptance of the bodily aspect of the daimons, we limit their impact and our access to the transformative potential they contain.

Our fear of these volatile realms, along with the traditional disregard of the body as integral to the unfolding of mental and spiritual life, reveals two central reasons for our ignorance. First, even though we are beginning to recognize the importance of the body, we must overcome a long history of disdain before we can fully acknowledge its central role in a meaningful, rich inner life that opens onto the invisible realities we normally consign to animality, hysteria, religion, or the spiritual world. I hope this study contributes to dissolving our disdain for the confusion and chaos that often comes with the unknown inner terrain.

THE DARK FEMININE AS DAIMON

Another reason that so few writers have focused on the body's role in the mind/body equation reflects the cultural rejection of the "dark feminine" energies associated with the Dark Goddess archetype. While we commonly associate relatedness, intuition, nurturing, and emotionality with the feminine, more recently the active, dynamic energies associated with the archetypal Dark Mother have been acknowledged as an integral, overlooked aspect of this cluster of qualities arbitrarily assigned to "the feminine." Debate continues to rage about precisely which qualities to include as the feminine, but consensus supports the need for reevaluating these typically undervalued, rejected or dark attributes.[6]

When we enter the realm of the Dark Mother or Dark Feminine we may experience visions, sacred sexuality, animal powers, as well as touches of madness, destruction, death, and rebirth. She rules the metamorphosis of nature, the relentless cycle of birth/death/rebirth. The hero's quest that has relegated these experiences to the shadow lands of the psyche is still the culture's guiding myth. But, if as some believe, an androgynous figure *drenched in erotic intensity*, born of the union of masculine and feminine, light and darkness, good and evil, is arising to replace him,[7] it is no wonder we are disturbed. Perhaps with the eruption of daimonic experiences we are facing more than a revolution in our individual psyche. In truth, we are facing a major revolution in our culture.

That we lack even a term in our language for the dark existential bookends of mortal life—we are born and we die—demonstrates how far we have distanced ourselves from the archetypal realities of the Dark Feminine. In combining the sensations of birth of the new with death of the old, daimonic states of consciousness resonate with these realities, revealing that apparent dichotomies such as beginning and end, union and separation, dark and light, contain one another and point to a deeper truth than the everyday. The numinosity of birth and death have the potential to lift us out of a dualistic mindset into a new state of consciousness, into states of wholeness and unitive vision. In these states of mind, we can recognize darkness as a necessary time of pregnant waiting before the cyclic return of light. The dark feminine aspects of inner life: destruction, decay, disorientation, darkness, night, and emptiness, once we move beyond our fears to realize they are drenched in erotic intensity, become a vehicle of a greater life force rather than something dreaded, feared, and avoided.

The implications for our inner life of this shift from an emphasis on the light side of Nature's processes to a more balanced view that honors her dark, hidden aspects, are only now beginning to be observed and documented. It is my contention that the energies of this dark, at once destructive and erotic principle are rooted in the body. When they come in the form of the daimons, they provide what has been a long missing ingredient in the unfolding of human potentialities. We come to a stage of individuation, or becoming more whole, when we must

9

go beyond the thrill of insights into ourselves to the integration of what we have learned. Our knowledge has gone as far as it can go without enlarging the container of consciousness. Here we are challenged to physically assimilate insights in order to effect any fundamental, lasting change in character and vision. For instance, the 'mother wound' we believe we understand, comes forward in raw, visceral fear, and we are faced with bringing the light of awareness to the transmutation of this pain, the actual dissolving of this piece of the psychic past. At this turning point from insight to embodied integration, dark daimonic forces appear to bridge the gap between body and imaginal soul, inviting our engagement. This is the point when we are challenged to deepen, to enter the darkness, where bodily sensation meets soul in an erotic, annihilating outburst of terrifying, potentially joyful, destruction.

Without the embrace of our own rejected dark feelings, sensations, thoughts and images, we may come to understand the forces moving in our souls, but we cannot act on this new understanding of ourselves. We are doomed to the talk of psychobabble, unchanged for all our spiritual, therapeutic, and creative efforts, except perhaps for our expanded vocabulary about our motivations, moods, emotions, and impulses. Assimilating, embracing, the daimons, we open ourselves to embody our best and worst moments, *living* our truths instead of merely espousing them. Human beings seem to have the unique potential of living in two worlds: the material and the spiritual. When we embrace the scary, erotic intensity of the daimons rising in us, we gain a more balanced vision into the potent invisible realities behind the solid life of the senses we usually inhabit.

AN EROTIC SOLUTION: EMBRACE OF THE DAIMON

When we *unite* with the daimonic image, we allow the image to transform, to alchemically alter our sense of self. Here we are really living at the edge, although it does not necessarily seem so at the time and is usually approached with no small amount of trepidation. Still, the unitive process is not an actual loss of self, but a sort of "cellular" metamorphosis, perhaps like the caterpillar as it enters the cocoon. It is subtly somatic, producing evanescent sensations seemingly within the depths of the bones, muscles and guts involving psychological death and rebirth. Along with this, the integration of insight brings this powerful metamorphosis in which we lose our old, limited identity and gradually drop into a new, previously unknown sense of who we are. A shaky time. If we learn to stay with the fear and discomfort of the transition, eventually we may become as the proverbial butterfly emerging from its cocoon. *Webster's Dictionary* defines metamorphosis as "change by supernatural means in an animal subsequent to birth or hatching."[8] The imaginal world abounds in a dynamic interplay of the animal, erotic, creative, and destructive energies of change. Abandon the familiar, all who enter here.

While we are beginning to recognize the centrality of the erotic as the core impulse in the subtle body, imaginal world, few seem to realize the dark implications of this revelation. Compelling unions bring pain as well as delight. They precipitate periods of liminality or transition when we feel pushed to our limits and must confront despair, depression and dissociation. In medieval alchemy, a language of the psyche we will explore more later in this book, this dying of old psychic forms always precedes the delights of union. Against our instincts, when we undertake the psycho-spiritual work of deepening, we need to learn to welcome, rather than run from, the pain, disorientation and horrors of dying. Our tendency will naturally be to distract ourselves at all costs rather than face the sensations and insights carried on these waves of symbolic dying. By continuing to allow ourselves to be distracted rather than attending to and assimilating these messengers of unfamiliar joys and pains, we avoid allowing ourselves to experience the *connection* between life and death, between union and separation, that is so central to a vivid inner life. In this realm of connectivity, where we feel we have no ground, we are quick to run back to grasp onto the familiar old ways of being. We dry up on ourselves, rigidify, stop living.

If we want to truly live, at some point, we find the dark facts of psychic life demand our full attention. If we want to break out of the stranglehold of the past, the familiar and the safe, we need to find the courage to allow our depths to unfold into consciousness, no matter how much they threaten our self-images, values and viewpoints. They will ask us to go beyond theory, beyond understanding even, to open to the sensations, emotions, and vulnerabilities of the most frightening, reviled and rejected parts of ourselves. The taboo drives of dissolving sexuality, aggression, and power integral to this realm contain keys to this strange relational world of ongoing unions and separations that we find on the imaginal plane. As we discuss the nature of the reunion of the soul with the outcast energies of the body, we will continue to return to this key mystery: the destructive creativity of *relationship itself*, a mystery so difficult for our minds to grasp, but self-evident to the soul in us. To unlock its full transformational mysteries, relationship requires us to meet its imperatives of strife, destruction, and parting, as well as its creative, melting joy.

CHAPTER 2

❦

The Subtle Body &
The "Unio Corporalis"

*The notion that the physical body . . . is as it were the exteriorization of an
invisible subtle embodiment of the life of the mind is a very ancient belief.*

—G. R. S. Mead [1]

THE TITLE OF CARL JUNG'S culminating work introduces
an important term for understanding the daimonic world
Mysterium Coniunctionis, Latin for "sacred union." Influenced
heavily by medieval alchemy, he came to see the sacred marriage
as process that lay at the center of inner life. This work of
bringing opposites together he envisioned as the ongoing
maturing of the limited psyche, the small self, into the greater
wholeness of the Self. He called the psyche's movement toward
wholeness "individuation." Jung describes three distinct stages of
individuating, each marked by a distinct union of opposites:[2]
1) the *unio mentalis*: the union of the higher mental faculties (spirit)
with the imaginal world (soul) to overcome the body, what we
know as insight,
2) the reunion of the individuated spirit/soul with the body, a
process to which Jung never gave a Latin name, but that I will
call the *unio corporalis* or embodiment of the image, and
3) the *unus mundus*: the union of the embodied image with the
world or 'enlightenment'. [3]

Most depth psychological work focuses on the first of these
three stages: bringing the unconscious image to awareness.
Anyone familiar with depth therapy will recognize this stage of

13

insight in which one confronts previously unconscious aspects of the self. This is a disillusioning process whose hallmark is a gradual increase in self-knowledge. Jung wrote prodigiously on this subject and, pathfinder that he was, discovered techniques to uncover these unconscious imaginal realms. Some of these methods he developed we take for granted today, such as active imagination and the use of expressive arts such as painting, dancing, sculpting, and song to bring the autonomous imagery of the psyche into awareness in emotionally vivid, differentiated, and comprehensible form. We can spend our entire therapeutic lifetimes involved in this stage, as there always seems to be more to learn about one's "issues."

But what happens once we have gained insight, the second stage or the *unio corporalis* is my main concern in this book. This stage may be thought of as the reunion of the imaginal soul with the body. What this embodiment entails I will explore in some detail. The creative potential that arises from allowing previously unconscious instincts and images to enter consciousness is first grasped as we gain insight in Stage One when we begin to better understand the genesis of our limiting behaviors. But nothing lasting occurs here, except perhaps a more psychologically sophisticated personality, if these insights are not then put into action, "integrated" through their actual embodiment. Who hasn't lamented the ongoing playing out of their own neurosis even after years or decades even of labor understanding the psychological dynamics involved? When times get tough, we tend to keep repeating patterns, regardless of our understanding. Thus, the idea that people do not really change with time.

In comparison with the first stage of psychological transformation, little has been written that addresses this second stage of individuation. Jung himself associated this phase of union with the necessary integration of psychological insights into daily living. In some of the most dense, obscure and difficult passages in Mysterium Conuinctionis[4], he examines the medieval alchemist Gerard Dorn's instructions for this stage. We are left scratching our heads trying to work out the meaning, as he concludes that the darkness of the process defies rational analysis. Therapists and laymen alike still stumble over the problem of the embodiment or integration of self-knowledge, of putting into practice what we learn through therapy, meditation, and other forms of self-inquiry. In truth, we know surprisingly little about it.

All three levels of the individuation process are said work together to unite the opposites in a new synthesis. The move toward wholeness may start with the mind, but it resonates through body and soul. I believe that when the body opens to the soul, this is when daimonic imagery is most likely to arise. The new levels of erotic intensity threaten to dissolve our conscious position, which they are intended to do, and our tendency is to distrust them and shut down. The dissolving, uniting forces *combine* what to us have been incompatible: attraction with repulsion, darkness with light, the erotic with the destructive. If we can allow these opposites to meet they move our inner resonance to a higher vibratory plane, expanding consciousness into new realms. It was exciting, through my explorations some of which I share in later chapters, to learn firsthand that the sacred marriage or *coniunctio*, the impulse to unite seeming opposites, does indeed seem to lie at the heart of the subtle body's imaginal world.

One important characteristic of the *coniunctio* is its paradoxical dual action. The creative process of each sacred marriage, or conjoining of opposites, involves not only the unitive moment of joining together in a new creation or 'third,' but also, as I have mentioned, a separating or darkening moment.[5] The idea that "darkness comes before dawn" captures this essential aspect of creativity. To state an obvious truth we as a culture are just beginning to appreciate. In alchemical language, when darkness falls, it is said to be the beginning of the inner work or the opus of transformation. The old king (ego) must die before the new reign dawns. The early alchemists called the dark, destructive side of these psychic unions the blackness or the *nigredo*. Chaos, uncertainty, disillusionment, depression, despair, or madness prevails during these liminal times of "making death."

The experiences surrounding these inner experiences of darkness and dying (the most difficult aspects were called *mortificatio)* may constitute our culture's ruling taboo. This taboo interferes with our moving naturally to Stage Two in the individuating process, a process that requires that we pass through a descent into the underworld of the Dark Feminine realities of birthing an erotic intensity that leads to dying. Entranced by our happily-ever-after prejudiced culture, we often do not see that in any relationship, project or creative endeavor or idea some form of death follows naturally after periods of intense involvement. When dark experiences befall, we tend to turn away, to move as quickly as possible to something positive or at least distracting, away from the negative affects of grieving, rage, terror, rotting and loss we associate with darkness and dying. As I came to see the extent of this cultural taboo, it shed a beacon of meaning on the horrendous imagery that initially aroused my interest in the imaginal. Were these shocking daimonic explosions announcing what the alchemists identified as the beginning of the work of inner union? Was I perhaps in the throes of a classic black or *nigredo* experience? I thought it must be so, but more about this later.

A CASE FOR THE SUBTLE BODY: A SIXTH SENSE?

Before we go any further we might as well tackle the challenging concept of the "subtle body". Since the goal of uniting the daimonic image with the body appears to involve incommensurable realities, we need to find a bridge between them. The notion of a "subtle body" suits this purpose: Originally used by the Greeks to mean part-spirit and part-body, the soul's own home within the corporeal body, the subtle body describes a place of liminality, an energetic meeting ground of mind and body that may be grasped intuitively.[6]

Why introduce such a term at all, associated, as it often is, with the occult, with auras, chakras, and spirits? Why not stick with "the imaginal" to describe this meeting place of image and instinct? Because the subtle body describes a specific area of the vast imaginal world—the specific area I am setting out to map. In the subtle body, word becomes flesh and spirit incarnates. It is the imaginal's realm of embodiment. I also like the term "subtle body" for its apt descriptiveness of the phenomena under study. The sensations and perceptions associated with the daimonic image are *subtle*, barely accessible to our five senses, but nonetheless real, intimately connected with the body. In addition, the subtle body has a history in the worlds of religious mysticism, philosophy, and analytical psychology, as well as the occult (the esoteric, what lies hidden). The newest explorers of the psyche—depth psychologists—have already found new names for this inner body where mind meets matter: the subjective body, the dreambody, the body of light or resurrection, and the body-self. Religious philosophers refer to it as the spiritual senses. Mystics call it soul.

Jung revived the old idea of the subtle body, to which he equated with the somatic unconscious. In *Psychology and Alchemy* and, especially, in his seminars on Nietzsche's *Thus Spake Zarathustra*, he explored the concept. There he alludes to G. R. S. Mead's 1919 *The Doctrine of the Subtle Body in Western Tradition*. Mead refers to neo-Platonist and early Christian writers on the subject, demonstrating how ancient was the belief that "an invisible subtle embodiment of the life of the mind" existed. Quoting Synesius, a neo-Platonist from the first century A. D., he describes the subtle body's role as intermediary between realms: "For this spirit is precisely the borderland between unreason and reason, between body and the bodiless. It is the common frontier of both, and by its means things Divine are joined with lowest things."[7]   Mead acknowledges the modern scientific skepticism regarding such a concept, but suggests, as I am confirming, that deeper investigation will prove the subtle body "a fertile working hypothesis" to organize an array of subjective data that would otherwise remain chaotic and undifferentiated.[8]

Henry Corbin, the French Islamic scholar and mystic, formulated a similar conception of the subtle body. In his description of the imaginal world, or *mundus imaginalis*, he refers to the subtle body as an essential element of the larger imaginal: "In short, this is the world of 'subtle bodies' of which it is indispensable to have some notion in order to understand that there is a link between pure spirit and material body."[9] He equates the subtle body with the "body of resurrection" and the "imaginal body" For him imaginal knowledge comes through subtle body perceptions. He describes subtle body faculties as "psychospiritual senses" sensitive to the dimensions, colors, and figures of "imaginalia." The latter have an immaterial materiality, a corporeality and spatiality of their own, which are not purely intelligible. Hearing, smell, taste, and touch have their correlates in the subtle realm, in the imaginal faculty.[10]

Corbin also called the organ that perceived the imaginal, "imaginative power". He says, "This world requires its own faculty of perception, namely, imaginative power, a faculty with a cognitive function, a noetic value which is as real as that of sense perception or intellectual intuition."[11] This imaginative power arising from the subtle body becomes an organ of knowledge whose function is to "produce symbols leading to inner intelligence."[12] An "organ of knowledge" is a phrase that captures the importance of the subtle body as a kind of sixth sense, the bodily basis of intuition that orients us through the maze of life's invisible realities. It adds an enriching dimension to life. As much as sight, or hearing, or touch, the subtle senses connect us with essential aspects of our existence.

Religious mystics appear to have highly developed subtle senses. In their literature, one finds a doctrine of spiritual sensation that describes five spiritual sense faculties that correspond remarkably with Corbin's conception of the subtle body. For instance, John of the Cross rhapsodizes on the subtle sense of touch felt as a caress, "Oh, then, thou delicate touch, thou Word, Son of God, who through the delicateness of Thy Divine Being, dost subtly penetrate the substance of my soul."[13] Teresa of Avila refers also to the subtle senses. She often explains that the soul seems to have other senses within itself that are similar to the exterior senses.[14] In keeping with the Christian tradition's rejection of the body, these mystics would disavow any relation of the spiritual senses with the gross physical body. Yet, their descriptions, full of convincing sensual imagery, which I will explore more fully later, make us pause at their disclaimers about the corrupt flesh and take note of their striking correspondence to subtle body phenomena.

In contrast to the mystics, I want to emphasize the concept of the subtle body here—not to diminish the importance of the corporeal body—but to encourage the dissolution of the recalcitrant body/mind dichotomy central to our Western conceptions. Because of our deeply ingrained tendency to reject the physical body, I want to emphasize that *the subtle body contains equal corporeal and psychic elements,* and maintains an extremely close relationship with the body. It can be perceived imaginally through "sight," or sensed kinesthetically. The words themselves— subtle body, somatic unconscious—point to the vital link with the body that we so easily let slip from our common conception of the imaginary as belonging entirely to the brain. Call it "subtle body," or "incarnate mind," it stretches our dualistically biased language to include apparent opposites in order to portray this arena of the psyche that serves ultimately as a medium for dissolving the boundaries of difference.

THE SUBTLE BODY IN DEPTH PSYCHOLOGY

A brief overview of the current use of the term "subtle body" in the practice of depth psychology may help clarify this concept that challenges our usual ways of thinking. Jung calls the subtle body a medium of realization that is neither mind nor matter, but the intermediate realm of subtle reality.[15] He, too, insists that imaginal processes are not to be taken as immaterial phantoms, but as "something corporeal, a 'subtle body', semi-spiritual in nature." [16] The distinction between psyche and body disappears when these two meet in an atmospheric body that he thought existed both in and out of space/time.[17]

A number of others have used some concept of the subtle body to elucidate their work. Jungian analyst, Nathan Schwartz-Salant, stands out for he recognizes the critical role of the subtle body in the therapeutic transference relationship.[18] He feels healing comes about between two people through contacting the imaginal symbol of union, the sacred marriage or alchemical *coniunctio*. In these moments of intimate contact, the subtle body serves as a medium for healing the split between body and mind in both people. He describes the subtle body as a palpable energy field that emanates from the physical body, invisible to the eyes, yet visible to imaginal sight. He sees it as a middle realm, a background subliminal field of energy, partaking of the physical as well as the psychic/mental/spiritual. Schwartz-Salant acknowledges, too, that the language of subtle body phenomena is open to misunderstanding. Since most people think of the subtle body as an illusion, one is faced with the "exceptionally difficult task of communicating this experience."[19]

Another analyst, Sylvia Brinton Perera, facilitates shamanic rituals for women, which encourage a spontaneous expression of a subtle body phenomenon she calls the emerging "bodySelf." Perera, while reiterating the impossibility of articulating the imaginal perceptivity of the body, manages to do a fine descriptive job:

> This knowing by the body is virtually impossible to articulate verbally, for it is an invisible energetic attunement with archetypal intent at its instinctual pole. It has integrity and precise accuracy, mirroring the form patterns with the repertoire of the preverbal body-Self, enabling the body to express archetypal events directly.[20]

She uses drumming ceremonies of sound and movement to reveal identification with inner "animal guides." These ceremonies are a means of contacting the subtle realms, transitional, necessary only until the body-self "can become conscious enough to become speakable, for the dark, compelling, instinctive and tabooed emotion and behaviors threaten to overwhelm . . ." The ceremony stands at the "border where the archetypal content seizes the body" (another apt description of the subtle body) and provides a safe container so the threatening energies can be eventually integrated.[21] Her work demonstrates well how the subtle body can connect us with a primal instinctual ground we both fear and desire.

Jungian writer and analyst Marion Woodman refers to the subtle body as the energy of the images. Following Jung, she believes we cannot long ignore the physiological component of the imaginal "complex" (or limiting emotional pattern) because it irritates the actual tissues and nerves, calling attention to itself.[22] She believes every complex has a bodily component that needs to be worked through until we are forced to bring it to consciousness. As long as the feeling tone of the image remains rooted in the body structure, the complex endures. Years of habitual tension prevent the body from releasing conflicts even after they have been resolved through insight.[23] Because the subtle body serves as a bridge between the mental and the physical, work on both bodily tensions and mental attitudes can be quickened by concentrating on the fertile meeting ground of the subtle body.[24]

Acceptance of the subtle senses as they begin to open hinges partly on the strength and orientation of the rational mind, particularly on the degree to which it serves as a barricade or a bridge to the irrational. Even as we start to register the tremors of imaginal perception, we may face a concurrent barrage of disdain, disbelief, and even outright hostility from our usual reasoned rootedness in the five senses. As the subtle senses develop, and we start to actually see energy fields or feel the edges blur between our body and the person next to us, we may conclude we are exhausted, have eaten bad food, are becoming ill, or must be falling in love. We call these subtle openings "chemistry," a funny feeling, the flu, or a waking dream. On the other hand, if we can suspend our disbelief in invisibles long enough, we may find ourselves roaming in imaginal fields for longer and longer periods of time.

Illness or crisis *will* often catapult the subtle into awareness. Arnold Mindell, another analyst, seems to have discovered the subtle body when faced with a prolonged illness. He articulates subtle body experience in his formulation of what he calls the "dreambody." In an attempt to surmount the difficulties of description, he offers numerous portrayals of the dreambody. He describes it as hovering "between body sensation and mythical visualization," as "spirit in the body," "inner body sensations and related fantasies" "a field-like essence extending beyond the real body," "energy vortices which possess archetypal experiences", and as "the psycho-physical process trying to dream itself into being." Mindell equates full development, or individuation, with the growth of dreambody awareness.[25]

Yet another closely related concept that can help validate the experience of the emergent subtle senses is the "subjective body." Analyst Donald Sandner describes the subjective body as an archetype that converts emotional states to bodily and sexual longings.[26] Sandner discusses Stanley Keleman's distinction between the body itself and the subjective body, described as an "inwardly felt body, charged with emotion and sexuality," more real psychologically than the physical body. The subjective body is an imaginal representation in the psyche of bodily emotion and sexuality—a structural archetype, on par with ego, through which psyche influences the actual body and vice versa.[27]

Hovering close to this description, we also find Donald Kalsched equating subtle body with the psyche itself, which he depicts with an apt metaphor as "the place where body meets mind and the two fall in love."[28] Contact with the subtle body gives a sense of animation, vitality, intimacy, and vulnerability. These qualities, Kalsched observes, are notably missing in people who have suffered a splitting of body and mind through early trauma. For these people, the emotional or affective component of experience lodges in the body, while the imagery itself stays in the mind, leaving a gap in experience—often an inability to even recognize what is going on with the feelings or senses. Kalsched's discussion revolves around trauma victims, but to me seems to broadly apply to the general tendency in our culture to split body and mind (and who hasn't been traumatized just coming into the cold world from the warm womb?).

This common internal split, from which we all suffer to some degree, implies both a lack of emotional awareness and an inability to differentiate among feelings, particularly those we have rejected as unacceptable. For instance, we say we are "angry," to describe an entire range of experience from irritation, to frustration, to indignation, to murderous rage. We do not handle our acceptable feelings with any greater delicacy. We use "love" to describe perhaps an even broader spectrum of experience, from love of ice cream, to love of the 49er's, to romantic love, to parental love, to love of God. Bringing body to mind begins to heal this split and to activate the subtle body senses capable of finer distinctions and richer perceptions.

We cannot leave this discussion of analytical reflections on the subtle body without hearing from James Hillman, the founder of archetypal psychology.[29] He describes the subtle body as: "a fantasy system of complexes, symptoms, tastes, influences and relations, zones of delight, pathologized images, trapped insights. . . .", and he speaks of body and soul losing their borders to each other, both metaphoric and literal at the same time.[30] In drawing a distinction between flesh and body, he describes the subtle body as "a union of incommensurables", "both immaterial spirit and physical reality" and a "meaningful system of body living within the flesh."[31] He also alludes to the subtle body (which he calls the imagination of the body), when he discusses "deliteralizing" the senses through imaginal experiences: "And all [imagery] involves the senses—though a sense beyond sense, a second sense of sense, a sensibility of the sensuous, not the sensuous, as such."[32] He encourages an intimate befriending of the subtle body to help counter what he recognizes as the well-established tendency to neglect this middle ground of the psyche.[33]

JUNG'S SCHEMATA OF THE UNCONSCIOUS

Since Hillman, as well as most of the writers already mentioned, has been inspired by Jung's conceptions of the subtle body, and because the concept plays such a large role in this study, we need to look more closely at Jung's views of the subtle body. Jung divides the unconscious conceptually into two parts—the somatic and the psychic unconscious. He pictures the unconscious on a continuum stretched between these two poles:

1. The instinctual, somatic unconscious of impulse and feeling, and

2. The archetypal, psychic unconscious of ideas and images.

He theorizes that if the entire psyche, including conscious and unconscious contents, could be viewed objectively, from afar, a continuum of psychic life would fit the following schemata, which he associates with the spectrum of light:

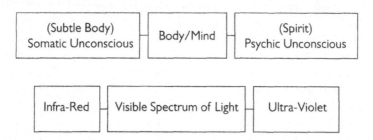

Consciousness corresponds to the visible spectrum of light, while unconscious material falls out of the range of vision into the somatic infrared or the psychic ultraviolet. Although for practical purposes he divides them in this model theoretically, Jung views the psychic and somatic unconscious as ultimately one unified field.

> You see, somewhere our unconscious becomes material, because the body is the living unit, and our conscious and our unconscious are embedded in it: they contact the body. Somewhere there is a place

> where the two ends meet and become interlocked. And
> that is the place where one cannot say whether it is
> matter {body}, or what one calls "psyche."[34]

Despite their fundamental similarity, when the unconscious is viewed from our usual vantage point—from the ego—the somatic and psychic ends yield considerably different experiences. When we descend into the body, the unconscious is, for Jung, associated with subtle body phenomena, which he equates with the somatic unconscious. This theoretical formulation of equating the subtle body with the unconscious body appears to contradict his statements about the subtle body's role as a semi-spiritual meeting ground of body and mind. But, Jung is well aware of the difficulties the concept of the subtle body presents and how easy it is for contradictions to arise. It is for this reason that he largely avoids speaking of it, describing it as exceedingly incomprehensible, growing darker and darker as it contacts the body, ending in the "utter darkness of matter."[35] He writes of the subtle body only theoretically, since in his mind, it does not consist of matter at all, or if it does, it is exceedingly fine and difficult to perceive and affirm.[36]

Although Jung writes little of the body or the somatic unconscious in his *Collected Works,* he was apparently forced to speak of the subtle body at length in his seminar series on Nietzsche's *Thus Spake Zarathustra.* Schwartz-Salant believes Nietzsche pushed Jung to grapple with the subtle body because Nietzsche so often included the body in his experience of the numinous.[37] Jung, in commenting on Nietzsche, remarks that when considering unconscious phenomena one must include not only the psychological unconscious or shadow, but also the physiological unconscious: "the so called subtle body"[38] This example from *Thus Spake Zarathustra* gives a flavor of Nietzsche's treatment of the subject: "Behind your thoughts and feelings, my brother, there stands a mighty ruler, an unknown sage—whose name is self. In your body he dwells, he is your body."[39] Jung commented that *Thus Spake Zarathustra* was "written in blood," and anything so written "contained the notion of the subtle body, the equivalent of the somatic unconscious."[40] I took note of Jung's point here, for, I believe, the daimonic images do come forth in metaphoric blood, reflecting the instinctual unconscious pulsing through the body as the image reaches consciousness.

The psychic unconscious carries images, symbols, and dreams, and is much more accessible to us than the somatic, instinctual component of the image we have relegated to the underworld. Our cultural rejection of the body encourages us to split off the instinctual unconscious, and with it our more primitive impulses and feelings, for the sake of the psychic or spirit realms. Even in psychoanalytic work that acknowledges the centrality of the image, the image has been spoken of as though it were predominantly mental, influencing attitudes, understanding, and insight. Jung believed that focus on one end of the continuum of consciousness necessarily reduced the contact with and clarity of the other pole, yet he encouraged focus on the psychic end.

Despite this emphasis on the psychic aspect of the image, Jung understands the importance of the body,[41] saying that images "arise in the depths of the body and they express its materiality every bit as much as the structure of the perceiving consciousness."[42] Discussing the religious conception of the resurrection of the flesh, he describes the subtle body as the numinosity inherent in the body.[43] For Jung, the subtle body actually appears to be another description of the Self, that enduring aspect of each person that exists beyond space and time and guides each individual life. Thus, the subtle body is mainly theoretical for him, in its local sense as the somatic unconscious and also in its larger use as one description of the Self. Today, despite Jung's recognition of the importance of the instincts and the body[44] and their connection to the whole being, Jungian thought still typically continues to be distinguished by its emphasis on the psychic end of the archetypal spectrum.

SANDRA LEE DENNIS

AN EXPANSION OF JUNG'S SUBTLE BODY CONCEPT

The daimonic images of this study have an energetic, kinesthetic, sensual component, corresponding to the body, and a conceptual, mythic, symbolic component relating to the mind. The subtle body, as I use it here, does not conform so precisely to the darkness of the somatic unconscious as Jung seems to suggest, nor does it correlate with the guiding Source or Self. It is more accessible to us than we might have imagined. Through the gathering of the senses, we may step lightly into the subtle sense realms. Here we discover the meeting ground of the somatic and psychological unconscious, that "edge" of preconsciousness for both the somatic and the spiritual aspects of the psyche.

When we play the inner edge of consciousness, we invoke the daimons into our world, and open our subtle eyes. An image that brings both the body and mind into consciousness becomes daimonic. Written accounts of psychological exploration tend to stop here, at the description of the powerful images that arise *(unio mentalis)*. But it does not stop here. The daimonic embrace with body and soul encourages an amazing unfolding of the psyche. For this affect-laden, soul-infused image now moves to reconnect with the body in a further, more profound union of body and soul *(unio corporalis)*. *This second meeting takes place in the containing medium of the subtle body.* Following Jung's schema, the subtle body, rather than being aligned with the somatic, is thus better represented as falling *between* the two poles of unconscious material—the bio-instinctive and the archetypal.

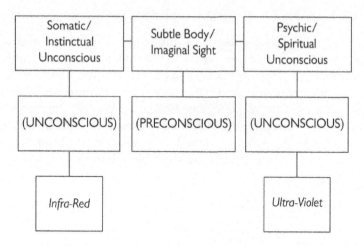

The subtle body contains as much mind as body. It distills and mixes these two opposites. Through its action, soul comes to Earth, and we glimpse the "heavenly" realms of the archetypes. The opposites combine to render images perceptible to our imaginal vision, a faculty that perceives the subtle body as being as real and as three-dimensional as the world of the five senses. The infrared and ultraviolet tones of the subtle body correspond to those twilight hues barely discernible to sight, perceived almost as a hallucination, yet still recognizable to physical sight. They appear to imaginal sight in the liminal terrain where consciousness meets the unconscious.

A delicate equipoise of these two poles of unconsciousness materializes the subtle body as an imaginal field that may be sensed as well as perceived. The resulting images arise with a striking reality that contains both instinct and spirit. These images may be experienced sensually as a color, sound, smell, or feeling when they manifest more of their instinctual origins. Or they may appear more formally as an animal, person, god, or geometric design when their psychic components predominate.

SANDRA LEE DENNIS

Therapeutic Change Through the Subtle Body
After "one hundred years of psychotherapy" more and more people are recognizing that insight into a recurring emotional pattern barely changes associated behaviors. Body-oriented therapists now argue for the inadequacy of insight alone (the prevailing therapeutic methodology), and believe they have found an answer to the problem of integration: behavior must have roots in body structure. No real change takes place unless it takes place in body and mind.

The psychodynamic approach offers one explanation. According to analyst Anita Greene, the split-off body complex originates when the self is a body-self in infancy and childhood. The wounds of childhood are then repressed into the body structure.[45] In adults, there remain highly-charged negative energies, most likely stored in the tissues of the body, associated with images that require release through specific body-centered methods, including body focus, cathartic release, breath work, or touch.[46]

According to this approach, body focus must accompany the insights gained through verbal therapy, spiritual disciplines, or creative work, to effect the healing of destructive, life-limiting behaviors. We now know that bodywork alone can be as one-sided as talk therapy, as it often releases the somatic unconscious without regard to the corresponding psychic image. We are left open and energized, but without the understanding necessary to effect lasting change in our destructive inclinations. We distinguish bodywork, such as Rolfing, or bio-energetics, from work on the subtle body, which involves the imagination as well as body sensations. When we engage subtle body perceptions, we affect both our physical and psychological inclinations.

Our inclinations, especially our pathologies, help define our individuality, and can point us toward the most creative sources in ourselves. From addiction, perversion, and madness, to our everyday irritability, these pathologies hold promise to unfold our destinies when followed as the daimonic spirit-infused guides they

29

can be. If we pay attention, we find that each pathology has an abiding imaginal counterpart waiting to be acknowledged and brought into the world. Our recurring fantasies, dreams, and images deserve our respect and attention, as they are the guardians at the gates of connection to an Underworld of sacred beginnings, a wellspring of meaning that nourishes our souls. We are also learning that regardless of origin, the "healing" of our pathologies—rather, following the pathology to its daimonic core—occurs most effectively through the subtle body in its capacity to integrate the physical and the psychic.[47]

Our tendency to concretize and to think dualistically obscures our awareness of the centrality of the subtle body realm, and gives the impression that we need to work on either the body or the mind.[48] Body therapies alone may breakdown physical armoring, and analysis may establish insight about our illusions, but work on and through the subtle body causes a shift in the fundamental sense of self that colors our way of being in the world. Conscious work with the subtle body first heals splitting and defensive projections, then it begins to mend our alienation from God, love, cosmic consciousness, the Self, call it what you will. Through the subtle senses we may experience the cyclical series of alchemical unions and deaths that eventually wear down the individual sense of self, and along with it, the tendency to picture the world as a concrete, separate object. We restore our link with the *participation mystique*. Subtle bodywork strengthens us by connecting us with the numinous backdrop to both mind and body.

Subtle body faculties then allow us to perceive the larger realm of which they are a part, the realm of the imaginal, the *mundus imaginalis*. The development and appreciation of this much apprehended, but little explored, realm is critical to the tasks of our time. For this unitive visionary realm, revealed through the subtle sense body, offers this vision of the union of All: a meaningful framework that can ultimately contain the nihilism and chaos of our postmodern times.

CHAPTER 3

The Mundus Imaginalis

Perhaps, then, a Western nirvana would require that the West first lose itself in the immeasurably vast and dangerous caverns of the imagination before it may reach the heights of Eastern spirituality, for otherwise there is a risk of a monistic adulation of the spirit principle.

—Robert Avens[1]

DURING THE PAST TWENTY YEARS, it has become common knowledge that "point of view" has an enormous impact on our interpretation of events, particularly intrapsychic events. Hence, there are as many explanations for the imaginal as there are worldviews. These views range from philosophical relativism, for which the meaning of any experience is determined by the theory through which it is viewed, to mysticism that sees in the image the forces of heaven and hell at play. For example, psychologist Jeanne Achterberg in her study of imagery in healing describes Lillian's experience of suffering years of chronic pelvic pain, finding no relief until she began to practice visualizing a concrete block dissolving in her lower back. One night, when practicing her imagery at home, she was seized by an imaginal episode that finally cured her.

> A coyote named Wildwood flashed into her mind. He advised her to stay by his side, and watch what was about to happen, and told her that what she saw would be related to the fire in her body. She then sensed herself sitting by a campfire in the midst of a hostile tribe of Indians who held her captive. She experienced the horror of being brutally gang-raped and murdered. "At the instant of my death . . . I woke up and was back in my body in the room, only my pain was completely gone and hasn't returned since." [2]

EMBRACE OF THE DAIMON

We can speculate that a shaman would explain this as a death/rebirth experience guided by a power animal, a psychologist would attribute it to the mind's ability to precipitate a powerful psychosomatic healing, a neuroscientist would question the abnormalities of her brain chemistry, while a fundamentalist would marvel at the grace-filled exorcism of the demon. Lillian herself attributed the cure to reliving a past-life experience, though she hadn't believed in reincarnation before the incident.

We must admit we do not know whether or not spirits or daimons exist beyond the images we have of them. As Roger Walsh puts it, Lillian's is a case of "ontological uncertainty," since we have no known method to determine the source of these phenomena. "The only honest position may be an agnostic view of spirits and channels in which we confess their indeterminacy and our ignorance."[3] The way we interpret a phenomenon will be largely determined by our prior assumptions about reality— personal beliefs, values, worldview, and philosophy. This relativistic outlook has become an integral part of the postmodern mind.[4] According to Sam Keen, "Human consciousness, it seems, is able to create or to discover almost any reality it focuses on long enough. We make the world in the image of what fascinates and terrifies us."[5] From this perspective, no explanation is more valid than another.[6] Truth wraps itself around our assumptions; we create our own reality.

Each camp has its own version of the importance of the image. For example, in religious life, a realm we might suppose open to imaginal reality, we find a long history of distrust of the imagination, we regard it as a source of deception, we deny it as a route to true knowledge. By emphasizing the "spiritual" Christianity has often dismissed the image as unreal. Imagination has been viewed as "a bridge for the demons, over which these murderous miscreants cross and recross,"[7] which devotees aimed to eliminate entirely. Consider these directions to new monks from *The Philokalia:* "Since every thought enters the heart through imagining something sensory (and, moreover, the sensory hinders the mental), so the light of the Deity begins to illumine the mind when it is freed of everything and totally empty of form."[8] Under Christian influence, the pagan *daimons* especially were seen as the powers of chaos, forces of negativity, a pandemonium. Opening to inner voices meant courting Satan, serpent worship, possession, black magic, or sickness.[9] Here in the Christian West, we still collectively carry this legacy of disdain and distrust of images.

Against the grain of his time, C. G. Jung acknowledged the significance of the vilified daimons of the imaginal world, and gave them significance through his formulation of the archetypal structure of the psyche. Discussing the archetypes, he noted they often manifest themselves "as daimones, as personal agencies."[10] Hillman, characterizing Jung's move toward the irrational images in the early days of psychoanalysis as "bold, courageous and heretical," credits him with reconnecting the daimons that Christianity had cast out of the soul. "By means of these daimonic realities, Jung confirmed the autonomy of the soul. His own experience connected again the realm of the daimons with that of soul, and ever since his move soul and daimons imply, even require each other."[11] Jung's pioneering work began to "undo the grip of the ancient ecclesiastical fingers upon our imaginary hearts."[12] Still, we ought not underestimate the impact of this pervasive worldview on our relationship to the imaginal, particularly to its darker occupants.

Recently, Western religious practitioners have begun to be influenced by Buddhism, and have incorporated aspects of Buddhist meditation practices in many spiritual and psychological methods. Most forms of Buddhism (the Tibetan tradition being an exception) reject the imaginal even more emphatically than the Christian tradition.[13] The imaginal is viewed as a delusion that Buddhist practitioners attempt to "deconstruct" along with all experience. In Vipassana meditation—"mindfulness," for instance—all phenomena are observed and eventually reduced to insubstantial, ephemeral waves of energy. Despite the ultimate focus on "emptiness," meditating does open doors to subtle imaginal realms. Acknowledging this, Jack Kornfield in his writing about imagination in Vipassana practice, emphasizes that deep concentration brings all manner of intense visions. "We can sense ourselves as other creatures, in other bodies, in other times and other realms. We can see and encounter animals, angels, demons, and gods." He notes the autonomy and numinosity of the images also. When such visions arise in the most compelling form they become as real as our day-to-day reality.[14] From the Buddhist perspective, these imaginal presences are seen as part of a process of purification of the mind that comes with spiritual exploration, nothing more than mere side effects of a practice aimed at liberation from the suffering caused by the illusion of sense-based reality.

Kornfield presents a dilemma for the Westerner involved in mindfulness practice. He explains that the images must be engaged to be felt and come to terms with.[15] If, however, their reality is denied, they cannot be truly engaged. Thus a real risk of bypassing the imaginal realm exists. A "spiritually trained" mind, by denying the validity of the dramatic, mythopoetic imaginal mind, declining to follow the path of the unfolding image, undermines its vital importance as the intra-psychic bridge between spirit and matter.[16] An exalted spirit in an emotionally stunted body can result. Such an approach can also limit the action of the creative muse. Creative inspiration thrives on the free play of the imaginal realm that can be discouraged by these religious practices.

It is not only in the field of religion that the image has been devalued. Cognitive psychologists, those we might assume to be the most interested in subjective mental processes, have only recently begun to recognize imagination as a valid category of study.[17] Early experimental psychologists under the sway of the scientific outlook tried to make the data of the psyche fit the scientific model. Influenced by the popularity of behaviorism, the image was considered an epiphenomenon of unconscious neural processes,[18]"a private, unobservable mental entity" therefore unreal.[19] A great battle was said to finally be won in having mental imagery accepted as a fundamental aspect of human cognitive behavior at all.

SANDRA LEE DENNIS

In this field today, imagination is still notoriously difficult to define, "despite a contemporary revival of interest in the topic, it remains an essentially contested concept: no generally acceptable theory even of the main subsets of the concept of imagination is presently available."[20]

The legacy of the psychoanalytic view of the psyche still exercises a strong hold on more common psychological interpretations of imaginal experiences. Freud painted a picture of the child teeming with instincts at birth. As we mature, he thought, the *it* or the *id* contains these aggressive, sexual, and antisocial impulses, often associated with daimonic imagery. But when the controlling mechanisms of the culturally conditioned superego or ego break down, early, repressed material from the *id* may break into consciousness in the form of dreams, images, or compulsive actions. He thought defense mechanisms normally keep these primitive threatening impulses outside conscious awareness.

"Projection," or assigning our unconscious motivations to those around us, is one defense mechanism that presumably operates to protect us from acknowledging these instincts. We merely project the unacceptable inner impulse outside ourselves to avoid facing it internally. The more vivid the image, the deeper and further away from consciousness the impulse. Possession by the devil, for instance, is explained as hatred of either parent cast into the devil image. Thus, in this view, daimonic images simply picture repressed instincts.

Earlier in his life, Freud posited that sexual impulses were involved with what he called demonic imagery, later he believed it was the fear of death.[21] Emphasis in psychoanalytic circles today has changed from the repression of instincts as the major cause of "pathological" imagery to a focus on the quality of early relationships. Object-relations theory and self-psychology, first formulated by Heinz Kohut, prevail in psychoanalysis today. From this vantage point, the apparently demonic "object" may be an exaggerated mythical form of an early punishing parental figure that has been incorporated into the self-image or introjected.

35

Another approach of growing importance with psychoanalytic roots has emerged out of post-Jungian attempts to combine body awareness with imaginal work. Here the concern lies with unearthing the underlying bio-image that contains experience of earlier trauma embedded in body armor. I agree with this approach, which points out that the body expresses in energetic form, such as over or undercharge, what the ego represses. This energetic patterning results in a body "complex."[22] These theorists also see the image as a product of the body-mind. According to this view, a more integrated flow between mind and body will produce more healthy, life-enhancing imagery. Naomi Goldenberg's interest in "resurrecting the body," exploring what she believes to be the "corporeal ground of our intelligence" puts her in this group. She uses Winnicott's definition of psyche as "the imaginative elaboration of somatic parts, feelings and functions" advocating a return to Freudian theory as a way to reestablish the primacy of the physical body in the emotional and mental life. From this perspective, symbols and images are, simply put, bodily feelings in picture form.[23]

The work of the archetypal psychologists bridges the views that grant absolute otherworldly autonomy to the image, such as the Christian, and those who see its genesis in individual psychological history. To Jungian and archetypal psychologists, image ranks as the first principle.[24] In the world of archetypal psychology, the imaginal is envisioned as a multivalent reality with repercussions on many levels of existence. From this point of view, reality includes a non-material spatiality known through intuitive apprehension that enlarges the realm of human experience. In the archetypal vision, the imaginal connects to the creative ground of psychic reality, wherein reside the gods and goddesses of religion and myth. Symbolizing worlds of being and meaning, these images are metaphors for the experiences of our personal lives. As the ranking present day champion of the imaginal world, James Hillman sees the image as the god of a mythopoetic psyche predisposed to characters, symbol, and metaphor. He says, "There are gods and daimons and heroes in our perceptions, feelings, ideas and actions, and these fantasy persons determine how we see, feel, think and behave, all existence is structured by imagination."[25]

Apart from these overarching theories, in clinical practice the concept of the image turns out to have vast history and importance. Since the publication of Freud's *Interpretation of Dreams* at the turn of the century, dream images as signs of unconscious libidinal forces have been a subject of continuing interest to the clinician, who aims to help and heal, as well as to theorize and understand. The "waking dream" and other imaginal phenomena have enjoyed less popularity than the dream, until the past fifty years. A quiet revolution began when Jung initially broke with Freud around the issue of the reality of the imaginal. To Jung, Freud's *libido* always appeared as images, the stuff of the soul.[26] Since Jung's pioneering days, interest in the image has grown to become a central concern for many therapies.

More and more practitioners with diverse orientations acknowledge the impact of the images of the psyche on psychological and physical well-being. In her study, Jeanne Achterberg includes no less than forty-seven psychotherapeutic schools of thought or techniques that rely on imagery. The reintroduction of the imaginal into Western psychology has even been called the "next great event" after Freud's insights about dream interpretation.[27] James Hillman has suggested it is "the major task now confronting psychology to differentiate the imaginal. . . . its laws, its configurations and moods of discourse, its psychological necessities."[28] He expresses one of my interests in writing this book—to further differentiate and map the imaginal world in order to help myself and others who are drawn to this fertile inner terrain.

NAMING THE TERRITORY

After centuries of neglect, imaginal subjective realms have not yet been differentiated enough to discuss them with precision. In current usage, "imaginary" and "imagination" still often refer to the unreal. We have been conditioned in the West to conceive of the world in pairs of opposites—mind/ body, conscious/ unconscious, light/ dark, rational/ irrational, masculine/ feminine, good/ bad—denying legitimacy to the "lesser" halves of each pair. The imagination, as a subset of the lesser "irrational," has been rejected and devalued by our culture to the point that we acknowledge its existence, if at all, as a deviation from psychological health and normalcy. To get a taste of our cultural prejudice, just look at these synonyms for "irrational"— unsound, untenable, absurd, foolish, inane, silly, crazy, demented, insane, and mad. What about the wonder, awe, Eros, creative pulsing, energetic vitality, and meaning brought forth by the irrational aspects of the psych? We continue to face a poverty of language that limits our experience when we try to speak of these faculties that have been marginalized for so long.

The French scholar and mystic, Henry Corbin, helps establish the most fundamental differentiation necessary in setting a framework to explore the realm of daimonic imagery. First of all, we owe him credit for coining the term *imaginal*. He writes eloquently, with experiential conviction, about the realm of the imaginal, calling it the *mundus imaginalis:* "a world that is ontologically as real as the world of the senses and that of the intellect". Corbin recognizes immediately the problem of naming the imaginal realm. He sees how necessary accurate terms are if this realm is to be properly conceived and experienced. He is adamant about the problem of terminology. At one point in his frustration at being misunderstood, he admits being tempted to use the term *imaginatrice* to set off the visionary imaginal world from the connotations of fantasy or secular figments of the mind.[29]

Like Corbin, Jung understands the importance of naming. He knows that *unnamed experiences tend to remain unconscious.* Correctly naming an experience is tremendously important. Jung says that when you give an experience a wrong name "you qualify it, you put it in prison, into a drawer or a cage, and you can no longer handle it because that name is all wrong."[30] A right name can save us from "disintegration, demons and chaos." I believe

Corbin's and Jung's concerns are well founded. They are right about the need for completely new words to help rouse us from unconscious ingrained patterns of thought that make no room for these matters. To this end, Jung employs scores of Latin terms to describe the results of his explorations into the imaginal psyche, some of which I also use. In this study, the terms "daimonic," "subtle body," "coniunctio," and even "imaginal" may sound odd or obscure, but I use them to help bring the unfamiliar into focus. To grasp their meaning, we are forced to create new ways of thinking that may seem bizarre to our ordinary mindset, but which are imperative if we are to recover what has been denied. For to be explored, described, and understood, the imaginal requires a shift out of ordinary consciousness. New terms can aid in that shift out of the old and into new categories of thinking and perceiving.

NUMINOSITY AND THE IMAGINAL

For Corbin, the *mundus imaginalis* and the sensible world symbolize one another. The imaginal faculty, he knows, has the capacity to transmute inner states to outer reality. He conceived the power of the imaginal as a religious power that cannot be produced intentionally, but comes of its own accord from outside space and time. For him, ecstasy is inherent in the images of this realm. He describes active imagination (encouraging the unfolding of imaginal scenes) as the "ephiphanic place" that allows for the full development of the image.[31]   Corbin's conception of the imaginal resonates with that of the Romantics, who recognized the spirit in nature, and who worshiped creative imagination. Coleridge explains creative imagination as the active conversion of the unknown order to the known, much as Rilke does when he calls us the "bees of the invisible". William Blake writes extensively of "imagination" the term he uses to describe his visionary experiences:

> The Nature of Visionary Fancy or Imagination is very
> little Known & the Eternal nature & permanence of its
> ever Existent Images is considered as less permanent
> than the things of Vegetative and Generative Nature....
> This World of Imagination is the World of Eternity. It
> is the Divine bosom into which we shall all go after the
> death of the Vegetated body. . . . There Exist in that
> Eternal World the Permanent Realities of Every Thing
> which we see reflected in this Vegetable Glass of Nature.[32]

Jung called the quality of eternity or religious power
associated with the imaginal *numinosity*, a term he revived from
Rudolf Otto's original conception of religious experiences in *The Idea
of the Holy*. Otto's term helped describe the autonomous, compelling
qualities of the image that Jung encountered when the imaginal
began to intrude spontaneously upon his world. In 1937, Jung
described the *numinosum* as "a dynamic agency or effect not caused
by an arbitrary act of will. On the contrary, it seizes and controls
the human subject, who is always rather its victim than its
creator . . . The *numinosum* is either a quality belonging to a visible
object or the influence of an invisible presence that causes a
peculiar alteration of consciousness"[33] Jung viewed encounters
with the numinous as enigmatic, deeply impressive, and mysterious,
defying explanation.[34] Though not proving the existence of God,
Jung described imaginal encounters as "godlike."[35] He assumed, as
does Corbin, that numinous images gain their potency from their
connection to a greater truth that we normally only dimly
recognize, and considered an encounter with the *numinosum* a part
of all religious, as well as psychopathological experience.
Summarizing Jung's thoughts on the *numinosum*, Andrew Samuels
concludes that a confrontation with numinous images not only
compels tremendously, but has teleological implications, foretelling
"a not yet disclosed, attractive, and fateful meaning."[36]

Late in his life, in *Answer to Job*, Jung spoke of the importance of
taking the trouble and patience to understand imaginal numina. He
believed we are possessed by them for a reason and owe them our
attention. Yet, we have been conditioned in the West to look at

Jung's reflections on numinosity and Corbin's statements about the *mundus imaginalis* with a raised eyebrow. We find little encouragement in our ordinary lives to give much thought or attention to the appearance of the imaginal, shrugging it off as a silly fantasy, a bad night, the result of poor food, or too many action movies. If we do surmount the initial hurdle of granting attention to the image, we are then faced with totally unexpected difficulties in engaging it. "It is altogether amazing" Jung says, "how little most people reflect on numinous objects and attempt to come to terms with them . . . and how laborious such an undertaking is once we have embarked upon it"[37] (I agree with him entirely on that point.)

Hinting at why numinous images challenge us so, Jung discusses how trying it can be to integrate such experiences into our understanding with any objectivity. An encounter with numinous images can change our lives, since the interpretation, fueled by the inherent transformative power we give them, can potentially shatter or enhance our worldview and our very sense of self. "The numinosity of the object makes it difficult to handle intellectually, since our affectivity is always involved. One participates for or against [the meaning of the images], and absolute objectivity is achieved here more rarely than anywhere else."[38]

This power to effect such deep change explains our touchiness and defensiveness, our tendency to simply turn and run away rather than to confront the imaginal. Should we decide to engage these images, we implicitly agree to open ourselves to a kind of psychic surgery, the outcome of which cannot be predicted in advance. As we begin to come more fully into contact with the instinctual components of the numinous, we stand to be dramatically changed. This is obviously not a path for everyone. But for some, the imaginal imperative cannot be set aside without injury to their well-being. Addiction, dissatisfaction, emptiness, or illnesses sound the daimon's alarm. We ignore them at our peril. They are calling to come more fully into our lives.

THE DAIMONIC IMAGINAL

I am describing the imaginal here with a broad brush as a realm of numinosity, a world of liminality where consciousness meets what has been unconscious. As a connecting medium, the imaginal itself has much in common with one of its components or processes—the "daimonic." You may recall that the Greeks conceived of the *daimons* as connective forces or spirit intermediaries between the human and the Divine.[39] In standard English usage we often use "daimon" as the equivalent of "demon" to represent an evil force, which is a degeneration of the original connotation of the term. In its literary sense, however, "daimon" still contains elements of its original definition as messenger of the Divine. The combination of its literary and common usage suggests to me that it contains the opposites that underlie imaginal union. Consequently, I use the term *daimonic* to help set off these sensation-laden, autonomous images that appear to connect psyche and soma from other forms of imagery with which they are easily confused, such as active imagination (in the sense of directed or controlled imagery), directed dreaming, creative imagination, visualization, hallucination, and fantasy.

Although some descriptions of the archetypal image may be similar to this definition of daimonic, the word *archetypal* has been used to describe such a wide spectrum of experience that its usefulness for making finer distinctions in the subtle realms I am exploring here is limited. The daimonic image is a specific kind of archetypal image that has been especially maligned and avoided, but is central to the opening to unitive unconsciousness. The term *daimonic* also calls forth the underworld, the dark, tumultuous numinosity of these instinct-laden images, while *archetypal* can easily leave us too much in the conceptual clouds.[40] From the point of view of the individual, the daimonic always includes arousing sensation and emotion as part of its impact. While the archetypal image assumes the existence of an instinctual driving force, its presence does not necessarily pull the instinctual to consciousness.

The daimonic image may indeed be archetypal, but it arrives on the scene somatically supercharged. Such an image must also be distinguished from intense feelings that overwhelm consciousness, but occur in the absence of a spontaneous, self-regulating image. Connecting these feelings to an image helps to calm the chaos to reveal their deeper meaning. The daimonic may emerge as madness to the unprepared psyche, or as creative potentiality to the prepared. Above all, the daimonic image reverberates with a three dimensional reality, appearing to the subtle senses as an autonomous presence connected to powerful sensation and feeling.

Unlike the daimons of the Greeks, who lived in ethereal realms, our embodied daimons, affiliated with the tabooed underworld, come to consciousness, stirring their counterparts in the realm of the subtle senses. These images are underworld gods, connected with numinous instinctual forces that, if properly held, allow us to resonate with the psychic territory they occupy, territory we generally associate with the outcast Earth, the body, and sometimes with Hell itself. Here, for instance, analyst Claire Douglas offers some of the flavors of the daimonic underworld encountered by Christiana Morgan, whose visions we will discuss more fully later. Morgan was Jung's patient, whose imaginal journeys are recounted in his *Visions Seminars*.

> They [Christiana and Jung] traveled . . . down into an exotic world of chthonic initiation, where Christiana united first with a black god and then with a dread matriarchal realm. As Morgan descended into the unconscious, she engaged in powerful shamanic acts: swallowing, then being swallowed by a snake, passing painfully through fire, bleeding, then immersing herself in a river of blood, experiencing violent, sometimes terrifyingly orgiastic rituals of union. She encountered many fierce and transformative animals on her journey, including a ram, a black stallion, bulls, goats, and snakes.[41]

In this passage we can see the motif of transformative change or metamorphosis that dominates daimonic processes. During metamorphosis the old gradually gives way to the new, each change a death, a step in the total unfolding process. Everyday metamorphic processes go on around us regularly and yet they remain remarkably invisible in our culture: sexual unions, births, destruction, death, decay and rebirth, all go on outside the mainstream of life. Shielded from contact with these ongoing undercurrents of our earthly existence, it is no wonder we avoid the inner events that reflect our own propensity toward metamorphosis.

The daimonic image stirs deep and troubling questions for our Western mindset, with its fundamental belief in the goodness of day, the clear light of reason, and the illusory permanence of our sense of identity. This prejudice couples with our suspiciousness regarding underworld darkness, irrational instinct, and the flux underlying our fragile identity. All this interferes with our ability to accept the visiting daimon. Furthermore, our lack of familiarity with imaginal realms leaves us prey to literalizing or to acting out their contents. We easily lose sight of their metaphoric quality. Confusing imaginal scenes with their enactment shakes our conscience, our sense of ourselves, and our securely anchored relation to what we have always taken for granted. With this attitude, when these images arise, in horror, we may fear we are about to become the next serial killer. No wonder we struggle to keep them from awareness!

DAIMON OR DEMON—PASSION OR PATHOLOGY?

As we will see, incomplete union in the imaginal world brings on the alchemical apparent opposite of growth, of union, that is the dark night of the *nigredo*, with all manner of despair, depression, chaos, bad luck, illness, and accident. The erotic daimon, when it first appears to us, announces a dual imaginal process, mixing union with destruction in a stunning paradox that strains our discriminating faculties. I will return to the difficulty of drawing distinctions in imaginal realms—recognizing, for instance, a fertile destructiveness or a self-centered expansion, for instance—throughout this discussion.

Uncovering unconscious, archetypal images always involves some element of numinous darkness. But in this daimonic realm of imaginal life—when the image actually incarnates in our bodies! —we must not only face the paradoxical attraction of such taboos as incest, scatology, sodomy, rage, cannibalism and madness, but also actually allow ourselves to enter into, though not enact, their metamorphosing energies. It is no surprise, then, that daimonic processes have been, at best, systematically ignored, but more often demonized. According to Hillman, every repressed image that comes to light has Hell or Hades as its source:

> There is an intolerable aspect to every image, as image.
> Its habitation in the undersense of things is their
> underworld and "death" An image as a simulacrum is
> but a shadow of life and the death of concretist faith.
> Imagining implies the death of the natural, organic view
> of life and this repels our common sense. Hence, the
> underworld stinks, dung and corpses, brimstone.
> Images are demonic, of the very devil, keep a distance.[42]

Are we not right then in our reflex to ward off the daimonic forces? I suggest that the difference between the daimonic—the numinous carrier of deep, enriching transformation—and its cousin, the demonic, derives, first of all, from their respective degrees of integration, the degree to which we fully embrace the image. The daimonic image encourages transformation of itself. Further developments in the content of the image are always implied. Despite their often horrific themes, they continue to unfold. But when the images are merely demonic, they have lost their connection to the body. The image tends to repeat, as in a recurring nightmare or destructive sexual fantasy. The repetition implies a loss of contact with the numinous source of the image. To act out of instinct without connecting to its imaginal context, or to move from image without regard for its bodily source is to fall into a demonic way of life. Any split between these two sides of human nature encourages either the animal or the computerized, mass-market robot in us—both demonic in their dehumanizing tendencies.

A daimonic image weds instinct with its guiding image. It lives in us as a guide, a direction, and a creative muse. Images cut off from their bodily counterparts can sell, manipulate, intoxicate, and incite to all manner of atrocity. At the other extreme, giving free rein to primitive instinct generates a sociopathic personality. In either case, we spend significant parts of our lives in hell, in demonic realms. On the other hand, when image meets body with respectful regard, the psyche opens to the subtle body, the visionary realms connect. The two sides meet in our most satisfying experiences: in inspired creative work, connected relationship or those embodied contemplative moments that bring us to the shores of vision where the daimons reside.

Another pitfall besides this habitual splitting faces us as the daimon comes into awareness. As the daimon moves to unite more deeply with us, it threatens our sense of self, which will be dismantled, or at least shifted, by its action. As this occurs, the temptation to identify with the energies of the daimonic image looms large. If we slip into identification with the daimon, imagining we are the Serpent Goddess or Magician of the Night, its action turns particularly demonic, and we may set ourselves apart, specially chosen, from the rest of humanity. Deluded, inflated personalities wreak all manner of havoc, as cult leaders and demagogues in the extreme, or simply as isolated islands of grandiosity that isolate us from any real contact with our neighbors, family, and friends.

Even when daimons appear in a positive, wise, or "angelic" form, if we identify with them as savior, Good Samaritan, or philanthropist, we block their transforming potential. Once we *realize* their damning potential, we may find we distrust the reality and intent of any powerful image. Hillman points out that all daimonic images violate our usual conception of reality. They conflict with our commonly agreed upon parameters of the known, and we experience them as a violation, against which we arm ourselves for our peace of mind. This natural arming, however, exacts a high price. For we reduce the daimonic to the merely demonic when we suppress, act out, drug, or otherwise try to exclude it from consciousness.

Stephen Diamond, a psychotherapist who has recently written about the question of anger, madness, and the daimonic, suggests that we need a concept that includes "the creative side of this elemental power."[43] (His use of the term daimonic is more broad than mine and closely follows that of Rollo May as "anything that can take us over.") Careful study of what we originally consider demonic imagery indeed reveals its creative qualities. Many nuances of texture, taste, and tone connect these images to what we normally consider to be positive—a particular vitality, power, clarity, and above all, numinosity can be felt in the midst of "possession" by the daimonic images. They mix the beastly with the sublime, to lead us to the farther reaches of our nature.[44]

Nevertheless, these daimonic images can be scary. They keep us at our edge, engage us in a fervor of existence that can exhaust us and exasperate our associates, often arising as "dark" figures that evoke fear, disgust, lust, anger, shame, or anxiety. At best they confuse or compel, shaking us out of the complacency of our everyday existence. The dark aspects of the psyche come vividly forth as the daimonic, sensation-laden image arises. In addition to the violent, sexual, animalistic, and scatological energies mentioned earlier, sensations of elemental bodily processes, such as orgasm, illness, pain, bleeding, lactation, pregnancy, and dying often accompany their appearance.

James Hillman considers such a "tortured psychology" and pathologizing fantasies prime movers of the soul, without which we are doomed to superficiality. He says, "If the soul is to be truly moved, a tortured psychology is necessary. For the soul to be struck to its imaginal depths so that it can gain some intelligence of itself . . . pathologizing fantasies are required . . . these pathologized fantasies are precisely the focal point of action and movement in the soul."[45] The daimonic displays an erotic, Dionysian character that links the best in life with its apparent worst. In the face of this attractive, apparent torture, we have a right to be confused and wary.

It makes sense that, traditionally, we have misnamed these eruptions of instinctual daimonic presence, as we have the imaginal subtle-body realm itself. We have named reports of the daimonic hysteria, incest memory, satanic possession, Oedipal strivings, psychotic breakdowns, negative impulses, carnal lust, or sexual perversion. Even Jungian and archetypal thinkers, who ought to be familiar with this territory, sometimes denigrate these experiences, as animus possession, negative shadow, or demon lover, thereby hobbling them, limiting their supposed sphere of action and our understanding of their importance. This panicky tendency to marginalize the daimonic image should alert us to its importance. It threatens the hegemony of our prevailing values and worldview. We fear the unleashing of instinctual forces that have been kept in check in our culture for perhaps thousands of years, whose purpose in the unfolding of the human drama we must admit we do not understand, but are now required to face.

Daimonic images today are impinging upon us with apparent urgency as evidenced through the explosive increase of images of violence, disease, and explicit sexuality in every form of media. Demanding our attention, they are breaking into the collective psyche, materializing in the empirical world as well as in the imaginal. To better understand what he considered initially to be the pathological, primitive imagery of his seemingly normal "upright" clients, analyst Thomas Moore even launched an in-depth study of the Marquis de Sade, culminating in his early book, Dark Eros.[46] He found these dark images important, not only for their power to move the imagination, but also because they allow entry into an underworld where "the Divine logos, the deep design within events" is to be found.[47] Echoing Hillman, he believes the "undeniable tendency of the soul toward the outrageously dark" is a necessity for the soul, a sign of transformation, a process that moves the soul, allowing her to "embrace more and repress less."[48] (His recent popularity on bestseller lists may also indicate a broad-based readiness for archetypal thinking, including the embodiment of the daimonic that concerns him.)

Daimonic images deserve our respectful attention as harbingers of our future. They hint at our unlived selves, as they surge to inseminate consciousness with their transformative force. No wonder we stand in nervous awe at their arrival. An encounter with the daimons of the imaginal world forces us to face the tentativeness of our sense of self, our solid world, and our rationality. We can no longer escape the natural destructive, separating force set in motion when body and mind meet. Arising from a world of creative process bathed in Eros, the daimon appears to demand our intimate involvement. In action, it is ravishing in the most positive sense, precipitating an inner death and regeneration, sinking itself into our bones as a permanent resident through an alchemical magic we are just beginning to discern.

CHAPTER 4

Alchemical Unions and Separations

Marriages may be made in heaven but they are
hatched in hell.

—Thomas Moore [1]

THE STUDY OF ALCHEMY offers us a symbolic language that is
uncontaminated by current usage. The alchemists offer a
description of sacred psychic rituals: they describe how the *prima
materia* of human unconsciousness is transformed to release "gold"
through confrontation and eventual union between warring
aspects of the psyche. These medieval alchemists offer a language
that enables us to further answer the modern day challenge to
map and clarify subtle-body phenomena. "Alchemy", C. G. Jung
says, "describes not merely in general outline but often in the most
astonishing detail, the same psychological phenomenology which
can be observed in the analysis of unconscious processes."[2] The
richness of this detailed description helps explain Jung's lifelong
fascination with the subject of alchemy.

Edward Edinger credits Jung with the single-handed rescue of
the arcane alchemical texts from the "rubbish heap of history."[3]
Jung devoted three volumes, two-thirds of his writings, two
thousand pages[4] and the last thirty years of his life to the alchemical
opus or work.[5] He understood alchemy as a map of psychological
development, an exact description of the individuation process,
and a reflection of the inner mystery of the union of opposites.[6]
Schwartz-Salant describes the alchemical process as "a series of
unions and deaths, aimed at purifying away the concretizing
tendency."[7]

The two central alchemical concepts I will discuss in this
chapter are the *coniunctio,* or union experience, and the *nigredo,* or

the dark dismemberment or dissolution process. The dark night *nigredo* purifies away all elements that mitigate against the union. The darkness reflects a mourning for the loss of union in which the soul must sacrifice and enter the dark night in order to regain vision of the liminal world of unions.

I rely particularly on the language associated with the alchemical symbol of union, the *coniunctio,* which is Latin for "joining" or "bringing together" to describe the reunion of the daimonic image with the body. Characterized as the culmination of the alchemical work, the *coniunctio* is most often symbolized by sexual union, referring as it does to a chemical combination of bodies drawn together by affinities.[8] Known as the main secret of the Western underground mystery religions, the *coniunctio* may be conceptualized as a process occurring outside the parameters of our usual space/time existence, accessible in altered states of consciousness in imaginal realms. Foreign to our culturally supported notion of empirical reality, it slides disruptingly into our awareness to begin its process of incarnating,[9] erupting in mystical moments, feelings of peace, harmony, oneness, as well as anxiety, chaos, and despair in its darkest forms. Although the mysterious and irrational *coniunctio* seems contrary to everything we ordinarily take for granted, it may afford us some comfort that modern physics is not entirely ignorant of such things. Schwartz-Salant, for instance, argues that the *coniunctio* is the central archetypal structure (or process) of physicist David Bohm's "implicate order"—that invisible source of the "explicate order" or the world of the senses.[10]

The *coniunctio* also reflects the Dionysus/Christ motif of communion with the god, which reveals a hidden link of the Christian tradition with earlier pagan rites. The culmination of the rites of Dionysus involved eating the raw flesh of a freshly killed animal, often a bull, which represented the god himself. As we shall see, this communion ceremony plays out the process of imaginal reunion with the body. The muscle and blood of the animal was thought to convey the divinity of the god to the initiates. The Christian communion ceremony in which one partakes of the blood and body of Christ reflects a similar motif. The longing of Christian saints for possession by the bridegroom, Christ, also resonates with the Dionysian orgiastic rituals when the celebrants enter a mystic union with the god. Both god-figures suffered cruel deaths, Dionysus by dismemberment, Christ by crucifixion, and both were resurrected. (Yeats's play, *The Resurrection*, traces Christ's life as a reenactment of the myth of Dionysus.) Those who resisted worship of Dionysus were overwhelmed by an elemental force causing possession, madness, and hallucinations; while those who turned away from Christ suffered the torments of Hell. The alchemists knew that rejection of the *coniunctio* impulse to inner union can bring on a surge of the blackening, hellish *nigredo*.

In Jungian thought, the analytic transference relationship is said to activate a *coniunctio* between analyst and patient, as well as between the opposites in the patient's psyche. Jung used a medieval alchemical text depicting the *coniunctio*, *The Rosarium Philosophorum*, to demonstrate phases in the development of that relationship (and these phases seem to apply to any intimate relationship). In *The Rosarium*, twenty archetypal portraits of Sol and Luna, which Jung characterized as opposite aspects of the psyche (masculine and feminine, rational and imaginal, conscious and unconscious), depict the stages of relationship leading to the divine marriage, the goal of the alchemical work. Jung also understood this culminating marriage of opposites as representing a "phenomenology of the Self."

Self is Jung's term for the natural organizing principle, the source or center of psychological life, typically symbolized in divine images.[11] Thus, this relational process of union and separation, and all stages between, may constitute the *essence of being*, itself. At the least, it represents a key to the hidden, transformative mysteries of existence. "Nature not only contains a process of transformation—it is itself transformation. It strives not for isolation but for union, for the wedding feast followed by death and rebirth"[12] *Coniunctio* processes then offer "the fragrance of immortality" They bring death, but also a culminating point of life—a new beginning.

Whenever we drop into a unitive moment—in nature, with friends or lovers, in a creative "Zen" moment, we directly experience this impulse to union described by the alchemists. We shift into subtle-body awareness.

THREE STAGES OF UNION

Let us look more closely at Jung's three stages of the *coniunctio*, the wedding feast: 1) the union of the newly freed soul with spirit or unconscious image (the *unio mentalis*), 2) the reunion of this liberated, insightful presence or spirit/soul entity with the body (the *unio corporalis*, our newly coined term), and 3) the union of the embodied image with the larger world (the *unus mundus*}. All three involve not just unions, but the inevitable separations characteristic of opposites meeting. Usually we find it difficult to contain two opposites in our mind at once, in this case, union and separation, yet all lovers know that anguish and ecstasy are integral to their love. A conscious relationship to the daimonic image, not unlike the relationship to a lover, demands that we make this stretch beyond our usual habits of dualistic thought to include its forces of generative bliss, along with its annihilating force. Here is a closer look at these processes, in reverse order.

The Union of the Embodied Image with the World
The union of spirit, soul, and body with the world, the *unus mundus*, represents the culmination of alchemical work, the last of the three stages of the *coniunctio*. This is far away and theoretical for most of us. Still, I want to start with this final stage to help us establish the intimate relationship between union and separation. The theoretical existence of this ultimate state of existence establishes the context for understanding the inevitability of the destruction inherent in human creativity. This final union describes the state of transcendence, the ultimate synthesis of consciousness with the whole world, what Jung describes as the "potential world of the first day of creation." He called this mystic union with the empirical world the "One and Simple."[13] Spirit and matter, body

and soul unite to reach the ineffable spiritual world of the religious traditions, a world that has, oddly, been granted more reality in the Western tradition than the imaginal.[14]

What is important for our purpose is that in the canons of alchemical knowledge only this ultimate union with the world qualifies as the "greater" *coniunctio*. All unions that come before it represent but partial versions of this culminating union. This next point deserves special attention: *Partial unions always precipitate the dark night or alchemical nigredo*. The destructive *nigredo* dissolves all structures that limit a full embracing of existence. In practice, this means that each time we have a creative surge, a moment of close communion, a psychological insight, or a successful integration of what we have understood, we can expect a period of disorientation, depression, or lack of meaning to follow until all obstacles on the way to clear seeing, pure love, and god consciousness, are dissolved.

The alchemists explained that substances brought together before they are thoroughly separated and differentiated are thought to be poisonous or caustic to one another. (How many married partners can attest to the truth of this?) Intense conflict ensues from such "premature" unions resulting in the black, or psychic dark night, the darkness that Jung referred to as "the original half-animal state of the unconscious."[15] Edinger characterizes such unions as the naive embrace of maternal unconsciousness: honey followed by the stroke of a viper.[16] Thus ever our taste for bliss is tempered by experience. Despite such frightening associations, the process of "making black" the *nigredo*, was viewed by the alchemists as a glorious sacred or religious work, as the true beginning of the transformative work and each new stage to follow. While much has been written about the *nigredo*, its necessary and frequent occurrence in psychologically creative work is little acknowledged.

The separation of the unconscious pair involved in a premature *coniunctio* feels like a death. That this defeat or death was thought to mark the true beginning of the next phase of the inner work, shows how inextricably are end and beginning joined at this level of the psyche. The imagery of this phase symbolizes a severe defeat for the conscious ego, precipitated by the inevitable loss of union, or rather the loss of direct contact with the numinous. This defeat ironically leads to greater contact with the numinous imaginal ground that flushes to consciousness new areas of the unconscious amidst feelings of failure and fractured identity.[17]

The most common alchemical processes connected with the blackening include *divisio* (division or dismemberment), *mortificatio* (death, killing, or mortification), *putrefactio* (rotting), *separatio* (separation), and *solutio* (dissolution). *Mortificatio* is the most negative operation in alchemy, having to do with darkness, defeat, torture, humiliation, death, and rotting.[18] This phase, especially, involves the contradictory imagery of the *Liebestod* or love/death, including images of blackness, sexual violence, putrefaction, dismemberment, and death, all with an erotic edge.

In alchemy, Sol disappears into the well of Luna, the paws are cut off the lion, the body is dismembered, the wings of the Eagle are clipped, or the royal couple lies in a coffin.[19] In outer life, marriages break up, bankruptcy threatens, life-threatening illness sets in, the house burns down, or the IRS sends an audit notice. Yet, some strange meaning calls out from these apparent calamities. As long as the ego unwittingly identifies with the contents of the unconscious, it precipitates the *nigredo* experience in which deeper unconscious material rushes to the surface (commonly known as "pride coming before the fall"). Whether at the stage of insight, bodily integration, or mystic embrace, experiences of union—influx of life force, new love, completed project, fresh outlook on life, surging prosperity, ingenuity, productivity, or understanding—are followed by dark periods, by the *nigredo*.

The close relationship between the *coniunctio* and the *nigredo* is reflected in the phenomenology of the daimonic images we will be exploring. The inherent connectedness of the two processes and our tendency to avoid the unpleasant *nigredo*, I believe, give the daimonic image its compelling, yet frightening, quality. If we do not confront our unwillingness to embrace the pain, despair, rage, and confusion of the transformative process, inner union stops, yet we cannot escape this death in life. Even as we run from these psychological imperatives, we feel ourselves dying in another way, caught in an extended darkness—with meaning, soul, vitality, love ever fading away. We are brought to the truth that we must embrace our inner demons to truly live.

The Mental Union (Unio Mentalis): Disillusionment

As I have mentioned, Jung wrote extensively about the union of insight, that meeting of opposites we experience when split-off contents of the unconscious are recovered.[20] Many have tasted the bittersweet flavors of this initial stage of union when the ego meets the unconscious image in the *unio mentalis*. Disillusionment is sprinkled throughout these experiences. The rising of the previously unconscious to consciousness often shocks us out of a lifelong illusion about who we are, and introduces us to parts of ourselves we have never acknowledged. These may include such unpleasant parts as our anger, fear, and hatred, which we experience as the "dark night", but can also include strengths we have cast aside to shore up our current self-image. Depressing as these experiences may be, they still deserve to be called a "union" insofar as working with them in creative endeavor, meditatively, or psychotherapeutically, leads to insight, which is the fruit of the meeting between awareness and unconscious image.

Through contact with our unconscious "dark" side, we gain insight into ourselves. Life itself gives us opportunities to confront hitherto hidden parts of ourselves, whether or not we are formally in therapy or engaged in explicitly spiritual or creative work. External events seem to conspire to wake us to ourselves. The shocked husband whose wife is leaving their "happy marriage" after twenty years, the loyal employee who is given her termination notice, the devoted church member who learns of the lies and improprieties of the priest or guru, the vibrant dancer diagnosed with cancer. All have come to a disillusioning point of insight. A series of such events may lead eventually to greater maturity, a more realistic self-assessment, and more peace with the forces of life, or to bitterness, anger, and disappointment.

Jung equated the experience of the *nigredo* of insight with encountering the castoff, despised, aspects of the shadow.[21] He said of the *nigredo* in this initial phase of psychic unfolding: "It is a bitter thing to accept the darkness and blackness of the *umbra soils* and to pass through this valley of the shadows. It is bitter indeed to discover behind one's lofty ideas, narrow, fanatical *constrictios.*"[22] As we have seen, however, the alchemists hailed the blackening as a glorious occasion, for it signaled the true dawning of the *opus*, the transformation process. Unfortunately, these experiences can also present a formidable obstacle to the continued growth of consciousness. We are not pleased when we discover, for example, a sadistic manipulator residing in our very heart. After a time of confronting these reviled aspects of ourselves, we may give up, ready to settle for any distraction that will relieve us, that might help us forget these terrible truths about ourselves. Truth can be tiring and we need a rest, especially as we discover that insight does not necessarily bring change. Tired of all this, we would be gone from the turmoils of inner change. No more opposites please, we cry, as we move toward some middle ground of suburban security—at least until the stagnation suffocates, and we garner the courage to jump back into that drama of passionate unfolding that life continues to offer.

During this phase of insight, as with all conjunctions short of the ultimate union, we still encounter the devil as the dark night, that is, we feel despair, depression, and futility. Death motifs often accompany crumbling illusions, but now perhaps we do not take them quite as seriously as before insight began to dawn. We begin to step back. Disturbing dreams, illness, anxiety, depression, or psychosomatic symptoms may all signal rejected unconscious material edging closer to consciousness. The dark side of the union of insight comes with the disenchantment that accompanies a shift in self-image as the previously rejected (and usually condemned or feared) aspects of the self are gradually acknowledged as being part of who we are. During this darkness, we seem to be losing everything we once were, which often evokes a full-fledged existential crisis.

Awakening insight is characterized by a separation of our identity from what we thought we knew of ourselves, a differentiation from the imprints of the past. While it involves a union of opposites, its nature exposes more the motif of separation than that of union. When we can objectify our feelings and instincts, coming to know them as "not I," we gradually strengthen the sense of a separate "I" and, at the same time, expand the breadth and depth of the *"I."* We accomplish this expansion through the incorporation of previously unconscious aspects of ourselves and from the separation from the unruly life of feeling. Insight and disillusionment teach us to stand alone. We learn the existential truth that we have always been alone. Many associate this insightful union with the first half of life, a time of establishing a sense of self, separate from the family matrix.

Insight further describes a conceptual understanding that may be marked by "ah-ha" experiences, along with self-recognition, as when we take back aspects of the self we have projected onto others. For example, Ann and Barry Ulanov describe a man who had a recurring nightmare in which a woman stabbed him to death. The frightening memory stayed with him as a confirmation of his belief that women are dangerous for men. He said, "They pierce your heart, they get you, and then they leave you." Through work on this image, he gradually uncovered the emotional theme of his rage toward women. When he finally could acknowledge his hatred, he began to see how he enacted it in his life in the veiled form of passive withholding.[23] Good beginning though it may have been, the insight alone will not necessarily lead him to give up his habitual withholding behavior. Such a change will probably require another round of nightmares, waking dreams or confrontations with avenging women, to bring the hot passion of rage into his felt sense, in short, a daimonic episode will need to usher in the change in behavior.

The term *unio mentalis* can be misleading. Although the emphasis is on the mind or ego uniting with previously unconscious material, this is not strictly a "mental" task. This initial stage of *coniunctio* surely does involve freeing the soul from its imprisonment in matter, extracting elements of soul from their identification with the body.[24] But it is also more than this, for it awakens body consciousness, insofar as it brings the psychic and somatic unconscious together. This coming together of the image with the instincts in the stage of insight is sometimes referred to as "integration of the image." But this is *not* the sense in which I use the term "integration." The meeting of image and feeling does not involve the daimonic reunion with the body. For me, "integration," properly so called, refers to the second stage, when the already ensouled image reconnects with the body. Nevertheless, the daimonic image is first encountered in the stage of the *unio mentalis*, at once the end result of insight, and the nascent embodiment of that insight. We need to have the insight before we can integrate it.

In this first stage, the mental representation acquaints us with feelings that have been unconscious. The image of a murderer arises, for instance, along with bodily experiences of rage and hatred. A longstanding, habitual dissociation ends as the ego comes to terms with the image and these feelings. When a murderer comes to consciousness, the one-sided sweet image we have maintained of ourselves must go. Our self-image must die. In these death throes (that come as a byproduct of the ego's confrontation with elements of the instinctual unconscious), we give birth to the daimonic image (which may take any number of unexpected forms, not necessarily related to the murderer) that may eventually be integrated, united with our being, reconnecting the power associated with the rage and hatred to the body in a life-affirming way.

By the time the daimonic image comes to consciousness, insight has strengthened the individual ego, as well as the field of conscious awareness. The ego has learned to stand aside from the wants, needs, and drives of the body we thought we knew, and insight has endowed it with a new breadth and flexibility through incorporating the previously rejected aspects of personality. Such insight is the hallmark of maturity: a regenerated personality, and a more realistic self-image. Jung himself acknowledged that while the ego's encounter with the image brings an increase in self-knowledge and maturity, it is still merely a potential. It is made real only through the next phase, the "union with the physical world of the body."[25]

The Reunion of the Soul with the Body

Tellingly, Jung never names the second phase of the *coniunctio*, referring to it only as the reunion of the *unio mentalis* with the body.[26] I have given it the Latin name *unio corporalis* to help remedy this lack. Ideally, during this phase, insights are brought into the body, into action, into the world. The impact of the daimonic image upon our instinctual body-centered life has been little explored, though many speak of its necessity.[27] Integration of insight, of the vivified, ensouled image with the body is little understood and remains a major stumbling block in therapeutic, spiritual, and creative work. Failure to put into practice what is learned during the time spent exploring the inner world sometimes leads to a ridicule of these important endeavors as ineffective, self-centered pastimes. I believe the troubling images that drove me to write this book, and make up the phenomenological heart of this study, help explain why so often "personal growth" stops at insight, and attracts such disdain or discouragement.

In *Mysterium Coniunctionis* Jung devotes more than sixty pages to the second phase of the inner union that must qualify as one of his most confused and obscure discussions.[28] He follows Dorn's claim that a certain substance with magical properties lies hidden in the physical body, the "quintessence of the philosophic wine."[29] It is this magical substance that makes "the fixed volatile and the volatile fixed" in the reunion with the body.[30] (This mysterious quintessence plays a central role in this stage.) The "spirit must be changed to [fixed] body and body to [volatile] spirit".[31] An interweaving of spirit and body must be accomplished before the complete conjunction or wholeness can be attained.[32] Here Jung says the alchemists referred to this magical quintessence released in the *unto corporalis* as truth, the *imago Dei,* Mercurius, the supreme chthonic spirit, the devil, and blood.

Jung is concerned with the soul image "getting out of hand" during the *unto corporalis,* as he believes it inclines naturally toward the body. Since the resolution of opposites is always an instinctual, energetic process, when the tension of opposites is great enough, unions activate spontaneously.[33] He cautions that insight gained in the *unto mentalis* may easily slip back into its former unconsciousness if union with the body takes place before "light of the spirit" has become a solid achievement.[34] He recommends the use of "active imagination" "a dreaming the dream forward that aims to objectify the affects and confront consciousness with them" as his principal method of establishing contact with and stabilizing the unconscious image.[35] He seems to imply that active imagination is the psychological counterpart of the second union that will eventually bring about integration of the daimonic fruits of insight.

Even when enacted through expressive movement, however, active imagination falls toward the psychic end of the unconscious spectrum. It appears to depend far more upon insight, upon the direction of the mind, than upon shifting the bodily roots of the sense of self. Perhaps because he favors the psychic end of the unconscious spectrum, or because he deems the accomplishment of bodily integration an "insoluble *task*", Jung concludes that insight cannot stand the clash with reality. In any event, he never seems to come to terms with this stage. Reading his comments today, one senses Jung's discomfort with the energetic process of reuniting with the body. His concern with the daimonic images "getting out of hand" seems to reflect the then prevailing cultural attitude of deep distrust of the instincts that predominate in this phase.[36]

In contrast with the psychic activity that dominates gaining insight, the emphasis during the *unio corporalis* must be placed on the body. This represents a radical reversal—and is not at all obvious. It is a turning point against a previously held position that requires violating our previous orientation. Now we must immerse ourselves in the very irrationality of sensation and feeling that was discouraged as insight dawns on the witnessing mind. When we take our new insight seriously by taking to heart the daimonic realities (the rage and hurt) of our inner selves, we actually strengthen our imaginal, subtle senses. This deep acceptance of the validity of the daimonic promptings toward the feelings and the body is the necessary precondition for bodily integration.

At this point, when the daimons encourage immersion in their reality, we must forget all we learned earlier, when we needed to separate ourselves from the chain of instinctual drives, and allow ourselves to fall into an intensification of feeling and sensation. This movement will naturally signal all sorts of dangers to us, as we have been involved in separating our sense of self out of the instinctual, feeling realm to bring it to awareness. This identification of feelings brought on by insight brings out the full symbolic expression of these daimonic energies, hence the predominance of what is considered "lower" or instinctual imagery: themes of primitive animality, aggression, and sexuality.

After years of objectifying the psyche through meditative practices, active imagination, creative pursuits, expressive therapy, or simply trying to be a "good" person, we have strengthened our defenses against bodily forces. To seriously take on the daimonic makes us fear we are leaving the path, abandoning what has given meaning to life, or entering into a self-indulgent morass. It takes a radical shift of mind to face up to the daimonic in ourselves—much less to reunite with it. Edinger comments on this phenomenon:

> What is a crime at one stage of psychological development is lawful at another and one cannot reach a new stage of psychological development without daring to challenge the code of the old stage. Hence, *every* new step is experienced as a crime and is accompanied by guilt, because the old standards, the

old way of being, have not yet been transcended. So
the first step carries the feeling of being a criminal.[37]

What kind of commitment to the source of life does it take
for us to *realize* that what opens a door on one level, closes it on
another? Who wants to feel like a criminal? The discriminating and
objectifying stance of the ego, or witness-consciousness, permits a
deepening and strengthening of the personality, a growth of self-
knowledge, but this very strength at some point becomes a liability.
If the ego cannot release its separateness and accept the
discomforting lead of the daimonic energies, its rigidity limits our
contact with yet deeper, more maturing, levels of the psyche.

Aside from fears of sin or crime, and our long habit of
holding fast to what we have always known, we are sure to find
the daimonic image, itself, rather forbidding. In keeping with its
predominantly somatic nature, the daimonic may bring us
physical and subtle-body torments in the form of aches, pains,
tensions, and particularly distressing sensations, including dizziness,
fragmenting, hollowness, expanding and contracting, falling,
madness or being possessed. It often involves themes of sexuality
and violence, death and decay. We naturally want to escape these
things. That is why it is so important to place them in their
larger transformative context.

Yet another obstacle presents itself when we face the
daimonic, regardless of the form it may take. The entrance of
daimonic energy into the body is a rather "feminine" process. Our
culturally sanctioned heroic and "masculine" ego ideal stands in the
way of the "feminine" receptivity required in our interaction with
the daimons. We believe we need to "take action" on these imaginal
promptings. We equate "just being" with laziness or down time, and do
not appreciate the impregnating potential of this state of mind.
Indeed, this stage of inner work toward union tends to be
relational, erotic, for the darkest material is colored with
passionate overtones. Feminine erotic receptivity and the union it
makes possible contrasts sharply with the separative "masculine"
move that emphasizes the first stage of work marked by rationality.

Moreover, I believe the common themes of sexuality and violence proliferate when the daimonic emerges as a result of *the overlay of sensations of erotic union with the dismantling of our limited self-image.* The daimonic encounter potentially brings an ecstatic body/mind experience charged with Dionysian energies of sublime sexuality, but for it to do so we must release our existing self-image to allow a penetration by the daimonic energies. We experience this penetration as a change in the bodily constituents of our sense of self. We feel fundamentally different, flooded with new, unusual, sometimes disorienting sensations.

We rarely realize how deeply our sense of who we are rests on a bodily foundation. The way we carry ourselves, the strength and weaknesses of various muscle groups, habitual tensions or chronic illness add up to determine our innermost experience of "I." To truly embrace or integrate the daimonic image, our fundamental bodily identity must shift to include new qualities inherent in the image, different perhaps for each person: qualities such as strength, sensuality, clarity, loving-kindness, and vision. Alice in her wonderland of ever-changing shapes and sizes could commiserate with our plight at this point. The *unio corporalis* entails the loss not merely of the mental image that was challenged in the first stages of self-awareness, but of a biologically based sense of who we are.

In the initial stage of the *unio mentalis*, the *nigredo* or darkening reflects our attachment to a particular rational self-image. We do not care to see ourselves as rageful, weak, conniving, greedy, powerful, or possibly vulnerable, or, for some, creative. We cling to our familiar idea of ourselves, reluctant to grieve the loss of our illusions, so we suffer. In the second stage, if we can let go further and begin to trust the taboo, ego-alien instinctual energies, the full daimonic presence will emerge. It is into a space of fractured identity that the daimonic heralds our deeper being come forth. The second stage of union, the conscious acceptance of the recently emerged daimonic image into the body, is a rare event that requires exceptional physical and psychological openness from us. At this stage, we no longer cling to illusory mental pictures of ourselves, rather, we must be ready to stake our fundamental being on the bewildering promise and threat of the previously unacceptable chaos within. Such an encounter with the daimon seems to tear down and rebuild our cells, finally altering our being in the world. The good news amidst the ruins is that while we are not who we suppose ourselves to be, we discover we are incomparably more complex, richer, multidimensional beings.

CHAPTER 5

The Dark Goddess Rising

Just ask yourself whether the Real might not be some very repressed—censored—forgotten "thing" to do with the body.

—Luce Irigaray [1]

AFTER BREAKING INTO AWARENESS, the daimons strive toward a state of annihilating union with the body, strongly charged with the destructive, erotic overtones associated with the sexuality/birth/death motifs. Historically these are qualities aligned with the archetype of the "Dark Goddess." Rational consciousness has been built on the rejection of these instinctual energies. They are considered taboo and disturb us both on account of her darkness and on account of her despised feminine traits. Whether witch, harpie, or siren, she embodies dynamic energies that include eros, sexuality, birth, death, and destruction.

Symbolized mythologically by Kali, Lilith, Ereshkigal, Sekmet, Medusa, and Hekate, her energies correspond remarkably to the numinous, connective daimonic. The Dark Feminine attributes represent a particularly reviled aspect of the somatic unconscious: the loathsome instinctual feminine of the primal bodily depths that remains well buried and undifferentiated in both men and women, its numinosity seen usually only as negative. Guardian of birth and death, the instinctual feminine includes violent, ecstatic urges to destroy the old in the service of life and to create the new. Blending of the transformative energies of birth with those of destruction, in fact, is one of her distinctive characteristics. The daimonic realities of the subtle body we are exploring here appear to be the very realms the Dark Goddess traditionally rules.[2]

EMBRACE OF THE DAIMON

The hierarchical scheme of being embraced by our culture since the time of Aristotle places the realms of the Dark Feminine forces—nature, irrationality, and the body—lower than the rational mind, and denies these forces any connection with the legitimate aspects of human nature, let alone its sacred dimension.[3] Within our Judeo-Christian sphere in the West, the corruptible, untrustworthy body cannot be a true spiritual source, rather, mystical embodied experiences have been depreciated: dismissed as misfired neurons, regressive illusions, or the work of the devil. We find admonitions against body-based states in most dualistic religious traditions. States of erotic union or numinous vision mediated by the body through sexuality, pain, disease, birth, or death are trivialized or pathologized. As well, we marginalize the intuitive who sees into the subtle-body realm of auras or energies or has imaginal prescience. We medicate for childbirth, postpartum blues, sexual compulsions, depression, or grief, effectively blocking the connective, visionary power of the forces being released.

Since Western culture has for so long revered the image of the male hero and relied upon it for guidance, these potent, instinctual, relational, and bodily realities evoke powerful resistances. The collective derogation of the Dark Feminine in service of the development of the heroic ego has left us with unbearable anxieties when called into the cauldron of death and rebirth she symbolizes

One of the first writers to develop the idea, introduced by Jung, that the dark side of the Great Mother has been repressed and subjected to collective derogation in order for masculine, heroic consciousness to develop was Edward Whitmont. He contends that her body-based energies evoke intolerable anxieties that we've had to distance ourselves from in order for egoic awareness to separate from the *participation mystique*—an intimate interrelatedness with the cycles of nature they represent. Whitmont calls up images from the *Book of Revelation* to evoke the dread and horror of the Great Mother—devouring, starving, engulfing, drowning, and dying—as typical of the apocalyptic representations in our mind of the return to her womb/tomb, associated with the body and Earth.[4]

The dark goddesses symbolize also the animal maternal instincts, which may include destroying her young or slaying her mate after copulation. When these animal instincts do emerge, we do not easily recognize or tolerate such taboo energies. However, we still project them and may uncover our attitude toward them in our revulsion toward the unfortunates who act on these impulses—the mother suffocating her newborn or leaving her toddlers to be drowned in a locked car and the woman turning on her abusive or betraying husband with knife in hand. Yet, the insistent rising of the daimonic to consciousness is calling for the resurrection, recognition, and integration of these most denied and repressed aspects of human nature.

THE MAIN MYSTERY OF THE "FEMININE PRINCIPLE"

Because the imaginal world is a world of relationship, and relationship—along with other 'feminine' values—has been devalued in our culture, we inherently distrust unifying, relational, daimonic encounters, tending to write them off as unreal or threatening. Despite our cultural rejection of the Eros associated with daimonic energies, states of union mediated by the body may be the primary vehicle for those with a strong feminine principle, whether men or women, to know the numinous. The riddle of relationship itself may have its roots in the archetypal dark feminine aspects of the unconscious that we are exploring. Nathan Schwartz-Salant suggests that the uniting processes central to the instinctual unconscious are the main mystery of the feminine principle,[5] just as individuality, the sense of "I am," is for the masculine. Jung expresses a similar idea: "The original wholeness remains a desideratum for which Sophia longs more than the Gnostic Christ. Discrimination and differentiation mean more to the rational intellect than wholeness through union of opposites."[6] With the ascendance of the rational intellect, we have learned to openly deride the unitive experiences that underlie the numinosity of the body, to the point of denying the existence of these subtle realities. This is especially true with regard to the devaluing and repression of sacred sexuality.

THE REPRESSION OF SACRED SEXUALITY

The enmity of body and spirit we find in Western religious thought may be a relatively new development. Riane Eisler, in her studies of early goddess mysteries, discusses how sexuality was connected to death and renewal as the link with rebirth and regeneration.[7] Sex was the sacred rite of the goddess in which priestesses, as channels to her power, would have ritual intercourse with community members who came to the temple to worship. Ritualized sexual union was primarily intended for ecstasy, spiritual illumination, and regeneration. In these rituals, the intensity of dying was also recognized as intimately connected with sexuality, especially as death was viewed as a passageway to rebirth into another bodily form (in contrast to the Christian resurrection into spirit). Sexual passions aroused by the Dark Goddess were thought to move the dying into death during their final moments through orgasmic contractions not unlike the labor contractions at birth.[8] Millennia ago, nature's night goddesses may have represented the power to renew and regenerate through ecstatic sexuality. They presided over the erotic mysteries and initiations in the transitional passage from death to rebirth.

Should we be surprised that with the coming of the sky gods, and the gradual shift from a matriarchal to a patriarchal focus, this sacred sexuality was the first power apparently cast out to establish the domain of the new god, Yahweh? Freud expressed what happens to old gods when new ones appear, "One thing is certain: gods can turn into evil demons when new gods oust them."[9] Indeed, in early Christianity sexuality became an evil temptation, especially forbidden to representatives of the church. St. Augustine taught that the excitement of intercourse transmitted original sin from generation to generation.[10] He condemned the Great Mother in her dark nature goddess guise as the most formidable enemy of Christianity.[11]

It appears that following on millennia of the ritual connection of sex and spirit, extreme measures—such as the Inquisition and the medieval witch-hunts—were finally needed to successfully demonize sexuality. The prosecutors in the witch trials seem to have aimed their accusations at the sexual mysteries of the old religion, for the "craft" contained the last remnants of the pre-Christian religion, in particular the fertility rites.[12] In the *Malleus Malificarum*, the bible of the witch hunters, "sin" became virtually identical with carnality, especially sexual pleasure.[13] Dionysian pagan celebrations of union with nature divinities of course would threaten the new order, and needed to be systematically demonized along with women. Trial records demonstrate that women were thought to have had an erotic propensity for devil worship. ". . . All witchcraft comes from carnal lust, which is in women insatiable."[14] The nature gods of the pagans, with whom the women entered into ritual union, were not imaginary beings in the eyes of early Christians, but real, hostile, evil powers. Demons were seen as fallen angels, not figments of imagination. The idea that they had angelic origins even helped to explain their numinous power and confirm their influence over the fallen soul.[15]

Seduction by the devil, submission to intercourse and "marriage" with him, was a common motif of the accusations.[16] Women actually admitted, often in great detail under torture, to having sex with the devil. According to Barstow in her study of witchcraft, ". . . we find women accused of flying to the sabbat on phallic broomsticks, being seduced by demon lovers, joining in orgiastic dances, kissing the devil's ass, copulating indiscriminately with other men, other women, relatives, demons, or the devil himself." Amazingly, women confessed (albeit under torture) to having sex with Beelzebub in all manner of ways and places: in their cells awaiting trial, in church, or at the market. He came as cows, birds, spiders, serpents, dogs, or goats.[17]

EMBRACE OF THE DAIMON

Regardless of the truth of these vivid accusations and confessions, we know they originated in someone's mind. Their striking similarity to the daimonic images in this book helps to support the contention that a fusion of the sexual and the religious impulse in the daimonic image springs from deep within the psyche.

A CURRENT DAY DAIMONIC ENCOUNTER

The modern-day daimonic episode that follows could well have provided evidence for burning at the stake during the Inquisition. It is my own material. Here, and in subsequent chapters, I place my imaginal experience in *italics*. In later chapters, I discuss external events in parenthesis when they provide a context for the images. Often I grabbed a piece of paper at the time of an imaginal breakthrough to write a description of the images as they unfolded. Some images were so vivid that they have stayed clear in memory. Because so many people have asked me, I will confirm that the only "drugs" I used during these years were coffee and, occasionally, a glass of wine. The imagery also did not emerge during any formal meditative practice, but appeared spontaneously during apparently unrelated ordinary events. It was only later that I began a methodical practice of working with the images. The following image typifies the early stages of the daimon rising to awareness. It ends, not in a reunion with the body, but with my merging with the daimonic presence.

The scene is a dark redwood forest. The man finds the child curled up in the hollow of a large old tree. He calls his sons to her. Each in turn unfolds her small body and rapes her, then returns her to the hollow. . . . As they leave, a rat bites hard into the leg of the older man, who grabs a log and begins to pummel the rat to death. The rat rejoices in its death throes knowing he has poisoned the man.... Inebriated with the rat's bite, the man transforms into a horned creature, full of black energy. He falls into a swoon, emerging as a magician. A magenta star-burst sparkles through his blackened aura. As a dark prince, he seduces women, who are irresistibly drawn to him, embracing them with his velvet cloak. They dissolve into him.

Typifying the mix of attraction and repulsion characteristic of the daimonic image, I still find this image troublesome because of its disconcerting impact. The scene is a dark redwood forest. To start with, it appears as a vivid, real life scene, as though dropped out of some other place in time into this reality. *The man finds the child curled up in the hollow of a tree.* This otherworldly quality alone arrests my attention and engages my respect and curiosity. Then this seductively numinous image betrays my expectations of its honorable intent with the unthinkable violation of the lost, innocent child. *He calls his sons to her, each in turn unfolds her small body and rapes her, then returns her to the hollow.* Moreover, the rapes themselves have a sexually stimulating effect I am loath to admit into awareness, with the result that my attachment to the image takes the form of internal judgment, an impassioned denunciation and rejection. Visceral repulsion and sexual pleasure combine to confound my best intentions about a relation to the image. Whether I accept or damn, I find myself not knowing which way to turn. Is this not a demonic force at work, I wonder?

In the midst of the instinctual pandemonium brought on by these irreconcilable feelings, the abstraction I have been suggesting, that the child may symbolize my own vulnerable feminine nature being inseminated by daimonic forces seems distant and irrelevant, hardly the sturdy container I need to hold this image without ambivalence, to let it flow on. Yet, eventually, flow it does. That the image flows points toward its daimonic promise. Still, I remained in the demonic prison of this image, which initially repeated itself in various forms day and night for some months. It trapped me in a tormenting double bind, until I could relax into the conflicting repulsion and attraction enough for the rat to appear.

As they leave, a rat bites hard into the leg of the older man, who grabs a log and begins to pummel it to death. The rat rejoices in its death throes knowing he has poisoned the man. The rat, another repulsive image, came finally as a force of numinous Otherness, avenging the wrong done the child. Here again, I am disturbed by the mixed themes of violence and pleasure, death and ecstasy. Yet I see that as the man and his sons served as transforming agent for the child, so the rat transforms the man. The aggressive, violating energies of the man dissolve him, through the inebriating poison of the rat's bite, into a superhuman, devilish form. (Throughout this unfolding again I did not consider the symbolic potential of these images as indicators of forces of my own psyche.) I may yet have gained insight into myself from this image (e.g., rage at men), but symbolic interpretation feels particularly inappropriate and lame in the face of such a vivid presence, the radical Otherness of the emerging daimon. I did finally begin to trust the unfolding, following the storyline with interest. I dimly may have recognized these were forces of erotic transformation at work. This shift in attitude seemed to allow a relaxation of the fear and loathing of the rape and the rat.

The emergence of the black magician followed soon after the rat's bite, and stopped the unfolding for some time, raising a number of doubts and fears, more inner turmoil. *Inebriated with the rat's bite, the man transforms into a horned creature, full of black energy. He falls into a swoon, emerging as a magician. A magenta star-burst sparkles through his blackened aura.* Now I am really sure Beelzebub is on the scene. What if this presence *is* a demon insinuating itself in my very body? He is not even in disguise, but blatantly obvious in this prince-of-darkness display of magenta star-burst aura and black cloak. Surely, this devil must be banished, exorcised in whatever way possible. But, no, then I lose the grandeur of his presence, its promise of immersion into unknown delights. Rather than banish this presence, I unreflecting merge with it. *As a dark prince, he seduces women, who are irresistibly drawn to him, embracing them with his velvet cloak. They dissolve into him.* In this grand gratification of identification with the emerging daimon, I again stop the unfolding, this time by inflating myself to feel I embody the power and seductive allure of the magician.

Identification with the daimon at this juncture is demonic, dehumanizing, limiting, and deluding. Sensations of power and sensuous appeal abound with this shift. I see myself as specially anointed, unique in the world, carrying a power to captivate whomever I please. I imagine myself adored by all, held in awe as a particularly entrancing presence. I do not recall how long this inflation continued. These are weak imaginary pleasures though, as we have seen, compared to the fundamental shift in the ground of Being that can occur when we extricate ourselves from this premature mingling with the instinctual flow of the daimon as he yearns toward the light of consciousness. But that shift requires yet more time, more preparation.

Were any images similar to this episode appearing in the minds of the inquisitors, or the poor "witches," during the trials? I suspect so, but with little psychological understanding. Instead daimonic encounters were summarily condemned as works of the devil. Apparently, the daimons needed to go underground at this point in history. For, during the three-hundred-year period of the witch craze, representatives of the official church not only demonized instinctual aspects of the religious imagination, but also enforced their position with terror, torture, and death. Never mind that in doing so they acted out the very forces they were intent on repressing. They combined public humiliation, torture, and death with lascivious spectacles, such as stripping women bare and inspecting them for signs of the devil. In so doing, they pushed the Great Mother forces, the remnants of the old religion and awe of the rites of Nature, into the collective cellar.

THE SACRED UNION SURVIVES

Meanwhile, the Christian mystics—always held in some suspicion by church authorities—actually perpetuated the pagan mystery of union with the divinity. Though pushed to an underground existence in the culture at large, the daimonic soul found its way into life through this cache of devotees of inner life. The mystics, of course, bathed their imaginal visitations with generous portions of religious attitude. The "bridal mystics," especially, envisioned God as a bridegroom who takes the soul in sexual embrace. In ecstatic rapture, God and the soul "melt into each other." They described such meetings as "storms of love."[18] Given the prevailing fearful atmosphere surrounding sexuality, it is remarkable that they used such a blatantly sexual image at all. Nelson Pike, in *The Phenomenology of Mysticism*, comments on the paradox of the frequent use of bridal imagery in a cultural milieu that debased and demonized sexuality:

> It would seem surprising that the mystics, who were themselves subject to the same tradition, and who for the most part, regarded themselves as strict followers of orthodox opinion, would choose the bridal metaphor as a means of expression in the present context. The mystical experience is thought by them to be the highest and finest experience one can have short of the beatific vision of God that will come in the next life. Didn't they themselves find some sort of discrepancy here?[19]

Justification for the bridal metaphor stemmed from the Old Testament *Song of Songs*. In their hands, the erotic "kiss of the mouth" is not a mere metaphor, but is worked so closely that it is hard to remember it is not literal.[20] Here is one example, quoted by Pike, from Jacques Nouet's *Man in Prayer:* "The soul . . . holds Him, embraces Him, clasps Him closely, and all on fire with love, she flows, she plunges, she buries and loses herself deliciously in God with sentiments of inconceivable joy."[21] The prevalence of these reports of erotic union with God should not be underestimated. One scholar of Christian mysticism concluded, "If one were to judge solely on the basis of the primary literature of the Christian mystical tradition, one would suppose that the *Song of Songs is*, by far, the most important book contained in either the Old or New Testament."[22] John of the Cross describes the soul's union with God boldly as an embrace:

> Oh Night, that led me, guiding night,
> Oh Night, far sweeter than the Dawn,
> Oh Night, that did so then unite The
> Loved with his Beloved, Transforming
> Lover in Beloved.[23]

St. Teresa of Avila's visionary experience of penetration by a fiery angel is even more explicit:

> The angel carried a long golden spear with a fiery tip. "With this he seemed to pierce my heart so that it penetrated to my entrails. When he drew it out, I thought he was drawing them out with it and he left me completely afire with a great love for God. The pain was so sharp that it made me utter several moans, and so excessive was the sweetness caused by this intense pain that one can never wish to lose it . . ."[24]

Bernini made this episode famous with a rendering in marble of an orgasmic St. Teresa receiving the plunging spear of the angel. Given the Inquisition with its negative attitude toward sexuality, it is not surprising that Teresa was distrustful of, and embarrassed by, such blatantly erotic transports.[25]

Undaunted by the reign of antibody, antisexual terror, the mystics' references to sensual union dominate their contemplative experience of God. Although they dutifully deny the carnality of their experiences, how rich must their imaginations have been to conjure up such enduring reports of sensuality? The ecstatic sexuality associated with mystical union, although colored by the context of the Middle Ages, resembles in many aspects the erotic encounter of daimon with body that I attempt to report here, now making its way into consciousness on a broader scale. For reasons beyond our current grasp, the Middle Ages isolated spirituality from sexuality. The spiritual components of orgasm became the exclusive preserve of the mystics, while their instinctual aspects appear to have been projected onto suspected witches. Sexuality was eventually depotentiated as a source of religious ecstasy and was considered legitimate only for procreation in the context of marriage (for those so weak they had to indulge), thus completing the final demonization of an instinctual force that was once recognized as the Divine.

The desacralizing of ecstatic, sexual energies was only one part of the cultural rejection of the forces of the Dark Mother.

EMBRACE OF THE DAIMON

Her destructive potential as death-giver was also condemned. In her role as destroyer, she has been cast in myth as the serpent, dragon, or sea monster to be killed by the hero in his quest. So reviled have her chthonic, destructive energies been in myth and legend that we take our aversion to these forces as a natural repugnance. For most people in our culture, these body-based daimonic energies evoke intolerable anxieties, and we tend to avoid allowing them into awareness by denial, diversion, or drugs. And yet, as Edward Whitmont suggests, these Dark Mother forces have been repressed and devalued collectively. Images of the Great Mother evoke our dread and horror—devouring, starving, engulfing, drowning, and dying.[26] Today, sexuality, along with other instinctual energies associated with the sex/death/ rebirth cycle—the daimonic—constellate the shadow, or most rejected and unacknowledged aspects, of our culture. We need to reclaim these energies we carry if we are to open wholeheartedly to the annihilating embrace of the daimon.[27] We begin to resacralize sexuality by acknowledging its shadow side of destruction and death, the dark Eros whose importance we may yet grasp.

DENIAL OF AND ATTRACTION TO VIOLENCE

We rarely consider the impact of this collective denial of the numinous daimonic on the instincts. The religious philosopher Antonio de Nicolas suggests that over time we incarnate the philosophies that guide our lives through "interiorization, linguistic behavior and the systematic use of [sense and perceptual] faculties."[28] That is, our ruling beliefs become part of the *structure of our bodies*, influencing the way we stand, breathe, walk, and speak. Likewise, when these beliefs are challenged, we feel in our bodily depths the anxiety and disorientation associated with their dismantling. Following this argument, we may have inherited a body pervaded by a tension that is part of our culture that results when natural destructive impulses meet the body armoring.

A paradoxical craving for violence for its own sake to release this tension may be one result. Edward Whitmont

SANDRA LEE DENNIS

noticed this phenomenon, which he associates with repressing the numinosity of destructiveness, "Violence, the urge to the destruction of form and the inflicting of bodily harm and death continue to exert a forceful, exciting, and invigorating attraction upon the ego." The undue excitement we get from this suppressed violence fuels the popularity of the hero or warrior image, that famous "butcher of his opponents" intoxicated by a satisfying of a sadistic power urge,[29] which has reemerged today in movie roles, for instance, played by Sylvester Stallone or Arnold Schwarzenegger. In computer games such as "Doom" and "Fury," these heroes proliferate. In cartoon land, they rule as Batman, Spiderman, and the Power Rangers. This repressed archetypal constellation may even help explain our propensity to go to war. In war, we project our destructive impulses onto the enemy. Sam Keen's *Faces of the Enemy* details this phenomenon of casting our destructive urges onto our latest foe, rather than acknowledging and claiming them as our own. These are but powerful rhythms of birth and death in our relation to the larger invisible worlds in which we participate.[30]

The mysterious, creative interplay of sexuality and aggression was portrayed in prehistory through the recently discovered images of the Sumerian underworld goddess Ereshkigal, and by the Greeks in the Gorgon-Medusa:

> The transformative Ereshkigal-Medusa dynamic is an expression of the deepest mystery of the life force, in which creation, destruction, change and recreation are but variations. . . . In the midst of the pain it inflicts, it instills its own peculiar ecstatic satisfaction. It gives birth to the forces of the dark twin, of Dionysus, aggression and destruction that were to be contained in the ancient sacrificial rites. Hence it is closely akin to, and often indistinguishable from, the rapture of religious ecstasy or sexual frenzy.[31]

This innate connection with the numinosities of regeneration constitutes the real daimon of violence. Whitmont believes the denial of this transpersonal, daimonic quality of sexuality, aggression, and the subsequent vulnerability of the human condition has led to their demonization and continued repression. Unfortunately the daimon becomes dangerous when denied and secularized. The ancient mysteries may have created ritual space for the enactment of orgiastic ritual, animal sacrifice or sexual congress as ways to collectively acknowledge and allow for the symbolic expression of these energies. In our culture, however, our destructive surgings have little legitimate collective outlet, except in projected form: war, political protest, threats toward "international criminals" the death penalty movement, and of course our fascination with media violence.[32]

In the evolutionary unfolding of human consciousness, differentiating ourselves from the matrix of life (the Dark Mother with her embodied sacred rites around sexuality, death, and rebirth) may have been part of the development of individuality—that heroic sense of *"I"* separate from the group and nature. This theory suggests we have had to distance ourselves from our ancestors' *participation mystique*, in the cycles of nature the Dark Goddess forces represent. Like a child separating from its mother, we had to turn our backs on Mother Nature until the seed of individual or heroic consciousness took root in us and grew strong. Richard Tarnas elaborates this idea as a conclusion to his intellectual masterpiece, *The Passion of the Western Mind:*

> For the evolution of the Western mind has been driven by a heroic impulse to forge an autonomous rational human self by separating it from the primordial unity with nature. . . . the evolution of the Western mind has been founded on the repression of the feminine—on the repression of undifferentiated unitary consciousness, of the *participation mystique* with nature: a progressive denial of the *anima mundi*, of the soul of the world, of the community of being, of the all-pervading, of mystery and ambiguity, of imagination, emotion, instinct, body, nature, woman.[33]

From this point of view, the hero's task may now have been accomplished, making room for the reemergence of nature's engulfing darkness as an active player in the psyche.[34] Tarnas concludes that reconnection with this repressed feminine has all along been an underlying goal of Western intellectual and spiritual evolution, the dominance of the masculine being merely a necessary step along that path. Heroic individuality now faces perhaps the most challenging evolutionary imperative of our time as it readies at last for a renewed inner relationship to the Mother Goddess's instinctual depths as "source, goal and immanent presence."[35]

But this separation necessarily calls forth a longing for a reunion with that which has been lost. . . . It is visible in the widespread urge to reconnect with the body, the emotions, the unconscious, the imagination and intuition. . . . *For the deepest passion of the Western mind has been to reunite with the ground of its being.* The driving impulse of the West's masculine consciousness has been its dialectical quest not only to realize itself, to forge its own autonomy, but also, finally, to recover its connection with the whole, to come to terms with the great feminine principle in life.[36]

CHRISTIANA MORGAN'S VISIONARY DESCENT

We owe a debt of gratitude to C. G. Jung for reintroducing the symbol of the Great Mother and writing at length about the importance of reclaiming the rejected feminine pole of the psyche as a necessary component in our growth toward a unified center or Self. Undaunted pioneer that he was, it appears that when it came to embracing the depths of instinct, Jung may still have been influenced by the distorting lens of heroic consciousness prevalent during his time. Claire Douglas has written an account of Jung's relationship to the archaic dark instincts in *Translate This Darkness*, an exploration of the visions of Christiana Morgan, who was one of his clients. Douglas claims that Jung drew heavily from Morgan's visions to formulate many of his conceptions of the psyche, such as the anima and animus, the Shadow and the Self.

He also used her visions as the focus of a lecture series he gave over a period of four years, now famous as *The Visions Seminars*, in which he concentrated on the unfolding of her extraordinary daimonic imagery.

In Christiana Morgan, Douglas believes, Jung found someone gifted with perfect imaginal "pitch" like his own. In her trances, marked by chthonic sensuality and erotic power, she delved into the collective unconscious and then surfaced to coherently translate what she found there.[37] In her imaginal descent she entered primal, matriarchal realms where ritual union seems to have occupied a central position. Douglas describes Morgan emerging daily from her world of dark gods where she engaged in "congress with bulls, green-eyed satyrs, libidinous stallions, golden youths, grape-leaved priests and writhing snakes", to each she opened herself, "drinking the wine and lifeblood they offered her."[38] The terrain she journeyed through resonates with forces of the daimonic, with unions and separations with the Dark Mother.

Jung characterized some of her visions of the archetypal Dark Mother as remnants of the animal maternal instinct, an instinct that is close to destructiveness.[39] One of her later images of a woman with many breasts sitting cross-legged, he described as a loathsome, archaic mother deity, remote, incommensurable, obscene and ugly, that reflected the horror and fear surrounding the tabooed instinctual mother. He believed the modern woman needed this horrid image to "increase her substance" and to balance the too-nice persona of the "good woman" of the time. However, he also acknowledged the personal and collective resistance to the forces the image represented. "One is absolutely against assimilating such a loathsome figure, it is too incompatible."[40] Douglas contends that images like this, along with Morgan's erotic encounters with animals and dark men, reptilian visitations, and recurrent birth and death themes, finally had a powerfully disturbing impact on Jung. She thinks he must have been shocked to discover in a woman this vast, dramatic, primitive unconscious, with its central goddess or anima figures.

She believes that although Jung was thrilled with Morgan's visions, he responded, understandably, through the gender-biased lens of his time that ultimately rejected the passionate, dynamic, annihilating feminine force, seeing it rather as an expression of inferiority that needed civilizing. Douglas shares these excerpts from Morgan's diaries to support her point. "You are like Brunnhilde," Morgan recorded Jung as having said as the visions came with more insistence, "You have never been broken in," implying the need to be tamed.[41] He suggested she drop all inner work and have another child. He began to restrain Morgan's imaginal flow, advising her to consult an etymological dictionary and to study myths that paralleled her visions. She reported that he told her, "to grow you must use your mind. If you only flow [with the image] then you reach a deep level where there is no tension—all levels become the same."[42] As if in response to Jung's reactions to her primitive erotic openings, her visions abruptly became detached and telegraphic, and Jung became more critical of her productions.[43]

We were not in the consulting room, so how can we ever know what Christiana, as client, needed to come to terms with in her upswelling psyche? Perhaps she did need to contain that tension. I have suggested, however, that when the flow of the image is stopped, one remains in the first stage of conscious relationship to the unconscious, the stage of mental understanding and insight, but arrests the daimonic eruption along with its assimilation into the body. Her visions reflect qualities of the *unio corporalis*, the meeting of the daimonic image with the body. They involve attraction and repulsion, the unleashing of tremendous energies of sexuality and destruction. In the process, the images themselves (animals, blood, sexuality, serpents) are transformed to reflect primordial nature. It appears that Jung's rational consciousness may have prevailed over the unfolding of the body knowledge fueling Morgan's imagery. Douglas speculates that Jung supported Morgan's journeying as long as she was going through a process similar to his own, but became tentative and threatened when he realized that she was involved in an unfamiliar, passionate landscape—"a woman's way"—an alternative world full of dynamic, loathsome images. She suggests these images simultaneously excited and repelled him but he ultimately chose to limit their force.[44]

Claire Douglas believes Christiana Morgan was laboring to bring birth to a new archetypal dynamic that is, as Tarnas so eloquently suggested, just coming to consciousness today—namely that of the heroine whose task it is on meeting the dragon of the dark feminine, not to slay it, but to keep it alive. This heroine[45] must, as the hero before her, separate from the unconscious fusion and then go on to enter into conscious relationship. Instead of defeating the primordial depths, however, she joins with them, as in this example of Morgan uniting with a Dionysian black god in a visionary blood ritual:

> I beheld a great Negro lying beneath a tree. In his hands were fruit. He was singing. I asked him, "What do you sing, oh Negro" and he answered me, "Little white child I sing to Darkness, to flaming fields, to the children within your womb." I said, "I must know you." He answered, "Whether you know me or not, I am here." While he sang, blood poured from his heart in slow, rhythmic beats. It flowed in a stream covering my feet. . . . I followed the stream. . . . Then I was afraid and walked about like one demented. At length I heard the Negro say. . . . "Now you are wedded to me."[46]

Her contemporary environment that called for restraining the so-called primitive must have colored Morgan's descriptions. Still, the implication of erotic union is clear. Since the dark erotic forces Morgan contacted are just beginning to be understood *in our time* as positive elements of the creative life force, we can hypothesize that neither Morgan nor Jung were ready to embrace these daimonic energies. Perhaps Morgan's capacity for the passionate feelings that connected the forces of death and destruction with the heart of the erotic needed to be curtailed, as the time had not yet come for the conscious acceptance of these archetypal currents. While Jung may also have had good reason to fear a psychotic break and turned Morgan away from her visions for this reason, I feel Douglas' analysis has intuitive appeal in giving a fuller picture of the dynamics involved.[47] Morgan's visions were clearly pointing her toward the annihilating forces of the "flow" when Jung counseled her to stop them, directing her instead, to the research and study of books on related subjects. Jung understood the daimonic intellectually, even intuitively, being so far ahead of his time, but it seems likely that he was not yet ready to provide the emotionally accepting, *somatically oriented* container necessary to continue to explore these daimonic initiations.

Thus, in the end, Morgan's visions remained "untranslated." Although she, with Jung's initiative, guidance, and support, appears to have discovered a new psychic territory, a path to creative integration of the spiritual and the chthonic, Morgan bequeathed to those coming behind her the task of translating and giving voice to this territory. Anyone exploring this terrain now faces the challenge of attempting to translate the messages by following the imaginal stream to its meeting with the cellular body. How do we communicate knowledge gained in the atmosphere of the nonverbal, irrational body through the medium of the rational, the written word?

As I mentioned earlier, the synonyms for irrational from Microsoft's Thesaurus include "unsound, fallacious, preposterous, inconceivable, inconsistent, specious, untenable, wrong." I find this list daunting, and an accurate expression of the prejudices one faces in attempting such a communication. Still, I offer here one translation of this darkness of the irrational—of the dynamic instinctual forces, the daimonic energies of Mother Nature—which are unleashed when the image unites with the body. For I also believe we live in a time when we are called to go beyond the metaphoric meaning, the conceptualization of the *coniunctio* image, to its depths of embodiment, to bring these numinous forces one step closer to conscious awareness.

EMBRACE OF THE DAIMON

SENSUAL KNOWLEDGE AND EROTICISM

Some realms of soul may be charted by ignoring the irrational body. But many lie hidden in its recesses, and must be *felt through* to gain deeper knowledge of human nature. For the daimon to incarnate, we must first conquer our distrust of elemental bodily processes—raw sexuality, sensuality, bleeding, pain, rage, lust, terror, grief—and engage the naturally-flowing body as companion in our explorations. Our bodies claim no lesser position, to use William Blake's phrase, than that portion of soul visible to the five senses.[48] The sensual carries its own unique connection to the transcendent and can lead us ever closer to the subtle senses capable of discerning the invisibles.

Before closing this chapter, I want to consider another alchemical description, that of "quintessence." The quintessence was the missing ingredient that came from the body necessary to complete the alchemical operation of the unio corporalis, the reunion of the soul with the body. This quintessence was also that elusive quality that Jung called the numinosity of the body. Hillman refers to it as the spark of Dionysus embedded in the body, and, I believe it is what Luce Irigaray calls this "Very repressed, censored, forgotten thing to do with the body." This numinosity of the body turns out to be the very thing we fear, but must learn to trust about ourselves. I suggest that this quintessence refers to the annihilating eroticism of the daimonic.

It refers specifically to the imaginal drive to orgasmic union with symbolic representatives of this Great Dark Mother inherent in each human being. We are unaccustomed to sustaining this level of eroticism except perhaps in an actual intimate relationship. But the daimons release waves of bliss as a byproduct of their reunion with the body, with or without a partner. In the Western tradition we put much attention on learning to cope with pain and suffering as a route to transcendence. The integration of the daimonic soul image asks something more from us. It asks that we increase our capacity for sustaining the other end of the sensual continuum. Our capacity for ecstasy, pleasure, and bliss must be stretched to accommodate the creative daimons being released into our inner world.

CHAPTER 6

Developing the Subtle Senses

We are bees of the invisible . . .
—Rainer Rilke [1]

SCIENTISTS AS WELL AS MYSTICS now affirm that we live in a world based on interconnectedness and relatedness. The imaginal opens on to this connective reality. When we enter this domain from our usual perch of rational "objectivity," the rules of engagement change, for we are entering a radically different realm remarkably similar to the one physicists now describe.[2] In her book "States of Grace," Charlene Spretnak discusses how difficult it is for our modern minds to absorb the implications of the bizarre worldviews of postmodern science that dissolve the familiar dualisms of matter and energy, particles and waves, into strange overriding interactive fields.

Integration of these new insights about the nature of reality requires a great leap that we are uncertain how to take. How can we come to realize that we live in an intelligent cosmos, in this relational, participatory universe the physicists describe? Quoting the Vietnamese monk Thich Nhat Hanh, Spretnak calls it the "palpable gestalt of unitive existence."[3] Since we have been taught to deny subtle perceptions that do not fit within a rationalist worldview, how can we ever even begin to develop subtle senses capable of perceiving the "dance of creation, disintegration and recreation?"[4] Spretnak argues, and I agree, that we need not just ideas but also experience to attempt this foray into a more fundamental way of seeing. We need *experiential* knowledge of this interconnectedness. To gain this knowledge, she suggests we engage ourselves in practices that will open our minds to receive subtle realities: practices such as yoga, meditation, contemplation, prayer, ritual, or artistic endeavors. We also need to develop better modes to express these realities, modes more congruent with their acausal, irrational quality, such as metaphor, poetry, and mythic narrative. These practices and modes of expression together may engage the imagination and help *reveal* this deeper reality in which we all participate.

Because of our deeply held commitment to a rational view of reality (defined by the reach of the five senses), we need to "suspend disbelief" in the irrational and the invisible in order to develop the faculties of imaginal sight, hearing, and sensing. You might even say that an element of "faith" is required to access this way of knowing. I am not using faith in the sense of belief, but a faith that is based on actual experience, "the substance of things hoped for, the evidence of things not seen,"[5] a faith built on recall of non-rational unitive moments, "peak experiences," if you like. Perhaps such a faith seeds the religious attitude that Jung felt essential for confronting the unconscious.

To explore the imaginal, we need training in the techniques of religion, psychology, or art that will give us experiences of connective reality. We should also apply these techniques to the point of developing at least a modicum of *experiential faith* based on *substance*, personal *evidence* for the existence of a numinous reality. In other words, a person must be ready to receive transcendent, subtle knowledge. The eye of the mind must be developed.[6] If we are still devoted to the Cartesian view that what we see is what we get, that higher worlds cannot possibly exist, neither these methods nor the "immersion" I will be discussing in more detail will open the doors of subtle perception.[7]

Another way to approach imaginal life requires that we learn to place doubt behind experience, realizing its crucial importance. This attitude assumes a scale of values that reverses the classic method of developing the intellect whereby we are taught to doubt everything before accepting it.[8] Our typical "modern" worldview explains away the entire visionary realm as merely one reality among many, and insists that we still have no way of knowing the truth of what we experience. Rationally, we may agree with this line of thought, but as we shift our consciousness through experiential practices, we enter a realm incommensurable with the rational, capable of more subtle perceptions than can ever be perceived by, and thereby proven, to the rational mind, as the colors of a sunset can never be "proven" to the blind.

DEVELOPMENT OF A METHOD FOR THE MADNESS

Wrestling with my own demonic explosions, my own baby daimons, I inadvertently stumbled on to a method for developing the subtle senses and encouraging imaginal unfolding. I came of age in the '60s, when the Siren's call toward expanded consciousness had reached a fever pitch. In my early 20's I began experimental meditative forays, took zealously to regular work on myself, and continued practicing for many years in and out of group settings. Certainly I was on my way to purity and enlightenment! Calamitously, my emerging sainthood came to an abrupt halt when I became pregnant in my late 30s.

As many women will understand, the turbulence of the first ten weeks of pregnancy can resemble a seemingly endless toss in a small boat on ten-foot squalls. Nauseating perturbations completely defeated my concentrative faculties, and, of course, with them went my witnessing meditative practices. By this time, these practices had become a lifeline I counted on for a sense of identity (spiritual seeker), meaning ("to wake up"), and self-containment (mindful focus). Without this lifeline, I was left adrift in disorienting forces. Flu-like sensations, intense anger, fear, grief, and weird imaginal fragments dominated my day. Apparently, mindfulness, "self-remembering," was a fine method for centering and exploring inner life as long as primal energies were in check, but woefully inadequate for the geared-up instinctual beast. My years of holiness and concentration evaporated into a fruitless and ludicrous venture at best—like trying to restrain a wild bear with a kite string.

By force of these circumstances, I figured I faced the following choices: 1) to try to regain analytic pointedness (an impossible exercise), 2) to boil with resentment at being helplessly tossed to and fro on the tumultuous sea of my changing body, or 3) to give up and throw myself wholly into my bodily woes. Though it went against my experience and training, eventually I chose the third option. Initially, my resistance to the irrational states of mind associated with these amorphous bodily states caused me much distress. I was convinced I was falling into hellish realms, losing my mind.

My inability to stay "present" to these primal upsurgings alternately angered, and then overwhelmed me with fright. But, gradually I was able to let go of my ponderous centering techniques and dive into the instinctual, emotional cauldron. I remember the first day I took an energetic plunge into the alien experience of my body. Lying on a dark green coverlet, between fits of running to our tiny bathroom to cope with waves of nausea, I finally just let myself "become" the nauseousness. Flowing into the sensations, I noticed, to my amazement that the (by now very familiar) sickening feeling had changed into an almost magical expansion and lightness. I had been rescued from the hellish realms and from that point on, my relation to my inner life took a new direction guided by immersing myself in sensation and feeling.

So began my "embodied immersion"[9] Embodied immersion, I learned, goes beyond the witnessing facility that forms with regular meditation practice. It develops the subtle senses essential for imaginal perception, the faculties I would need to explore the daimonic realm. Other approaches resemble this simple body-centered method. Mindell's amplification of body sensation, Gendlin's Focusing, and the Gestalt practice of identification with the image all suggest a similar process. I find that each nuance of a new approach can help in exploring these realms, so I add my own voice to the work of these pioneers. Many others have also recognized the importance of including the body in accessing the unconscious. As Joan Chodorow put it, "We may sense, as the alchemists did, that if spirit has been imprisoned in matter, then it is to matter we must go to discover and release spirit."[10] A sensate, body-based approach encourages the unfolding of the images inhabiting our "cells" in a way other approaches do not.[11] Someone as verbal and intuitive as Hillman even recommends a sensate reading of images, claiming we are all sensation types when we are seized by an image. "The moment you leave sensing out of imagining, it is imagining that becomes sheer fantasy, mere imaginings, only a dream."[12]

Contemporary scholars of religious studies have noted that the experiences of mystics prove that bodily exercises also are an indispensable precondition for gaining access to certain states of mind. In other words, spiritual practices "bear a particular epistemology,"[13] a certain route to knowledge. Discussing the meditation exercises of Ignatius de Loyola, de Nicolas describes how meditation dismembers the original sense of false security we gain from the parameters of sense-based experience. A meditator sensitizes the body by the exercises, thereby opening to new kinds of sensations. She imposes "a continuous violence in the form of nonphysical dismemberment" gradually becoming a "dismembered sensorium whose senses the primordial images may then use."[14] These primordial or original images may be encoded in our brain and tissue, and liberated as daimons through consciousness-raising strategies (techniques of religion, psychology, and art).

As the anthropologist goes to Trobriand to live among the Trobrianders, we go to the imaginal to learn its secret.[15] We participate, immerse ourselves, in the sense Richard Tarnas uses the term in discussing the relation of the psyche to the cosmos. He explains that the emerging unitive worldview implicates us as intimate participants in a cosmic greater mind. Our imaginal experience gives us a window on that greater mind or larger context. Tarnas describes what he sees as a grand, evolving archetypal way of knowing:

EMBRACE OF THE DAIMON

> The organizing principles of this epistemology are
> symbolic, nonliteral, and radically multivalent in
> character, suggesting a nondualistic ontology that is
> metaphorically patterned "all the way down."[16]

Okay, this is challenging. What he means, I believe, is that from this archetypal perspective, individual and trans-personal aspects of the psyche "radically interpenetrate." Since the psyche is a microcosm of the whole universe, we ourselves become a tiny organ of the universe's own process of self-revelation.[17] Thus, embodied participation with the image opens to an imaginal world we can interpret on many different levels. An image may impinge upon us from apparently different levels of the psyche: from an actual biographical memory, from the transitional birth experience, from the days of our ancestors, from past lives, or even from collective events, such as the Holocaust, Vietnam, or witch burnings. The level from which the image arises gives different nuances to the experience, but the multivalent image resonates through all these levels, bringing light to each. From the archetypal viewpoint, each part of the imagining body-psyche contains the sensations of the archetypal images of origin. Through these subtle-body sensations, we can begin to feel how the outer and inner worlds continually interrelate, creatively unfolding new possibilities.[18]

BODY-CENTERED IMMERSION

I had no suspicion of the potentials of this realm I was entering in my early forays into bodily states.[19] I began to simply focus on the most prominent sensation and allowed it to expand. I would allow it to expand to become as large as it wished. Often tension or a pain appeared to fill the whole world with one big ache until it dispersed into a play of delicious energies. This body-centered presence began to open new territory, territory with a more perceptual (visionary) and less conceptual (insightful) basis than that explored by mindfulness. It opened to a land of dramatic possibilities. I was exploring a new world of deconstructed sensation, my ego or sense-of-self being teased out of the fragments of sensation that dispersed all around me. I had arrived on foreign shores, yet some call of familiarity also beckoned, some feeling of home.

It was not until many months after my daughter was born that the shocking images associated with these fragments of sensation began to break through with a vivid insistence. At this point, I really thought I was a candidate for Bellevue.[20] After years of "witnessing," I was accustomed to dismissing any imagery as a mere byproduct of nervous activity. Well-practiced in ignoring images, I routinely withdrew my attention from them. But immersion in the strongest sensations associated with an image—the sharpness of the butcher's knife, the redness of a shirt, the bristling tickle of a rat's hair—compelled my attention in a new way. Tentatively, I decided to grant psychic space to these images arising from bodily sensations. I had learned to merge with my troublesome bodily experience only to discover a liberating flow. What if I related similarly to these dark, disturbing, strangely numinous images? As I slowly began to allow myself to mingle even with the horrible images, a more systematic approach to their exploration developed, and they began to reveal more of their nature.

I have formulated the following "steps" in an effort to communicate this process of sensate immersion. Of course, in outlining discrete steps, I violate the nonlinear quality of the imaginal, but I thought they may be helpful to other would-be explorers of daimonic territory.[21] These steps are:

1. *Attend* to the predominant sensation of the moment. Often this will be a sensation we normally avoid, some unpleasant feeling, hiding just beneath numbness, disorientation, or restlessness, revealed by focused attention.[22]
2. Let the sensation *expand* to fill the whole body.

EMBRACE OF THE DAIMON

3. *Open* to any imagery that forms in relation to the sensation. Ask, for instance, the sensation to speak or show more: "What are you trying to tell me?"
4. Once an image forms (it can be a sight, sound or smell), *permit amplification* of the sensation from the impact of the image, allowing a delicate titration from image back to sensation.
5. Attend mainly to the sensation, holding the image lightly, and *detect the slightest pleasant sensation* amid any discomfort, revulsion or pain.
6. *Shift focus,* "identity" to the pleasurable sensation (despite the pull back into the habitual identification with, or numbing to, the predominant discomfort).
7. Finally, *allow* the pleasant, expansive aspect of the phenomenon to grow and to carry the image and identity along with it.

When attending to these normally avoided sensations, I often panicked, encountering darkness, dizzying emptiness, or space. Immersion, however, implies "cooking" in these panic-inducing sensations. Sometimes in an effort to focus on impressions of "emptiness," for instance, body boundaries were gradually erased, until "I" became no more than the smile of the Cheshire cat in the sustaining blackness. Eventually, the emptiness would push against some new body tension or feeling that would not dissolve in its presence. *These were the points at which the daimonic imaginal was most likely to emerge.* Startling at first, the daimons seemed almost to dare engagement in a hide-and-seek game, elusively departing and reappearing once more.

These images do stir ambivalence, for when the daimon appears, one encounters the dilemma of Beauty and the Beast. As we have seen, imaginal counterparts of painful, agitated, or tense body states are not attractive. Violent, sadomasochistic, crazed, or scatologically inclined, they can be cruel and threatening. Often they come in the form of strange beasts, insects, reptiles, or

96

rodents, with demonic overtones. Naturally, we resist these images. Why should we embrace them?

As long as we mentally reject these images, or even simply watch them, the first steps toward immersion are not possible. Simple mental acceptance of their presence must precede engaging these images. This presents a larger stumbling block than we might think because of the taboo surrounding the dark content of the daimons. "No," we say, "too foreign, forbidden, frightening." As the torturing, murderous image, for instance, pushes to be released from consciousness, we fight back as it sledgehammers, stabs, rapes, and strangles its way through our unconscious attachment to it. Our resistance only increases its resolve. The sensations of the daimonic image alarm us, but we bring ourselves even more pain and tension when we fight the image. Fortunately, if we can allow ourselves to feel the beauty in the beast, that is, if we can locate the daimon's libidinous pull—that pleasure amid the tension—it offers a key to unlocking its potential and can serve as a hook that draws us into the frightening, strange sensations and their images.

Sensations and their images require time to build to daimonic proportions. These images do not come every day. They grow to maturity as the feeling tone and its image come again and again to consciousness, until we arrive at a certain understanding. The image may have to visit us again and again over months or years in dreams, waking fantasy, or imaginal episodes before all elements—thoughts, forms, feelings, sensations, memories—come together, and the full-blown daimon arises. Conscious immersion in an image of rape or torture, for instance, may take years because of the range of attitude, emotion, and body feeling that must be opened, including the entire spectrum of the experiences of both the rapist and the victim that the image implies.

Immersion in imaginal realms may develop as a conscious practice, or it may come more spontaneously. Some people seem naturally to immerse themselves as part of artful living. Coping with crisis: death, illness, war, assault, poverty, madness, or deep involvement with any creative endeavor that taps the unconscious, from raising children to house building to writing poetry, may spark an immersion in this turbulent world. Serious religious or meditative life opens onto these daimonic vistas, and the great difficulties of committed relationship also reliably activate archetypal forces. Any life open to the enlarging mysteries of human nature knows the taste of immersion at the edges of consciousness where we live with the daimons.

In practices aimed directly at immersion in the imaginal world, we amplify the sensations to help bring the image to light, so that it presents itself as clearly as possible in its visual, somatic, and affective components, becoming like a body within our body. Clarification and intensification constellate a tremendously charged energy pattern: a veritable presence with which to contend. At this point, our *relationship to* the energetic image counts for much and determines its impact upon us. The daimon can dement or enlighten, sicken or vitalize, destroy or nurture. If we, in the depths of the subtle body, accept and embrace its energy pattern, the unique presence of the daimon, it releases its "redeeming" aspects—the essential wisdom, or strength, or beauty, for example, at the heart of the image. At the moment we completely and consciously receive the daimon, the alchemical process reaches its culmination, and the lead of the aversive image turns to some hue of the golden numinosity at its core. This cannot be forced, as the daimon always takes the lead in opening us to the new. "Some hue of golden numinosity" represents my feeble attempt to describe what is always an unprecedented, surprising quality symbolized by the daimonic image. It comes into sight like a bewitching color we have never envisioned before.

THE REUNION WITH THE BODY

One day, when we feel we have finally come to terms with our depths, met and accepted the major demons we harbor—when all is seemingly settled, the emerging daimons come to make their claim upon us. Not bad enough that they have insinuated themselves in our minds and feelings, they begin to insist on reentering our bodily life. It is at this point—the point of the *unio corporalis*—that we, as members of a body-denying, reason and light-adoring culture generally fail to participate in their dark endeavor, even those of us committed to the inner life. For, the images require more from us now than cohabitation and tolerance. Now, to truly accept their insistent embrace, we must be willing to make a sacrifice, a sacrifice we are not eager to make, for that is the sacrifice of our fundamental sense-of-self.

Not that we are unpracticed at loosening the grip of our habitual self-image after years of insights requiring us to alter our idea of what kind of person we actually are. Insights help us change the inhabitants of the house in which we live. I am talking now about altering the frame and foundation of the house itself. Our sense-of-self rests firmly on the foundation of our habitual physical sensations. Because our normal sense of ourselves has been body-ego centered for decades, most of the time we feel that we are this body-based "I." As a byproduct of the immersion practice of letting sensations expand, our sense of ourselves begins to expand, too. Eventually, the sense of "I" shifts, if we allow it, if ego can let go, to the containing consciousness or soul, which we can detect as a quality of "presence." Such a shift unveils a delicate fragility, a vulnerability to experience we may never have suspected we carry within us.

This is the radical, subtle-body receptivity that encourages the reunion of the image with the body, that part of us that attracts and invites the daimonic presence into itself. As I discussed earlier, the quintessential "magical substance" that allows this union to take place, the numinosity of the body, appears to derive from this dynamic receptivity (Adam's pose receiving the touch of God the Father in the Sistine Chapel hints at the quality), a "feminine" quality. "Dynamic receptivity" cries for a new name—the connotations of "receptive" fail to describe the magnetic force that draws the image inexorably into this world of the senses. Not passively receptive, but luminously poised to participate, to receive whatever comes, this powerful receptivity reflects a curious, expectant welcoming of the unknown. It implies a predisposition toward emptiness, blackness, night, and the promise of change, death, and renewal. Such receptivity expresses nothing less than an articulation of our elementary particulate nature, a willingness to be torn apart in an instant as we meet the onrushing force of the daimon. (I am aware I could also be describing the erotic core of feminine sexual power. Deep in the belly of the woman, both physical and psychic, we find an elixir of receptive dissolution.) This radical receptivity receives the daimonic image in a shower of subtle-body orgasmic sensations to effect a metamorphosis—a profound alteration in our sense of identity.

Each daimonic union brings joy, and eventually grief. The joy of participating in this larger world, the joy of being "home" of belonging, the joy of connection, dissolution, ongoing change, the joy of knowing who we are in that moment, all amid grief at the loss of the dearly loved, familiar "I." To flow into a greater world that is announcing itself, a segment of bodily identity must be released, slowly transforming our sense not just of who we are, but what we are. Was Shakespeare not correct then, "We are such stuff as dreams are made on..."? As we have seen, experiences of union precipitate a darkening. Following our epiphanies, some hours, days, or more rarely, even weeks or months pass, and we begin to feel depressed, despondent, miserable, and empty.

For the loss of these parts of ourselves means a change in the configuration of who we feel ourselves to be. The "I" is not the same after these little deaths precipitated by the numinous infusion. We may go through dizzying disorientation, a sense of fragmentation, and other radically unfamiliar states. On returning to the body, the ego suffers these effects of reunion with the imaginal. It mourns over the little corpses of itself, and the necessary cleanup of the now mortified and putrefying inner beings it has been. The remaining sense of "I" gathers around and weeps and moans. As we change, our outer life, too, will change. Outwardly, we may become ineffective, dispirited, isolated, or depressed. However, a consolidation of the remaining aspects of self takes place. After some time, the bereft "I" becomes steady enough again, ready once more to fly into the arms of containing consciousness. It will still hold on to those parts of itself most reluctant to be let go. They will be subject to the purification ritual of the next stage in the imaginal nuptials. More on this darkening process comes later.

DIFFERENTIATING FUSION/MERGING AND IMMERSION

I think that it is necessary to address the technical problem of merging or fusion before going further with this discussion, because I know it is important to try to make a distinction between merging and the immersion I have been describing. Fusion with the image is generally discouraged in analytic practice. Such identification with the numinous power of the image supposedly leads to ego inflation and grandiosity—an unrealistic, eventually destructive position that encourages the building of new illusions, rather than fostering self-knowledge. Fusion is said to be a psychological defense, a way of protecting oneself from pain. To escape from the unbearable in our lives, we give ourselves up by merging with the Other.

I suggest that we take another look at fusion. The admonition against it may stem from our general preference for heroic individuality and separateness, and our suspicion of their antithesis—any sort of merging. All states of merging are not bad. Some are but a stage in an unconscious creative process, representing a rest and recharging at the deepest levels of our being, a rest that satisfies a longing to return to a pre-individuated cosmic oneness with the matrix of life. I contend that rather than discouraging these states, we ought to encourage them, for the capacity to merge contains elements of surrender and openness that constitute a central aspect of all expansive unions. More experience with these states could help balance certain people who find themselves isolated in their self-sufficiency.

Merging and separateness are both necessary for "immersion." Merging alone has more a palliative than a healing impact, resembling more an isolated experience than a life-changing encounter. Some traditions recognize the positive potential in merged states. Visualization and meditation on certain saints or deities encourage fused identification as a way to attain the object of meditation. This sort of fusion "practice" occurs as the image emerges from consciousness and may help activate the instinctual energies of the image as part of the process of gaining insight.

Still, as Jessica Benjamin points out, "The capacity to enter into states in which distinctness and union are reconciled underlies the most intense experience of adult erotic life."[23] How can we learn to recognize the difference between a restful, delightful fusion and an immersion that births the daimonic imaged? The difference is subtle. The distinction, I believe, turns on where we find the sense of "I." Has the "I" entered into the experience of the image (fusion), is it part of our own presence (immersion), or is it located in the "third" entity—that of the relationship itself (union or transcendence)? Although, ultimately, each person needs to develop the art of differentiating these states of mind through a practiced *feel* for such encounters, I offer a few further suggestions for recognizing the difference.

The experience of *fusion* resembles the relation of a small child to her mother. The mother subsumes the child. "I" am lost in her larger presence, which we may undergo positively (an engulfing divinity), or negatively (a harrowing tormentor), or some combination of the two. The sense of self or ego remains weak, not well formed enough to survive a dissolution in the arms of this larger consciousness. Danger signals flash. Signs that fusion is operative in inner or outer relationship include an obsessive hunger for the Other, a clinging, or desperation, and a tendency to rush into the relationship. These signs alternate with panicked flight, withdrawal, and distancing to avoid the seductive engulfment. Often we will need a "hit" of the adored person or a meditative practice to feel okay. Compulsivity sets the tone. Internally, the daimon tends to appear and reappear unchanged, with obsessive force. Finally, while the sensations of fusion may be blissful, the sense of an alchemical bodily alteration through the contact does not occur, nor does the sense of a third presence form, the presence of the relationship itself.

At the first stage in the process of union, as we build a more realistic self-image through insight, some tendencies toward fusion may need to be curtailed until ego-strength builds. However, we easily overemphasize the threat of merging. A related danger presents just as great a difficulty. The insistent warnings against merging (voiced in therapeutic settings), in combination with our collective history of rejecting the dark instinctual, instill such a deep distrust of the unifying urgings of the imaginal that we unknowingly may continue to block the daimon's eroticism, or impulse to merge. Again, what was appropriate at one stage to help keep a weak ego from fragmenting or blowing itself up, has now become a defense, hiding a deeper fear of alteration of self that the pending union threatens to bring. When insight needs to be integrated, our failure to surrender to the daimon's embrace blocks the contact we so badly need: the contact with deep strength, vision, love, and creativity residing in the image.

On the other hand, once the instinctual energies have been freed and the mature daimonic image appears, mere fusion with the image stands in the way of true union. Immersion with the energies of the daimonic image can collapse into fusion if it occurs before consciousness has developed sufficiently to bear the erotic tension between a separate identity and union. The entire atmosphere is one hallmark of sustaining the self-sense in face of the numinous other. Once the ego trusts enough to release into larger consciousness, however, *immersion* brings us into contact with the instinctual roots of the image without relinquishing our own ground. Such culminating unions are rare, often coming after long dark periods. Such an inner union occurs between "equals," as between two lovers in sexual embrace. A tone of surrender surrounds the encounter, and subtle alchemical changes appear to result for both partners. In imaginal realms, the daimon appears to change, too, through its union with the body.

EMBRACE OF THE DAIMON

The line between immersion in the image and union is then more theoretical than real. Once we enter into *union* with the image, the image often begins to shape shift. Classically (but not necessarily), the image gains more human features through the union. We are filled with the liquid presence of the daimon, and the sense of "I" now rests in the "third," a palpable presence born of the union that can feel like a god or goddess—a spiritual force (the Holy Ghost?)—forming a triangular relationship with the body-self and the daimonic Other.[24] This radical shift opens the doors to visionary awareness.

PERSONAL OR COLLECTIVE PROCESSES

Jung thought the personal Shadow—those hidden, repressed parts of ourselves—had to be integrated before we could contain images from the collective. We know now that the psyche doesn't always follow such linear processes. We seem to be like radio receivers, pre-programmed to pick up certain signals or archetypal patterns. From our earliest days, these patterns express themselves through our experiences, leaving their traces on our personal histories. The loud, dynamic, dominant child will attract a different life than the quiet, sweet, submissive one. Why? Environment, type or archetype? Perhaps all of the above. The personal becomes a way of illuminating the archetypal, and our recurring images, in turn, inform our understanding of our history and daily lives. Anyone involved in depth work knows how easily we mix the personal with the collective, the private pain with the existential dilemma or spiritual darkness. And regardless of how long or how deeply we plumb the depths, shards of biographical truth continue to emerge amid the archetypal material.

Still, differentiating the collective from the personal image hones our imaginal discriminating faculties. Is this an image we should watch, "feed" dialogue with, immerse ourselves in, submit to, act out? Or should we banish it altogether from awareness? For the bulk of the images that make up the subject of this book, we traditionally, perhaps unwisely, have chosen this last option, assuming that impersonal energies are personal. To the extent that we ban certain images in ourselves, we all qualify as iconoclasts.

We allow images and their feelings to develop if we invest too heavily in either the personal or collective interpretation of the image. We miss the richness a multi-leveled perspective can bring. Biographical material releases buried insights into our individual nature, while the impersonal deepens our understanding of the collective and our place in it. We need both to enlarge our humanity. Furthermore, focusing on difficult collective images, such as those of nuclear holocaust, war, genocide, or the suffering of innocents, can be a politically correct way to avoid facing personal pain. Facing personal pain requires integrating undeveloped emotions, such as terror or rage, and immature, pre-verbal parts of ourselves, such as woundedness and fragmentation, which may be highly ego-alien. Such personally tinged material threatens our sense of self in a way the impersonal does not.

Insight often wells up in connection with painful *personal* memories or intense feelings that need to be held, heard, expressed, and released. Such an insight is likely to come as a fragment of personal history, sometimes disguised in dream dress. The rejecting mother becomes a knife, the seductive father, a wolf. These images, as they connect with the affects and memories with which they are associated, gradually begin to melt away, losing their charge and their insistence in the psychic repertoire. Often, as they dissolve, a numinous presence will begin to appear, as though these personal images had been a veil, preventing the daimon from emerging.

The collective image has a different flavor, though it, too, may overlap with a personal image. The collective image may appear to be only personal at first. If we relate to the image as merely personal, however, its deeper implications, its call toward the collective, may be missed just at the point we seem to be called upon to act for the community. For instance, one client felt the image of a knife-stab to the heart as a child being abandoned. As the feeling began to expand into the subjective sense of the heart breaking open, she sensed the pain of "all abandoned children" and for that moment she opened to a numinous, timeless dimension of connectedness with the rest of humanity.[25] Tibetan practice encourages this taking on the pain and suffering of others that the collective image can stimulate as a means of going beyond our private, personal problems.

Too much focus on the personal dimension of the image blocks this connection to the numinous collective backdrop of our individual history. When everything is taken on a personal level, we spend our time in its limiting circle, never realizing how the collective may require us to hear its message and deepen our understanding of the collective and our place in its larger world. As another example, women have for too long accepted collective denigration, trivialization, and abuse in images of the bitch, or witch, or nag, and taken it as a reflection of their personal worth, rather than seeing through to the archetypal numinosity and strength implied by such powerful images. We may develop a more realistic, stronger ego by focus on the personal, but we block out the larger archetypal ground of commonality through which we taste our intimate participation in the world—the *participation mystique*—and from which develops a new, yet ancient, larger sense of self as part of the *anima mundi*.

Generational or family images also arise. When they do, we sense that the feelings and their accompanying images come not from our personal lives, but from the experience of our "ancestors." Like a psychic familial legacy, such images come forth in the form of the ancestors themselves, or through more impersonal bodily experiences. For instance, a man may experience the contractions and phantom pains of the final stages of giving birth, including pushing and delivery, throughout which he senses the presence of his grandmother. He learns later that his grandmother delivered his mother by cesarean section. Through his phantom delivery he seems to have gone through the final stage of the birthing for his grandmother. The physical and physiological relief that accompanies such experiences defies reason. The idea of a recurring family image at least fits these episodes. Who knows why we might be called upon to complete business, or resolve situations our forebears left undone? We only know the phenomenon occurs with some regularity in subtle-body work. We need to be willing to hold any powerful image that emerges on many levels at once, open to mine the full range of meaning-giving potential.

A NOTE ON THE SENSE OF "I" AND THE SUBTLE BODY

To allow the daimonic image to penetrate the body, and infuse us with its meaning-bearing presence, requires faith and openness, but especially it requires a letting go or a suspension of the sense of "I." Many have speculated on the nature of the "I." Most wisdom traditions acknowledge its presence and outline ways to deal with it. Whether a tradition supports the notion that we arrive for our earthly existence with a spiritual essence or soul, or the idea that we can develop in time a connection with a Divine source outside our usual sense-of-self, most agree that the individual separate sense of "I" represents an obstacle to connecting with a larger existence. Identified as the source of vanity in the Christian tradition, known as Maya in the Buddhist world, and recognized as the ego or self in the psychological, who is this "I"? Who is this "I" that inhabits our bodies, takes credits for our successes, laments our defeats, introduces itself to others, but primarily gives us that sense of ME, the peculiar flavor we associate with ourselves? Many—whole schools of thought—much more qualified than I have tried to answer this question, and I do not presume to more than glance at it here, and only as much as is needed to advance this discussion about the "I" relationship to the imaginal.

The sense of ourselves, we are told, takes time to develop. It seems that we are born with an undifferentiated, boundless sense of ourselves. Merged as we have been with our mother's body, we participate deeply in her existence, our individual psychological boundaries not yet formed. Later, painstakingly, a separate sense of "I" unfolds, passing through many pitfalls that may impede its development and leave us with a variety of wounds or weaknesses. The newly hatched "I" allows for a certain navigation in the world we could not accomplish without it. In this sense, the "I" is an ally, giving a sense of security, of psychological home base, from which we go forth to face the uncertainties of this cold world into which we have come from a warm encompassing womb. As we grow up, our entire identity gradually begins to adhere to a separate sense of "I" and we lose our connection to the larger, boundless world of childhood.

Once a participant in the unbounded matrix of the womb (and who knows what cosmic travels prior to that aquatic incarnation), we attach our sense of who we are to our caretakers and eventually to their images internalized in our skin-encapsulated bodies, accepting the images of those others as parts of our "I". Object-relations theorists, particularly, have developed a detailed map of the stages in the development of an ego-self and the ways in which ego as a "structure-building" process can go wrong. While secular psychological approaches see the development of the self as the last step in psychological maturity, the wisdom traditions indicate that, if we are to journey beyond the sense-based world in tandem with which the "I" has been constructed, we must eventually set aside this edifice that has required so many years to construct.

What happens to this "I" in the immersion process of imaginal reunion with the body? The embrace of the daimon goes beyond the "merging of the ego with unconscious figures."[26] In our ordinary state of mind, in which we are unconsciously identified with the body, the "I" occupies the entire body space. We and the body are one merged identity. Hurt my body, hurt me. There is no room for the mediating, receptive, subtle body in this unconscious identification. In our usual state, *when the separate "I" permeates the body, the subtle body remains phenomenologically unavailable.* Images have nowhere to roam. For the subtle body to breathe, for the daimon to emerge to rejoin the body, there must be some relaxing of the "I's" grip on the body. The ego must slip out of the

SANDRA LEE DENNIS

body field into a larger containing consciousness—that presence I have described as soul—to allow subtle-body space for the alchemical union. Although we are rarely, if ever, completely separated from the body-ego, there are degrees of separation. Each union or *coniunctio* experience sears off some of the connection of the ego to the body. This allows consciousness to permeate and slowly uncover that other center of bodily presence, of immanent numinosity, the subtle body.

When this larger consciousness absorbs the sense of "I"— which may feel like an out-of-body state, but actually heralds a further incarnating of daimonic forces—our ordinary exclusive identification with the body releases. We begin to sense ourselves as the larger field of consciousness, separate from the usual smaller, local sense of "I". Other people, too, begin to look more like the soulful energetic field that surrounds them than their ordinary three-dimensional form. This larger field of awareness creates a space into which the "I" may move, and it simultaneously sustains or "holds" the alchemical happenings of the subtle body. Without this shift, the protective mantle or oppressive suffocation, depending on your perspective, of the body-ego "I" impedes or prevents the subtle-body reunion of the daimon with the body from taking place.

These explorations—with "I" held as part of the larger consciousness—show that ego has a crucial part to play in the soul making, the enrichment of the psyche, that can take place as the daimonic image reunites with the body in the subtle-body field. The "I" is to the subtle body as the caretaker is to the grown child who is ready to leave home. The "I" must let the body go forth to meet the imaginal world without continually hanging on, but it must also be as sure as possible that the "child" is prepared, and the "I" itself must be capable of surviving on its own without living through the child. To carry the parent/child metaphor to another level, the "I" itself may be the time/space offspring of the larger containing consciousness, our share of the "true Self" and it will naturally come home to this soul presence if gently chided to do so. "Come along now, you are no longer needed there at your post in the body," we might say. In order for the "I" to willingly let go of its hold on the body, it must perceive the containing consciousness as strong, steady, and powerful enough to protect the soft animal of the body, its subtle permutation, as well as the "I" itself. If the containing consciousness is weak, we encounter enormous resistance. The "I" simply will not leave the body-field, despite our best attempts to deconstruct it through meditation, douse it with drugs, or inflame it through romance or creative activities.

We might succeed in shocking the ego into dissociation (deprivations, orgies, S&M practices, cultic obedience), or drugging it into fusion (marijuana, alcohol, ecstasy), imagining we have entered an ego-less state. In fact, these subterfuges simply fuel our spiritual materialism, identifying our ego as spiritual, creative, or psychologically integrated. In fact, we have merely stripped the body psyche naked without an adequate protective shield of consciousness. We have isolated or obliterated ourselves, while fancying, because it often brings a sense of safety, that we are high above the cares of life in a blissful reality. In this state there is no discrimination to recognize, no containing medium, no fertile ground to provide roots for the powerful energies of the daimon. The dissociated or fused psyche is barren soil.[27] While dissociating or fusing protects us from pain, it also prevents any alchemical connection with the world around us. A flexible connection with people and things and images only occurs through the medium of the individual soul. We have to be there to participate in this relational world. Daimonic encounters require the receptivity of soul without the protective illusion of an isolated "I".[28]

UNPLEASANT SENSATIONS AS PRECURSORS

I have been speaking a great deal about our relationship to inner imaginal life. What about the great majority of our days spent absent from the images, our ordinary days spent in the business of work, dishes, carpools, meetings, and shopping? Even when we stop long enough to attend to it, our inner life often appears barren of imagery. We can go days, weeks, or even months not recalling dreams, registering no images. In these sometimes-lengthy periods without imagery, we need to be on the lookout for unbearable sensations, as they may signal the presence of an unconscious image coming to consciousness.

A period of physical unrest or illness may *precede* the emergence of any new image, but especially of the sensation-laden daimonic image. As a deep shift in the sense-of-self is about to occur, these periods of trying physical discomforts resemble a subtle-body labor to bring forth the full-bodied daimon. If we recognize these discomforts as contractions signaling the impending birth of an imaginal presence, we can increase opportunities for ourselves (and those we are helping) to encounter the instinctual forces of the daimonic with more conscious awareness. We can become active participants in encouraging the imaginal to consciousness.

In the face of the perplexing contraries of difficult imagery, I have tried to think through the many questions evoked—often without success. This taught me that while some problems need to be thought through, *most imaginal material needs to be felt through.* To help birth the unconscious image into consciousness, we must allow ourselves to feel-through sensations we often avoid and disown. We need the self-knowledge that comes from claiming our full range of feelings and sensations. If we are unable to permit the full registration of bodily feeling, we will be left with numerous incomplete imaginal gestalts and physical holdings, unable to flow in any new uncomfortable direction ordained by the infant daimon coming to awareness. Bodily sensations and feelings are like tendrils coming up from the deep, feeling toward our surface consciousness, signaling the presence of the emerging octopus. Once the announcing sensations are fully felt through, the image, itself, will arise to be confronted by consciousness.

Sensations that are difficult to contain, even unbearable, rarely take the form of physical pain that cannot be tolerated. What is intolerable is usually the cognitive or subtle-body component of the sensation. That is, deeply held attitudes prevent us from fully entering into certain emotions or sensations. Some of the more common intolerable sensations that presage imaginal reunion experiences are listed below. This is not an exhaustive list, only an illustration. Since our tendency is to live our lives as comfortably as possible, it takes a concerted effort to train attention on these feelings rather than to distract or numb ourselves with TV, food, reading, sport, drugs, sex, or whatever works to turn us away.

1. *Body-Boundary Shifts: Fragmentation, Dismemberment, Expansion, or Contraction*— Union with the image brings critical changes in the sense of body boundaries. With our "I" so intricately connected to our bodily reality, the sensation of imploding, exploding, or disintegrating can be highly threatening. In such fragmented states of mind, shifting the sense-of-self to the spaces between the scattered particles of our being encourages connection with the larger matrix of consciousness, rather than the fragmentation itself. Resting in the arms of the containing consciousness, we can more easily let such fragmenting or dismemberment occur. We may resist the sensation of expanding to fill the room, the country, or even all of outer space. We may also oppose the sensation of growing smaller, into a tiny dot perhaps. These sensations are "ego-dystonic," not me. "I" am not that small or that large. (Lewis Carroll knew about these shape-shifting domains and described Alice going through them in Wonderland.)

Our identities are fluid and can stretch far beyond and beneath our usual bounded sense-of-self. Birth of the new may require us to expand or shrink to reflect the new presence. As with all novel sensations, boundary shifts require some degree of dis-identification with the body if we are to feel them through, since almost by definition they expand our sense of who we are and our relation to the world. For instance, women often have unconscious, culturally prescribed, prohibitions about the danger of taking up too much space that impedes energetic expansion. Being "too big" has become associated with punishment and dread. The cult film *The Attack of the 50 Foot Woman* played on this fear.

112

2. *Pressure in the Head or Eyes*—The head is sacred ego country. Often we stay "in our heads" for a feeling of security even when the rest of the body is allowed to expand, disintegrate, and so forth. When the familiar sensations of the head go, we experience profound disorientation, a true launching into the unknown. The impression that the boundaries of our head are changing in any way can be unendurable, producing pressure, or stabbing, anxiety headaches. On a more mundane, but imminently practical level, the fear of the pain of a threatening headache will arrest the flow of the daimonic image. The prospect even of this sheer discomfort may cause us to shy away from sensations associated with the head area. Neck and shoulder pressure often hold rage: the desire to choke, beat, or strangle. Since many people in our culture commonly cut off rage, it is wise to suspect it may underlie any tensions that present themselves around the head.

When the image unites with the body, it needs to unite with the whole body. Sometimes the imaginal union will seem complete, except for the head. This is a sign of partial union, at best, and probably indicates a split-off state of consciousness. In this case, the body/mind split is reflected physically as a sense-of-self located in the head, observing the body—down there—merging with the image. When the sense-of-self resides in containing consciousness, that larger field holds the entire body, including our precious head. For the daimon to reunite with and become present in the body, our identification with the head must go, for the imaginal partner will not consummate a headless union.

3. *"Hunger" or "Thirst" in the Throat, Chest, and Belly*—Early body-based "memories" often need to be cleared before the image reenters the body. Such memories relate to the foundational sense of who we are. Subtle body hunger or thirst sensations lead to "oral" feelings of vulnerability, dependence, and neediness—another group of feelings routinely rejected in the West. Often these feelings are intolerable to us (particularly to men). Involuntary

movements of the mouth to bite, suck, or nurse that may be activated as part of the daimonic flow are extremely ego-alien to most adults. These sensations may relate to early deprivation, an inborn pattern, or a religious feeling (hunger and thirst for contact with God), depending on what level we tap into. They often connect with a sense of longing, loss, or grief, and will disappear once we can endure the emotional pain of lack—of not having received what was once so desperately needed. Longing may also reveal a need for the nourishment of the daimonic source, which has been called to mind by the nearness of an emerging image. The temptation is always to act out the feelings and try to satisfy the longing with sex, food, drink, or drugs. Craving for a chocolate malted milk is always a giveaway for me that these feelings want to be acted out. Still, malteds taste especially good at these times.

4. *Strength: Tingling Energy Surges Throughout the Body*—As the numinous image reenters the field of the subtle body, sensations associated with power and strength naturally emerge. These tingling energy bursts, which may feel like body expansion, may be more difficult for women than for men. Feelings of strength can be frightening when we fear we may act them out destructively, or attract hostility to ourselves for emanating strength. Perhaps we have been attached to an unconscious image of ourselves as small, meek, and helpless. Perhaps we are not willing to face the responsibility such strength implies.

5. *Sensations of Falling or Dizziness*—The sensation of falling into an endless space commonly precedes imaginal episodes. Actually, we need to fall into the darkness of the subtle body, because it is there that the union with the daimonic image takes place. Thus we need to get accustomed to the free-fall of the mind. Falling sensations generate fear, disorientation, confusion, and lack of groundedness, as perceptual reality loses its substantiality. "Falling" seems to signal that we are entering into a space of unknowingness, where we will lose our bearings, the security of our ordinary world. A free-fall

that seems to have no end may also bring up feelings of fragmentation or despair. We need to be able to let ourselves "fall," remembering from within the containing presence that the fall is intrapsychic. The creators of *Back to the Future: The Ride* at Universal Studios in Los Angeles captured this inner geography of dizziness and falling and used it to produce one of the most popular attractions there. We yearn to confront this fear of falling into our craggy depths.

6. *Genital Excitement/Tension*—We may think we enjoy being sexually stimulated. Perhaps, but not as the annihilating daimon beckons. We commonly numb or restrict the sense of numinous sexual excitement that invariably accompanies the daimon reuniting with the body. We know that despite media images to the contrary, sexual desire and pleasure are deeply defended against in our culture that values self-sacrifice, work, and delayed gratification. Repressed desire may feel like anger or fear until we notice the heat being generated in our genitals. The daimon generates unitive sexual impulses, which connect our sense-of-self with a larger more permeable world. Surprisingly, many fears accompany the pleasure of such sexual excitement.

Might we not act on our impulses, unleashing some diabolical sexual fantasy? Or perhaps we will attract unwanted sexual advances. We may unknowingly fear that the sexual energy will reach the heart, its intensity breaking open levels of pain we are not yet ready or willing to handle. Most of us do not realize how much we block or move to act out sensations of sexual pleasure. Obsessive sexual attractions can drain off the pressure of these sensations that accompany the rising of daimonic images, and probably occur often as the daimons begin to arise. Falling in love, we project the daimon onto the attractive Other in order to avoid it in ourselves. If we can pay close attention to our attitudes regarding sexual excitement, we may discover our defenses. When we can be reassured that it is safe to feel sensations of delight, we may be able to allow the edge of sensual excitement to grow and the daimonic intensity along with it.

7. *Pressure or Pain in the Heart*—Pain in the area of the heart often signals unlived grief, the natural accompaniment to loss. By the time the daimonic image begins to reunite with the body, we will have become accustomed to grief. Insight, the *unto mentalis*, brings plenty of grief as illusions die, and we begin to accept formerly rejected parts of ourselves. The loss associated with integration, the reunion of the daimon with the body, provokes greater changes even than those experienced at the level of insight. The entire body-self is alchemized by the *unio corporalis*. Reunion with the body activates unpredictable changes in us. Furthermore, it may take years to open up to the bodily pain of the past. Historical events, such as trauma in infancy or childhood, may have frozen us on a deep "cellular" level. Unacknowledged grief freezes feeling. Unfreezing implies entering into rage, terror, and vulnerability that the frozen panic has successfully blocked for so long.

Thus, letting the heart break means death to a former way of life. Are we not as attached to our emotional outlook as we are to our familiar body patterns? We may profoundly distrust life, perhaps with good reason. We may severely limit our trust in certain people or situations. Or we may naively trust without discrimination. Each time the heart breaks, we crack through a way of being in the world to a new emotional perspective. The heart radiates as another center of our sense-of-self—probably more effective than the head—connecting all parts of the body. A new experience of heart requires a shift in the entire way we feel ourselves. The parameters of the heart, our capacity to feel the world, define deeply who we are.

Grief changes her, as we let go of a subtle pattern in our lifestyle. We may need to go through deep personal pain about our birth, childhood, lost possibilities, and people, the suffering of others, the fate of the planet, before we begin to feel more fully our connectedness. The expanded heart embraces our mysterious link with animals, nature, other people, and history. Stephen Levine suggests we cultivate the attitude "let it break," to help us stay with the stardust scattering of the breaking heart as part of our daily lives.[29] Such breaking may be deeply impersonal and subtle, connecting us to the most delicate inner archetypal realms, or dramatically personal and physical, as we relive abandonment, abuse, or betrayal.

We may be concerned for our physical well-being. We may fear suffocation as the waves of the breaking heart spread into the throat, or perhaps we fear a heart attack from throbbing chest pressures. We may resist the tears that often accompany a breaking heart, or the moans, the groans, the little animal sounds that seem so foreign to the mature adults we fancy ourselves to be. Or perhaps it is the uncontrollable body-shaking we fear. Will we fall apart? The fear is of dying, of not holding together. And perhaps we will actually need to be held to let this break happen, by an outer, as well as inner, mother figure. In times of heartbreak, let us allow ourselves to be held.

8. *The "Unbearable Lightness of Being"*—Finally, a floating, airy presence may intrude as we relax more into our bodies. Even this can be alarming, as we are accustomed to sensing ourselves as physical material beings. Deep relaxation, a loosening of major constrictions, can produce an allover lightness that threatens our sense of solidity. Can we allow ourselves to become air, unbearably light, wafting with the wind, dissolving so intimately into the world around us?

Images, as well as thoughts, may appear in conjunction with any of the above-mentioned sensations. It may even be the image, itself, we are avoiding, rather than the sensation. I have highlighted sensations because they are rarely included in discussions of powerful images. A machine-gun-wielding maniac, a sobbing toddler in a fetal position, or a rotting piece of human flesh on a cross, are some living images that might be associated with head pain and eye pressure, for instance. The images are getting less attention here because they have long captured our interest as center-stage participants in the psychic drama. We have overlooked, however, the backdrop, the scenery, the stage itself—the sensational precursors to the images. Any discussion of the visual components of the daimonic images must stress the critical part played by the underlying sensations that, through immersion, can truly bring the image into our flesh-and-blood world.

CHAPTER 7

~~~~~~~~~~

Dangerous Passage:
From Insight to Integration

This openness to being acted upon is the essence of the experience of the human soul faced with the transpersonal. It is not based upon passivity, but upon an active willingness to receive.

—Sylvia Brinton Perera [1]

ONCE WE HAVE GAINED sufficient insight that the image begins to extricate itself from its entanglement with our body-based sense of self, we enter a turbulent transitional phase. Often preceded by long periods of no imagery at all, this is the point at which the image and its affects have come together, but we have not freed ourselves from the daimon's peculiar grip on our muscles, nerves, and senses. Let us take a closer look at what happens as we move beyond insight.

PERIODS OF NO IMAGERY

Clinical reports show the most common problem in depth psychological work is not daimonic or frightening, but blocked imagery.[2] Most people will never have consciously experienced the troubling imagery under discussion here. Even for those with regular access to affect-laden images, periods of no imagery often occur. As we have seen, from the alchemical point of view, states of no imagery predictably arise as part of the darkening following a union experience. The darkening comes as veiled grief at the loss of contact with the numinous we felt during periods of insight, love, inspiration, bliss, or vision. The deadening that precedes the reunion of the image with the body often expresses itself as blocked imaginal capacity.

We have also seen how each feeling-laden daimonic image signals symbolic death for the old order of the personality. When the pre-conscious nascent image arises, signaled by the initial insight, it may pose a threat so great that no imagery at all can be tolerated until further ego strength (through further insight or bringing unconscious feelings to awareness) develops. As the imaginal process deepens, and the annihilating cosmic roots of the daimonic image begin to emerge, the problem of accepting these instinctual energies becomes even more critical.

These transitional states reveal any unhealed fragmentation or trauma we carry in the body that prevent our full contact with the depths of life. Feelings and memories from trauma may become such an absorbing foreground that bringing the difficult feelings to awareness is completely blocked. Nathan Schwartz-Salant associates the state of no imagery with infantile states, where what are known clinically as borderline, schizoid, and narcissistic states of mind abound.[3] These states overflow with infantile terror, rage, and fragmentation. Many people carry the "early wounding" (or original sin or mythic pain, depending on your ideology) that gives rise to these defensive stances as our inner world opens.

We naturally avoid the pain and disorientation associated with repressed instincts, and the concomitant loss of contact with the life-giving ground of being. A barely-hidden terror reigns as the daimon unveils these wounds, these strongholds of human separateness, hidden behind an array of more sophisticated defenses. It is during these dark periods of no imagery that we most need to focus on the pre-conscious sensations that arise. Attention to any unpleasant sensations expedites the imaginal unfolding through the days (weeks, or months) that look deceptively stagnant. The images remain underground in their winter phase, but the body speaks their emerging presence through its tensions, aches, pains, and strange sensations. The headache or stomach pain, exhaustion or cold, the flu or allergies or minor accidents—each asks for attention to the budding image behind the discomforts. Before we end up in oblivion with the help of painkillers that block these telling symptoms, it is a helpful practice to try to attend to the messages they bring.

If the necessity of attending to these primal feelings— often of rage, terror, vulnerability, worthlessness, emptiness, or despair— that accompany the daimonic image is not acknowledged, the process of integration shuts down. The now insightful client or creative artist continues living out the same old problems, the same old blocks, despite pools of understanding about their causes. The underlying feelings and sensations, as well as the concomitant imagery, must be contacted to constellate the subtle body, where a fundamental shift can take place. This is easier to understand as image and shadow feeling first come together in the ah ha, or insight, moment. But we are less prepared for facing the feelings and sensations at the edge of the abyss brought on by the daimon's destructive, dissolving, side or by the foretaste of its liquid light of union.

If we remember that states of no imagery signal the *nigredo*, we may recognize them as a sign of an underground image pushing to emerge into day. The numbing characteristic of periods of no imagery wards off such trying images, their affects, and the threat they pose.[1] As the numbing lessens, sensations I have described, such as falling, dizziness, or black emptiness begin to come into awareness. Body-centered immersion encourages detailed attention to these background sensations associated with fragmented foreground feelings.

Are the sensation and feeling I am stressing here really so central to reconnecting with the visionary world? James Hillman, for one, disdains therapy's current preoccupation with finding truth through underlying feelings, which he calls our "most heartfelt delusion" Instead, he sees feelings as secondary, as auras of the image.[5] As I have pointed out, the image may also be seen as the aura of the feeling. I believe image and feeling are aspects of the same phenomenon. We have seen how our inability to allow certain feelings and sensations greatly impedes the attendant image formations. The terror, grief, and rage typically underlying the phase of no imagery eventually unleash archaic energies into the consciousness necessary for containing further deepening, a more intimate connection with the imaginal source, and must be confronted as part of the dark-night side of self-knowledge.

The situation of an image arising without feeling also occurs with some regularity during this phase. The splitting of image and affect is the "natural" state of mind before the Eros accompanying insight begins to pull the image together with its instinctual feeling body. Feelings emerge with no connection to image, or images appeal with no feeling. For some people, establishing contact with feeling alone is a long and arduous task, for others, feelings flow without connection to any informing image. The same advice to attend to sensation holds when disembodied images arise unattached to feeling.

In order for a symptom to appear as an image in the first place, the ego must to some degree abandon its usual control. We have all experienced compelling imaginal or dream fragments; they may even haunt us with their regular, disembodied presence.[6] To encourage the assimilation, the meaning-learning potential of these images, we need to connect with the feelings and sensations associated with them as we would in times of no imagery. Often we spend hours lying awake at night, or in the therapist's office revisiting such images (hoping the affects will come along?) talking endlessly with or about them, when the simple movement of shifting to associated sensations brings the body of the image into play and reconnects us with our interior drama.

No matter which stage of the incarnating cycle we find ourselves going through, in periods of no imagery the way back to conscious contact with inner life is through the body. In times of stress, advice to exercise more, or simply to move—in gardening, cleaning, building, handicrafts—we half recognize this connection. When we move, we reconnect with our body.

122

SANDRA LEE DENNIS

THE PULL OF OPPOSITES

This transition I am describing (from insight to integration), can easily drive one for refuge into drugs, diversions, depression, or frenetic activity. When we do finally manage some inner focus, we may realize why we have been blocked for so long. The most dreaded, yet compelling, images and feelings begin to arise: blood, copulating couples, piles of shit, rotting bodies, child torture, rats, spiders, and snakes. The taboo themes come forth with a vengeance, justifying our strong feelings of resistance. Suddenly, we find ourselves on the rack, torturously pulled between the contradictory pleasures of numinous expansion and the pain of inner chaos.

The imaginal world begins to dance to an erotic rhythm. Eros calls us into an annihilating, black embrace, where the illusion of the outer world and the ground of our usual sense-of-self dissolve. We are unsure about this alarming shift. Have we danced ourselves into heaven or hell? Embraced love or death? Love or fear? That we must pass through burgeoning tabooed images discourages whatever mystical or healing aspirations may have brought us this far.

Besides befriending and relaxing into the bodily tensions during the portending periods of no imagery, we need to learn to recognize the signs of the daimon emerging. Recognizing these signs, such as no imagery, despair or stagnation, we are less likely to miss the path, or to linger longer than necessary at this infernal crossroads. For the hellish images that arise can become bearably purgatorial if we learn to hold them with a light touch and that religious attitude.

With the beginning line of the *Mysterium Coniunctionis* Jung offers this profound insight: "The factors which come together in the *coniunctio* are conceived as opposites, either confronting one another in enmity or attracting one another in love."[7] He suggests, counter-intuitively, though clear to any teenager, that what repels actually signals an unconscious desire to unite, that the sacred *impulse to connect* (Eros) may take the form of attraction *or* repulsion, enmity *or* love.

123

EMBRACE OF THE DAIMON

From this point of view, whatever strongly stirs our desire nature, for or against, somehow directs us, pointing us toward the mysteries of union. I have suggested that when we remain conscious of our aversive images, and reverently invite these demons "in for tea" we encourage their underlying uniting forces to come to consciousness.

Unaccustomed as we are to holding the erotic tension of opposites in awareness, we do not realize this is just what we need to do. The physical anxieties that correlate with the strain of simultaneously feeling attracted and repelled by the emerging imagery need to be brought to consciousness, despite the maze of difficult feelings. As we release our unconscious identification with these bodily tension patterns, we also begin to free the daimon to come fully into awareness. Earlier disillusioning moments, when our dark side inched into light, may have revealed these tensions. However, as Eros attempts to move image to body, he ups the ante in terms of what he requires of us to follow the daimon's unfolding. This is the moment we must become willing participants in the destruction of our old body-ego. Now we must allow the daimon to create an entirely new energy field. The images from this perilous passage are especially confusing. They can easily crystallize in demonic form. Unexpectedly, I report with great relief that to cooperate in dissolving ego structure in the body, we need only relax into some of the most exquisite aspects of our nature hidden in these images.

EROS THE CREATOR: REVIVING ECSTATIC SEXUALITY

The rising daimons test our capacity for ecstasy. Sexual images proliferate in imaginal realms, yet many sexual images fall into the territory of taboo, and repel us, especially when they involve violence or death. The erotic connection of love with death becomes clear in imaginal realms, and this connection may have even been recognized at one time. As we have seen, modern scholars believe that pagan mysteries culminated in an ecstatic union, a *hieros gamos,* with the god. Experienced as an initiation into death, this ritual sexuality may have been an integral part of worship ceremonies. Pictures on Roman tombs depicted the loves of gods and mortals, such as Jupiter and Leda, Bacchus and Ariadne, and Diana and Endymion. And the most blessed death was thought to be in the embrace of a deity. In our times, the *Liebestod,* the love/death theme of Wagner's *Tristan and Isolde,* affirms that in the dance of Eros, death is the culmination of love, and love is death's secret. We have seen how the ecstatic aspects of sexuality that mix loving with dying were forced into exile by the coming of Christianity, but we rarely consider today how firmly this split between sexuality and spirit, between love and death, continues to keep us from our innate ecstatic potential.

Sexuality, as it moves beyond the merely physical, becomes spiritual. It connects the physical with the spirit. In its wake, both our sense of three-dimensional reality and our place in it are changed. Ecstatic sexuality reminds us of the in-substantiality of the flesh, of the unfathomable mystery of existence. It brings the spirit into the body, accelerating the embodiment of soul. Deep body relaxation, the pleasure of merging, can break us open emotionally, obliterating our sense of separateness, and connecting us to a larger reality. However, for most of us, bliss ushers in anxiety. When pleasure spreads through the body, body tensions that reflect antique emotional blocks are activated.

Many of us need some kind of deep-tissue massage or body-centered therapy to even begin to realize the extent to which we block the flow of life with our physical tensions. The support of another person helps us bear the pain of allowing these lifelong tensions to dissolve, along with their emotional counterparts. Unfreezing these blocks is the mainstay of the unbearable sensations associated with the unfolding of the daimonic images of the soul. Until we allow ourselves to bear the seemingly unbearable, we block access to the inherent bliss of our nature.

We have a deep drive for ecstasy, a potential for bliss that is perhaps our most undeveloped capacity. To realize this potential, we must be willing to die to our old life, our existing sense of self. In these death themes we capture the subtle essence of erotic connection. New life is breathed into our days, fresh sights, more delicate sounds, and surprising scents. Arising daimons require no less of us in our relation to them. Erotic sexuality implies a relationship to all of life, not simply to the rituals of sexual intercourse. Those moments we live with our sexuality open and alive, we sense into our connection with nature, with the world around us. We taste the *participation mystique* as we die gradually to an egocentric sense of ourselves as a separate being. Most of the time, however, this unlived potential creates a vague dissatisfaction despite our attempts at happiness through conventional sex, money, drugs, entertainment, security, or success. Most of the versions of fun and pleasure we allow ourselves are shallow substitutes for the soul nourishment of deep connection that attunes us to the larger reality of which we are a part.

Dark Eros: Images Unfold

The association between Eros as a uniting and Eros as a destroying force brims with taboo. Although we rarely recognize Eros in the midst of destruction, the erotic component of violence and death helps to explain our fascination with them. As we have seen, when the ensouled daimon pulls away from the body, and we have to confront destructive erotic energies in ourselves, we lose nerve. We prefer not to enter this hellish place that can so easily trap us. Images of violence, putrefaction, and death bathed in an erotic glow threaten to undo us. I will share some examples.

The following image came from one of those periods when the underlying violence was so intense that I became numb to images, feelings, and sensations in order to protect myself from being overwhelmed. Following at least a month of restless sleep, depression, irritability and bleak thoughts, the following imaginal episode came into awareness. Characteristic of the early stages of the daimon's emergence, this image reflects my unwillingness to let it come fully into consciousness. The dismembering mirrors two forces at work: the daimon's destruction of obstacles to aid his escape from the body, and my resistance to his breaking away. This scene paints a picture of the torments we meet "on the rack" when we oppose the emerging daimon. It also shows an image that did not progress beyond the dismemberment and sexual violence it depicts. I have placed these images in the third person to give myself some distance.

A strange man rips her open and plunges his hands into her body to lift out her heart and other organs. Deliriously, he lifts soft, bleeding handfuls to his face, rubbing his cheeks, eyes, and mouth with the blood, muscle, and organs until he climaxes. He begins to gnaw at the heart. Meanwhile, she is still not dead. She feels the pain of his teeth in her heart. Then he begins all over again. He fondles her breasts, rips her chest open, and hurls her heart, lungs and other organs against a distant rock. He continues to rape and strangle her, profoundly frustrated that she will not die.

These pictures evoked subtle physical correlates of being opened up and torn apart, as well as being sexually stimulated. The woman in this scene refuses to die despite the worst mutilations. *She feels the pain of his teeth in her heart. Then he begins all over again.* I believe I was unable to let this image unfold, as I was holding on to the excitement it generated amid the torments. Even though I had the insight to see through the split sense of self as a victim, on the one hand, and a rapist on the other, I had yet to release the violent sensations of this split from my body. I was attached to the inner violence and excitement generated by the victim/violator split, thus I prevented the embryonic daimon born from this insight from emerging into consciousness. I was caught in the morass of numinous violence as the daimon strove to come to light.

Variations on this image occurred over a number of months, making it a good example of how we can get stuck in the demonic aspects of the unfolding image. Arresting an image (or its concomitant feeling or sensation) causes it to turn over again and again in our mind and body, demonically prolonging the pain produced by our conflict. We habitually stop this unfolding process in many ways: for instance through body armor, intellectual analysis, intense emotion, or acting out the image in some form.

127

How did I hold on to this image? The scene itself repelled me so that I often turned away, at its first dreaded glimpse, into some activity—a movie, a project, calling a friend, having a snack or drink. When I did manage to focus on this insistent image, my experience was one of relief, but I also felt repulsion mixed with thrill and shame at my interest in the scene. Did the local sensations of intense excitement enthrall me, charging me with just enough life force that I was reluctant to give it up, despite the grossness of the scene? Evidently I could not relax the deep body-holding related to this set of sensations. For whatever reason, the revulsion prevented me from truly following the dissolving impact of this image. I was not ready to allow its destructive, ecstatic potential to fully work its alchemy.

I may have intuited that opening to the level of destruction symbolized by the image would bring on a fragmenting change in my sense of myself. Where would this annihilating force take me? Would I ever regroup if I let myself be destroyed? Who would I become if I allowed myself to die to this dismembering maniac? These questions were not, of course, consciously formulated, but I believe they sourced my fears. *He continues to rape and strangle her, profoundly frustrated that she will not die.* Perhaps in letting go I would discover a lust for life, a surging of primal enthusiasm that would contradict a stoic moderation I spent decades cultivating. *Meanwhile, she is still not dead.* I can only surmise what might have unfolded because this image did not develop, but eventually faded away, its themes picked up in other, related episodes.

See how easy it is to remain stalled at this torturous crossroads, turning round and round, going nowhere. Resistance in the form of fear, disgust and shame fuels the natural violence involved *(rips her open. . . . gnaws at her heart. . . hurls her organs . . . against a distant rock)* in birthing the daimon from the body. At the same time, a drive toward ecstasy *(deliriously . . . climaxes)* resonates with the Eros of the image. Consequently, profoundly ambivalent, we flee in fear, or remain transfixed, awestruck at the scenes before us. This is the danger of arriving at this place.

SANDRA LEE DENNIS

Dismemberment, in this case of the inner body, appears frequently in daimonic imagery and myth as a grotesque, but apparently highly effective form of torture. Hillman describes Dionysian dismemberment as an almost delightful psychological process of awakening body consciousness. Dismemberment is also celebrated in alchemy. From this perspective, dismemberment dissolves the ego (or "Old King") activating the "sparks of Dionysus" embedded in the bodily aspects of our complexes, and leads us into archetypal consciousness of the body.[8] As we have seen, when dismemberment imagery appears with daimonic sexual overtones, a crazy-making mixture of dread and dissolving relief challenges our limits. If we can contain it all, the bodily aspect of the ego begins to die into the world of creative flux, and the image progresses, as in the following.

> *A grayish black wolf sneers and keeps falling asleep as the woman tries to engage him in conversation. Suddenly, he jolts up from sleep, grabs her, pulls off her clothes and starts to lick between her legs, then rapes her, biting off her breasts and head and pulling out her heart. . . . He continues until she is absorbed completely into him. . . . Now with human hands and face, the wolf grabs an ax and hacks the body completely to pieces. Each fall of the ax fills him with glee until he explodes in thousands of pieces of light.*

Here again, I confronted a repeating, initially disgusting, yet stimulating image that combined sexual violence, animality, and dismemberment. The deadly potion of aggression, lust, and vulnerability brewed up in a container of vivid presence imprisoned me in another self-made chamber of torments. In this instance, I tried to escape by allowing myself to be prematurely merged with the wolf. *He continues until she is absorbed completely into him.* This gave a temporary reprieve, as merging can produce a nonexistence that numbs us to our own feelings at the same time as it fills us with the power of the image. Still, the same disturbing image kept reappearing. I theorize that this merging produced a partial union that humanized the wolf, who then appeared with a human face and hands, which he used to hack me to pieces. *Now with human hands and face, the wolf grabs an ax and hacks the body completely to pieces.* When the image finally began to move (I believe, prompted by

129

my learning to relax into the mixed rage, lust, and despair of the wolf and woman images), I finally experienced the dismemberment as a fragmentation of my sense of self. *Each fall of the ax fills him with glee until he explodes in thousands of pieces of light.* A sense of floating above my body in hundreds of pieces disoriented and confused me. I gradually learned to focus on the black void between the floating fragments and began to feel into a surprising supportive cloud of sustaining warmth, a blissfulness that I now associate with an opening to the visionary medium of the subtle senses. The daimonic promise in this case began to lead through the destructive image to sensations of connectedness and support. This progression encouraged my continuing involvement with these images.

In today's world, it seems imaginal violence is erupting around us, bursting into film, print, and music. This imaginal violence we encounter daily in our news and entertainment is also reflected in the proliferation of weapons on a scale never before imaginable. Nuclear weaponry, notably, offers a chilling metaphor for the daimonic *nigredo*. The growth of our collective destructive potential may also epitomize the underside of the drive for the ecstatic. This drive takes us down to the purifying fires of Hades, where the creative powers of the emerging underworld can bring about a paradoxical renewal through destruction. Immersion in the destructive element of the psyche can take us through and beyond violence to connectivity in ourselves, and thereby offer an unexpected route to peace.[9] If we can only allow the full impact of the image to enter us, against our fears and shame, the inner violence typical of this transitional period from insight to integration works to clear away our attachments so that unexpected new patterns of connection emerge.[10]

Destructive Sexual Imagery: Torture, Violence, SM

Bridging worlds, sexuality takes us from the concrete to the imaginal and back again. The magical force of this erotic stream carries us along in a destructive rapture. As disturbing as it may be, the intense delights of sexuality regularly combine with sensations of violence to begin and end daimonic encounters, bewildering us, and arresting our attention. That humans so often experience erotic pleasure in combination with inflicting or receiving pain has baffled many minds. Freud thought sadism was the instinctual fusion of libidinal and destructive impulses.[11] Jungians speak of the demon lover[12] as a carrier of archaic aggression, addictive because hurtful sexuality offers "access to the ambrosia of Divine energies."[13] Thomas Moore writes of sadistic images as possibly some form of nourishment for (and as an essential ingredient of) the soul's nature.[14] Stanislov Grof points out that our first association with sexual arousal comes from our journey through the birth canal with its attendant anxiety, pain, and aggression, predisposing us to experience the odd mixture of the sexual with the aggressive.[15]

Masochism and sadism are said to reflect a psychic fusion, and are often described as opposite sides of the same impulse. But, since our culture places such a high value on power, we hardly grant them equal weight. Conquering seems so natural and right that we fail to see there are no winners without losers. Our accolades are reserved for the winner. In imaginal realms, too, for many of us it is easier to "identify with the aggressor" than to feel the vulnerability of the victim. Full immersion in a sadomasochistic image, however, places us in the crossfire of dominance-submission where we must feel both the control of the sadist and the helplessness of the victim. If we can stand the tension of these seeming opposites long enough, the image begins to transform into something new, as in this example.

The witch slashes the girl's eyes, blinding her and squeezing her heart until it is dry and hard like a rock. . . . Swooning with delight as she sees the girl's blood begin to flow profusely, she stabs her over and over again in the chest in an orgiastic frenzy. The girl dies, melting into the streams of blood flowing from her wounds. . . . As the last of her flesh dissolves, the pool of blood bursts into flames and rises up, laughing to engulf the witch in bloody living fire, burning her alive. Peals of laughter arise as the two come together as fire.

131

This image sequence did unfold, although it took a long time, many months, possibly a year, as I think of it, for this sequence to reach its final consummation in fire. The repetition of surging aggression and panicky recoil in an atmosphere of sexual arousal resulted in an anguished double bind, until the identification with this cauldron of conflicted feeling was released, and the image was freed from the grip of the body. I was more able to feel the rage of the witch and the surges of electric power that accompanied the tormenting cruelty. *The witch slashes the girl's eyes, blinding her and squeezing her heart until it is dry and hard like a rock.* In projecting the vulnerable side of this image, I protected myself from the helpless feelings of the victim girl.

Before the daimon emerges from sadomasochistic imagery, we must reclaim both sides of that pair—the perpetrator and the victim. Indeed, one naturally flows into the other if we do not stop the process. As victim, we are held not by pain alone, but by the state of surrender, helplessness, dependence, and merging with a powerful, sadistic Other. As aggressive sadist, our self-assured hardness actually merges with the victim's pain, opening the soul's vulnerability to forces larger than itself. The inflow of numinosity we feel in this merger enslaves us to the image and the attendant feelings. We begin to believe that torment and dissolving union are inseparable in the soul.

But we are misled. The closeness of death suggested by sadomasochistic images strangely teases the soul, as both sides of such an encounter actually offer an effective way to avoid death, yet stay close to its mystery. There is even a quasi-religious aspect to these sexually violent impulses. For is their ultimate aim not death in ecstasy, or the ecstasy of seeming immortality in the face of pain? But, alas, such an image does no more than tease, frustrating us in our ecstatic drive. For real release, the ego must trust enough for us to experience both sides of the sadomasochistic image, through the erotic dissolving violence that ensues from this held tension. At which point, the image, too, dissolves.

This repeating image of violent assault finally started to move with the blood beginning to flow. To see the blood flow at all required a shift in perspective from perpetrator to victim. *Swooning with delight as she sees the girl's blood begin to flow profusely. In an orgiastic frenzy, she stabs her over and over again in the chest. The girl dies, melting into the streams of blood flowing from her wounds.* The witch never consciously notices the impact of her actions on the girl, but is wrapped up in her own sensations, until she finally registers: "Blood? Ye, gads, the girl is bleeding" Even this slight shift to the experience of the victim opens up the metamorphosis—the witch swoons, *swooning with delight,* falling into a transformative trance that finally allows the girl to die. In the rising of the fire, the image finally reaches daimonic proportions. *As the last of her flesh dissolves, the pool of blood bursts into flames and rises up, laughing, to engulf the witch in a bloody living inferno, burning her alive.*

The next shift, of the flesh melting into blood and then bursting into flame, expresses the elemental leveling force of the arising daimon. The flesh-melting blood begins to take the bodily sense of self along with it into a flowing cohesiveness. The fire dissolves further the separateness and fear inherent in the body, expressed by tensions tightly aligned with images of helplessness, pain, and cruelty. *Peals of laughter arise as the two come together as fire.* The laughter rings with recognition of the ultimate marriage of the witch and the girl, an ironic coming together in a blissful annihilation. At the core of this difficult image, we finally discover its transformative source. Without the step of dissolving the distinction of the sadist and the masochist, then flowing into the unifying erotic current the coming together unleashes, we remain in the dry riverbed of Sade's landscape. Turned on by pickax intercourse or slashing tortures, the body gets a release, but the soul remains imprisoned.

The Christian fascination with the crucifixion (the *passion* of Christ) has insinuated itself in our souls, involving us in torture more than we care to admit. How many of us have held to the image of the crucifixion as a viable doorway to the spirit? We rarely even discuss the extent to which the motif of torture and death is united with sexual imagery in Christianity. Here, for example, we might mistake St. Augustine for an archetypal psychologist with this glowing picture of inner union amid the torment of the crucifixion:

> Like a bridegroom, Christ went forth from his chamber, he went out with a presage of his nuptials into the field of the world. . . . He came to the marriage bed of the cross, and there, in mounting it, he consummated his marriage. And when he perceived the sighs of the creature he lovingly gave himself up to the torment in the place of his bride . . . and he joined the female to himself forever.[16]

The crucifixion does seem to represent a station of the soul—the overcoming of the body. We, however, live in times that apparently call for a more conscious relationship to the Eros of such torments. Are we ready to let the arising daimon devour our long-suffering attachment to pain and initiate us into the delightful side of soul life—the resurrection? As a culture, we may be getting ready to move beyond the stage of one-sided crucified torment, into the redeeming heart of the erotic. To allow the daimon to incarnate, we need to face our fear of being seduced and destroyed by these primal erotic energies, trusting even the most destructive and taboo forms they may take. But that is not enough. We need to be willing to take the next step into a pleasure we also deeply distrust, even disdain, into the ecstatic embrace of the daimon.

Identity Shifts and Sexually Violent Imagery
The ubiquitous sexual violence of the imaginal world reflects the destruction of the old self-sense mixing with this erotic impulse to union. This mingling of the sensations of the *coniunctio*, the pending union, and the sensations of the destruction of the sense of self give rise to sexually violent images. The body begins to engage in a kind of foreplay with the newly hatched daimon, yearning toward union. These erotic sensations of attraction to the daimon mingle with the sensations of dissolution, deconstruction, and the dismantling of the structures of the old self. Thus sex and violence are inseparable in the imaginal world.

SANDRA LEE DENNIS

As we shall see, the actual reunion with the released energies of the image infuses the subtle body with a deep identity change. For the consummation brings new, unexpected qualities, such as strength, clarity, and joy for us to assimilate. The reluctant releasing informs the image with a violent struggle to separate, overlaid with yearnings to reunite. Like a final fling when a love affair ends, we cling to the image all the while acknowledging its imminent departure. That we finally release our physical identification with the energies of the daimon helps explain why the union of integration, though replete with such disturbing, violent, sexual imagery, results in feelings of liberation and the profound relaxation associated with bliss.

During this transitional time, we function caught between the conflicting energies of delightful union and violent separation. It is no surprise that we need to numb ourselves to distraction with work, television, and shopping. No wonder we are especially fraught with ambivalence toward our deep inner life at these times. As they inch toward awareness, images of erotic violence insinuate themselves in our consciously controlled fantasies, as well as appearing spontaneously. Imaginal ax murderers and serial rapists capture our attention with obsessive insistence and tempt us to identify personally (as Sade seemed to do) with these reflections of an impersonal process. We then face erotic torment as an afflicting attraction of the imaginal landscape. Rather than testifying to our innate delight in inflicting or receiving pain, however, the proliferation of sexually violent images reflects how profoundly the processes of death and destruction are connected with the ecstasy of creation.

Death, Rotting, and Rebirth

As we approach the liminal "dark night", the *nigredo* of incarnation, we also have the opportunity to witness the decay of those aspects of ourselves sloughed off in the dying process of the old self. Eros and excrement do not fit comfortably together in our minds, yet in the natural sequence of events, we die and then we rot (in imaginal realms, not necessarily in that order). Rotting, putrefaction, and the scatological in imagery, along with feelings of disgust, relief, vulnerability, and softness can also signal the *nigredo* of integration, as in this image.

> *The witch forces the woman to drink a brew containing old tennis shoes and turds. . . . After drinking she falls into a frenzy, her flesh begins to decay, until she shrinks into a cocoon and then expands to become an enormous caterpillar, and finally a gnarly penis. Crawling along, the penis gnaws at women like a slug devouring leaves, then falls into a pit with other odd-shaped members. The witch cooks them in a mixture of dog turds, shredded tampax, and menstrual blood. . . . Hot caterpillars crawl out of the brew and gradually become attractive, soft men. Each dives into the womb of a passing woman and merges with her.*

A brew of dirty tennis shoes mixed with turds, of course, disgusted me! *The witch forces the woman to drink a brew containing old tennis shoes and turds.* How could such a picture be encased in a timeless presence? No, no, no. I would not accept this image and its various permutations for a very long time. It was months from its first appearance before I began to grant it any attention. Once I made that critical move of accepting the revolting, foul-smelling aspects of the image, however, it unfolded with some ease.

With this shift toward acceptance, metamorphosis began to dominate this image. The decaying flesh, cocoon, caterpillar, and, finally, the slug-like, devouring penis showed the rapid shape shifts the emerging daimon passes through as he sloughs off and devours the ego structures that impede his coming to light. *After drinking, she falls into a frenzy, her flesh begins to decay, until she shrinks into a cocoon and then expands to become an enormous caterpillar, and finally a gnarly penis.* Accepting all that dizzying form shifting did not relieve me from another immersion in a repulsive brew. However, this time tampons and menstrual blood rounded out the potion. *The witch cooks them in a mixture of dog turds, shredded tampax, and menstrual blood.* Blood is one thing, but menstrual blood remains a potent taboo, associated at least from Biblical times with filth and the inauspicious.[17] A true openness to the numinous elixir carried by this fertile, distinctly feminine medium of birthing souls took many years of workshops and women's groups to come through.

Such a huge collective attitude gives way only slowly in the individual psyche, but eventually I felt its heady, intoxicating power.

The emergence of the daimonic, hot caterpillars signaled another shift. *Hot caterpillars crawl out of the brew and gradually become attractive, soft men.* These glowing creatures stimulated a lively sensuality, a relaxed, languishing warmth. *Each dives into the womb of a passing woman and merges with her.* This final union image suggests this image was also working to complete the healing of a psychic split between the masculine attitude and the feminine.

Physical revulsion, like that brought up by this image, produces distressing sensations, a feeling that we may be harmed by what we see, smell, or touch, even in imaginal realms. I wonder how drunken Sade must have become on his version of the disgusting brew; since scatological imagery mixed with the sexual was a device he used most often to offend. The mushy, warm softness we might associate with feces images suggests a quality that lets us relax into ourselves and feel our vulnerability as tender, fleshy, mortal creatures. Apparently from what we know, Sade was slow to accept his vulnerability; he rather lived out, in endless literary feasts on excrement, his identification with these emblems of our eventual decay.

Remarking on the strange sense of shame that is called forth when aspects of the chthonic, "the bug-eyed, toady, twisted, grotesque, slimy or hulking creatures," appear in our imaginal life, Patricia Berry laments our tendency to repress these carriers of our ugliness and deformity. She believes that with them we lose a natural, earthy level of ourselves.[18] And, I would add, we lose our connection to the mysteries they contain. (But, who considers mysteries when faced with drinking a foul-smelling feces brew?)

Decay accompanies dying, and imaginal death competes with sexuality for first place as we release the body patterns associated with our identification with the daimon. In our culture, death has just begun to emerge from its longtime invisibility, and we still do not trust it. We are blind to its erotic, connecting side, seeing only the separation it brings. In the time when Mother Nature was regarded as the death-giver, she "eliminated and consumed all that was old, rundown, devitalized, and useless." Of the many losses incurred since the days of the worship of Mother Nature, perhaps the greatest has been our trust in death as a natural passage into purification, healing, and rebirth. Formerly, the Dark Mother was also believed to transform the substance of the dead in her magical cauldron and offer it back as elixir.[19] She is thought to have ruled the underworld realm of formlessness where she took the soul after death, imparting there her secret powers of regeneration. We are badly in need of this image to counteract our fear of death—literal and figurative.

Having banished death from our lives and forgotten its intimate connection to rebirth, we find ourselves too often attracted to that intermediate field of violence where we unconsciously live out our inner lives. As death has again begun to reenter our lives so vividly with Hiroshima, the Holocaust, cancer, AIDS, Alzheimer's, the loss of the forests, streams, and wildlife, perhaps the planet itself, we are being forced to acknowledge and confront its presence as part of life. To get beyond violence, we are being called to confront our fear of death's call. Dying to our old selves in the embrace of the dissolving daimon may be just what we need to do in order to respond to that call and to follow his lead through this dangerous passage to our most authentic selves.

CHAPTER 8

❧

Imaginal Creatures as Signs on the Path

> *Jesus sayeth, ye ask who are those that draw us to the kingdom if the kingdom is in Heaven? The fowls of the air and all beasts that are under the earth or upon the earth, and the fishes of the sea, these are they that will draw you into the Kingdom.*

— Gnostic Oxyrhynchus Papyrus [1]

I HAVE CHOSEN THE imaginal serpent to illustrate the *unio corporalis*, the phenomenon of daimonic reunion with the body in more detail, and to attempt further to differentiate it from the more familiar *unio mentalis*, the process of gaining insight. Its affinity with animal nature, insistent imaginal recurrence, and symbolic history, make serpent imagery particularly well-suited, both to structure the discussion of the development of daimonic images that follows, and to impart, in this chapter and the next, a sense of the manner in which daimonic images break into daily life. Before delving into the serpent imagery, however, the broader category of animal images deserves discussion.

The instincts that stir when the daimon unites with the body often express themselves in animal imagery. In addition to destruction and sexuality, it is surprising to see how often animals appear in imaginal material. They stubbornly insist on participating in our inner lives despite our longstanding rejection of "the animal within." One analyst put it this way, "Considering the sterility of our technological culture, the persistence and vivid proliferation of animal life in the modern psyche stands out all the more remarkably"[2] In my own life, a few years before the imaginal animals associated with the daimonic began to appear, I had a vivid but reassuring dream in which a number of huge animals of the zodiac surrounded me. I recall at least a goat, bull, lion, eagle, crab, and two fish, all encircled by a giant serpent. They came as silent guardians or companions, and calmed my initial fears with their wild friendliness. I played among these magnificent creatures, each according to its disposition: with the fish I swam, I flew on the back of the eagle, climbed a mountain with the goat.

I wish I could say these charming companions returned in the waking images that came later, however, in the early days of daimonic intrusions, no grand creatures of the zodiac materialized. Instead, I was commonly visited by such lower orders as ants, spiders, maggots, bats, or scavenging birds. Later, the snake appeared in many forms—cobra, python, diamondback, king, boa constrictor. I was driven once again to question these imaginal events. What was the meaning of all these creatures marching into my mind? As the presence and power of these animal images grew, they added to the disturbance of my everyday equilibrium with their insistent, intimate appearance.

I learned that animals represent archaic, unintegrated aspects of the psyche, in Jungian thought, lower instinctual forces that must be passed through before the more human or godlike image appears.[3] Jung thought our instincts often used animal symbols to represent themselves. When images first break into consciousness, the animals do appear to correlate with split-off unconscious instinctual aspects of the psyche coming into conscious awareness. The serpent often signals sensuality; the bear, maternal protective strength; the dog, rage. Associated archetypically with the Dark Mother, the zoologically lower animals, such as reptiles and insects, represent the most archaic aspects of the instincts, and, according to this theory, those most demonized and rejected. As these previously repressed instinctual feelings, represented by the animal images, meet the conscious mind, and we acknowledge them as part of ourselves, we become more at home with our instinctual, feeling life. But, even after we have assimilated the animal instinctual energies, and we are more comfortable let us say with our sexuality, our aggression, and our tendencies to dominate, animal representations still abound in the imaginal world. The humanizing impact this theory should bring has not diminished the animal parade through the mind. I wondered why these animal images are still so active.

I came to believe that at the later stages of integration (as the image imprints on the body) the animal images, rather than representing split-off parts of a whole, appear in their own right as representatives of the imaginal world. Heralding their intent through the nightmares of the *nigredo*, these animal daimons come to participate in nature's ritual of incarnated union, the erotic union we see throughout nature, at the heart of her cycles of birth and death. Imaginal animals adhere naturally to this central *coniunctio* process and seem to arise from depths at which we connect with all of nature. Jung hinted at this possibility in *The Visions Seminars* where Morgan's visions are full of animal imagery, commenting that she was reunited with the animal soul as the deepest part of the collective unconscious.[1]

Despite the enormous strides made by Jung's work in counteracting our culture's negative attitude toward animality, he and his circle were still influenced by the rejecting attitudes of the time (many of which continue today), in regard to dark feminine forces, including animal instinctuality. An example comes from Tina Keller, who was an early client of both C. G. Jung and Toni Wolff, one of his early students who became a well-known analyst in her own right. Keller recounts a visitation by a recurrent imaginal companion, the dark man, Leonard. Leonard wanted her help in conveying secret knowledge, and insisted she open her mouth to express the knowledge. She feared and resisted this, intuiting that only an animal howl or groan would emerge. After much discussion with Toni Wolff, she decided this unspoken message coming from Leonard must be conveyed by him *in language comprehensible to the modern mind* before she should express it. Subsequently, it was not expressed at all.[5]

What could the incomprehensible howl or groan reveal that they both apparently so feared? Although she was protected from a dreaded merger with animality, the gentility of her refusal to express primal moans effectively prevented the sounds from coming to consciousness to be assimilated and understood. This repression of the primitive animal we all carry that permeates our culture effectively *stops the release of the instinctual energies necessary for the maturation of the daimonic image.* Until Tina Keller is willing to open her mouth in response to the daimon's urging, she remains ignorant of this part of herself, and Leonard's message remains unheard. Her refusal results in continued repression and probably projection of these instinctual energies of the self onto someone else.

"Projection," that is, seeing our own unconscious impulses in someone else without recognizing them as such, has been well established as a classic way the psyche defends against its own hidden tendencies. It is a common practice to project rejected animal-based images onto our enemies. Sam Keen, in his study of the archetypal enemy, confirms that across cultures, the enemy is depicted as all sorts of frightening and repellant creatures; from a rat to a shark to a snake.[6] With such baggage about the "animal within" we must overcome well-entrenched resistance to assimilate the instinctual aspects of animal images as they emerge into consciousness. Thus, it is not unusual to spend years encountering imaginal animals as representations of our feeling life (insight) before they begin to appear as autonomous daimonic forms (integration).

Visionary animals easily capture the imagination. Accounts of imaginal animals are found scattered throughout the work of creative writers, archetypal psychologists, mystics, and philosophers. Gaston Bachelard, the French phenomenologist who inspired Hillman, was so familiar with this terrain he developed an "animalizing phenomenology." He wrote of the "strange myth of metamorphosis" that began in Ovid, rigid and formal, and was now being brought to life by those returning consciously to their own primal animal impulses.[7] He theorized that metamorphosis—the sense of subjective shape shifts that includes identification with animal forms—was caused by an "excess of the will to love, a sign of animalized life."[8] It is a sign of a deep *biological experience* facilitated by the transformational power of dream animals.[9]

Hillman, along with Bachelard, thought a need to animalize was at the source of imagination, whose "first function" was to create animal forms.[10] Hillman ran an animal dream group in Zurich for years. Calling imagination an *animal mundi* as well *anima mundi,* he was fascinated with the exceptionally moving power of animal imagery.[11] Contrary to the traditional Jungian view, he stressed that these images do not represent our primitive, bestial nature, but are specific soul qualities, "essentials that cannot better present themselves than in this animal shape."[12]

To recover imagination we must first restore the preposterous sea-monsters and every winged fowl and every thing that creepeth. Only the animal can answer Descartes. Imagine—the subtle body is our brute awareness, and angelology, a logos of animals.[13]Hillman points out that in archaic psychology throughout the world, the animal is part Divine, and the Divine part animal.[14] Animal imagery submerges us in a lost nature, the archaic instinctual response, which we must touch to find the true place of transcendence.[15]

One of the earliest forms of archaic psychology that survives to some extent today comes from the great shamanic hunting cultures. In shamanic practices, the god manifested directly in animal form. Communion with the Divine occurred through these imaginal animals.[16] Sylvia Brinton Perera, who has been influenced by shamanism in her work on the recovery of dark feminine energies, speaks of a phase in inner development that correlates with daimonic when instinct meets meaningful symbol.[17] She describes the visitation of the animal powers as a transitional space (a dangerous passage) that heralds the emerging body-self:[18] a time when one is called by the "primitive pulsings of the animal brain to encounter the gods as animal powers."[19]

Jung himself thought, "the fire of passion belongs to animal nature."[20] To him it was that most paradoxical Greek god, Dionysus, who delivered the self over to the beast, as he took on many animal shapes. Jung believed the Dionysian mysteries may have been performed to bring people back to their animal instincts,[21] which he equated with both Dionysus and the terrible Mother. The Dionysian was the blissful and terrible experience of human distinction merging in animal divinity into the "abyss of impassioned dissolution."[22]

When the early pagan transformational mysteries were gradually outlawed by Christianity, the animal gods were demonized. Christians interpreted animal visitation as a dangerous sign of the demonic, a legacy we carry to this day. The devil, conceived as a supernatural, bestial angel,[23] was thought to mingle often with animal forms because his deepest appeal was to the animal in the human being. The Middle Ages inherited belief in the devil's animal shape-shifting abilities from the pagan world, but context and attitude dramatically changed the way these animal powers were handled. The typical "witch" of the 16th and 17th centuries was thought to have a number of familiar spirits, most often animal in form. She fed them her blood, implying a close bond, and these daimonic creatures acted, on her direction, to inflict harm. One study of the witch trials relays an account of a witch accused of sending animal demons to possess an 8 year-old girl. The witch admitted the devil had first lain with her in the form of a dog, a cat, and a bird.[24] In another story, a 13th century German visionary was attacked by animal demons, frequently in the form of a spider, beginning at age 15.[25]

We should not be surprised to learn that the Christian mystics, familiar as they were with imaginal domains, also confronted animal daimons in their contemplations. The demon's famous temptations of St. Anthony include vivid encounters with creatures: "across his calves he feels the trail of spiders, on his hands the chill of vipers, and spiders spinning their webs enclose him in their mesh."[26] Crowds of what he described as demons attacked him in frightening animal forms, including lions, wolves, panthers, snakes, and scorpions. He prayed for relief and for the discernment to know the difference between the visions sent by God and those of the Devil (as some of us are still doing). The vividness of the imagery apparently called for some supernatural explanation, which he attributed to the Devil. "Now it is very easy for the enemy to create apparitions and appearances of such a character that they shall be deemed real and actual objects."[27]

Teresa of Avila also sought consultation to be sure her visions, which at times included animals, reptiles, and insects, were not inspired by the Devil, stating the same theme, "for I tell thee truly, that the devil hath his contemplatives as God hath his...".[28] Still, she used irrepressible animal imagery to describe the onset of mystical rapture: it came on with a violent, "strong swift impulse, one is swooped into the air on the back of a powerful eagle."[29] The Christian demonization of animal images still predominates in the West, and we must confront it to achieve a more open relationship to the surging bestiary of the imaginal.

To help counter these long-held attitudes, Stanislov Grof, for one, has provided strong evidence demonstrating the role of prenatal and birth experiences in activating animal imagery. Through his depth psychological research using LSD and deep-breathing practices, he has established the profound impact of experiences in the womb, and especially the birth process, itself, on later psychic life. He has shown that imprints from the trauma of being born—being taken from the warm, dark womb into the cold daylight—gives rise to predictable symptoms, recurrent problematic feelings, images, and themes, depending on the details of the birth. Curiously, images associated with constricting labor and the turbulent journey through the birth canal often take animal forms. The following vision from my own collection offers one example that to me resonates with a difficult labor.

> *A black vortex sucks everything into itself. It is dark and musty. The hole begins closing in around me, a clammy moving creature. Terrified, I am falling through dark space. Bats, mice, and insects cover me, swarm around me like a*

blanket, biting and stinging, eating me alive. They burrow down my throat, in my eyes, in my ears. I want to scream, but no one can hear. Bats flap around my head. Paralyzed, I fall into a swoon and dive into a black chasm.

Grof suggests a holographic vision of psychic life, much like the archetypal, in which imagery resonates throughout various levels of existence. For example, we could interpret the above images biologically as a recovered memory of birth trauma, collectively as the poisoning of Earth's air and water, transpersonally as a past life experience of being buried alive, or psychospiritually as a *nigredo*, dying as precursor to psychic rebirth.

G. I. Gurdjieff, the teacher and mystic, advised that to learn to love, we must first love animals.[30] While he may have been referring to animals of the empirical world, the advice applies also in imaginal realms. Imaginal animals herald our intimate involvement with nature, effecting an alchemy that more human images do not accomplish. Embodying the animal short circuits our tendency to conceptualize and interpret. It crawls under our skin, into our muscles and veins, insinuating itself into our posture, our very being in the world.

THE BENIGHTED SERPENT

The entrance of the serpent into my imaginal life was heralded by a dream early in the period of my visionary eruptions:

A small, silver serpent emerges from behind the ear of the gray cat. I recoil and hide in fear. As the serpent slithers away into a floor heater, I watch, with fascination, from behind a door. Worried that the snake is roaming freely and will cause harm, I pursue it, aided by a black man. Though we look everywhere, it has disappeared.

This dream contained the repulsion and attraction, the approach/avoid syndrome that commonly accompany the daimonic. This silvery snake continued to compel my interest, reappearing on several occasions, then disappearing, as it had in the dream. For a number of years, "pursuing the snake" meant following the other imagery that seemed to arise from the same underground realms. I did so, as I have mentioned, entering into hidden aspects of myself with some fervor, privately, and in individual and group work. Finally, a few years after this dream, the serpent returned, this time as a recurring imaginal force.

Acceptance of the snake was always difficult. I had internalized the "enmity between woman and snake" dictated by the Biblical Yahweh as the punishment for woman following Eve's transgression with the apple of the Tree of Knowledge. Against this dread of the reptile which I assumed to be innate,[31] I was faced with the companionship of snakes of various sizes, shapes, and colors inhabiting what seemed like every corner of my physical being.[32] The cramp in my calf *this morning as I stretch on the bar yields to scores of small black, swirling vipers.* I could escape from this disturbing hoard through distractions, television, magazines, conversations, house cleaning, eating, or projects, but any time I tried to rest or quiet myself, vivid serpents greeted me immediately.

For a while, I stopped meditating, exercising, or drifting into contemplative reflection. Assiduously avoiding my inner world, I spent my time watching Clark Gable movies, making business calls, or choosing new wallpaper for each room of the house. Finally, I became ill for a number of months, a forced descent into the physical. *A diamondback snake lurks in my raspy throat, a cobra in my bronchial congestion and my stuffed head, adding to my misery.* When I realized that revulsion to these imaginal visits was actually making me more sick, I gradually began to accept the serpents into my body, although recurring fears of *Rosemary's Baby* proportions—that I was in league with the devil or courting incipient madness—continued to occasionally block this willed acceptance.

The cobra's flared hood pushes up through my throat into my head, bursting there into a large, white bird. The day this cobra transformed into a white bird, toward the end of my convalescence, I picked up Jung's *Seven Sermons to the Dead* to discover an entire chapter devoted to "The Serpent and the Dove." With this synchronicity, I finally decided to begin to read what I could find about snake imagery. Reading has always served as a raft to me when my mind is at sea. While I would like to share the amazing range of information I discovered about serpent symbology that would be a major sidetrack. But I will give a short sketch.

The serpent, it turns out, is the symbol for which there are several thousand interpretations. To name just a few, the snake represents: the primal life force, the instinctual aspect of sexuality, the dark underworld current, the regenerative principle, the gift of prophecy, male genitalia, and the Mother goddess.[33] It also stands as the guardian of the threshold between the inner and outer worlds, and as a medium that turns the inner world outward.

Characterized as the strongest and most common symbol, the serpent represents a great elemental being from which symbolic and spiritual life flows, as well as the ultimate symbol of instinctual life. The snake crawls on the ground, hence its association with the earth; moreover it burrows in the earth, making it a true underground creature. Meanwhile, the serpent invasions increased. *As I plant the begonia under the copper beech, scores of creepy green serpents spill out of the area of my chest.* In the Greek world, the serpent was companion to Asklepios, uniting light and darkness as the essence of its healing powers. In the Christian era, the Gnostics portrayed Christ as a healing serpent. They also described the serpent of paradise as the wild beast and as the instructor. In the treatise *On the Origin of the World* [34] the wild beast is the instructor.[35]

The history and importance of serpent imagery in the collective imagination surprised me. *The Bestiary of Christ,* which discusses an enormous variety of animals, real and symbolic, reports the snake as "the largest and most complex subject" in the study of religious or philosophical symbolism of former times.[36] As it turns out, the serpent occupied a central position in pagan ritual, and may well have been one of the earliest forms of the Divine. *Standing at the stove preparing the morning oatmeal, I notice a long, thin black viper lies coiled in my abdomen.* Earth-born goddesses were often originally snakes, and snake-goddess imagery appears in the Neolithic period, in Old

Europe, and in Mesopotamia.[37] In the religions of Greece and the ancient Near East, the snake was a well known image of deity.[38] According to Jung, in a ceremony from the Eleusinian mysteries, the initiate had to kiss a loathsome snake as a sort of union ritual. In another, a golden snake was passed down through the initiate's collar and garments, then pulled out at the feet to symbolize "complete penetration by the Divine serpent."[39]

According to Joseph Campbell, "Serpent Gods do not die,"[40] although prodigious efforts have been expended to destroy them. They shed their skin and transform. Indo-European myths abound of the slaying of the Serpent/ Dragon/ Dark Mother by various heroes: Zeus and Apollo kill Typhon and Python, Perseus slays the serpent-haired Medusa, and Yahweh destroys the serpentine monster Leviathan. Knowing that the introduction of new gods commonly involves the vilification of the old, it is no wonder that the snake was selected as the creature to have brought sin and death into the Judeo-Christian world. The snake, once a common symbol of the creative source of all, into whom all return, came to be reviled as a dangerous agent of darkness and, subsequently, of the Devil.

As we might expect, Christian mystics viewed snake imagery, along with animals in general, as an essential symbol of Satan and rejected it with vehemence. Teresa of Avila sprinkles her luminous prose with allusions to what she calls "so many bad things"—reptiles, lizards, snakes, and poisonous vipers—that come to cloud the contemplative's visions of the light divine.[41] Sometimes her references are clearly allegorical, as when she describes the snakes as worldly things,[42] but she also discusses imaginative visions and the capacity of the devil to send these images. She speaks of the gift of discernment among images, by which one would quickly be able to ferret out those images sent by Satan,[43] the merest hint of reptilian nature was an immediate giveaway of devilish authorship.

This legacy continues today. Though very few snakes are actually venomous or harmful to humans, we have learned to fear them all, although it is still a real question whether we were taught or whether the aversion is archetypal. We must confront this aversion to enable the snake's reemergence from the unconscious depths. Only then can we incorporate its instinctual energies and eventually unite consciously with the daimonic serpent. Yahweh's punishing enmity between the woman and the snake meant women (and, we might add, the "feminine" in man) have been cut off through fear and aversion from these instinctual powers and their elemental wisdom. As long as we continue to equate snakes with feminine wiles, with slipperiness, with cunning and guile, with betrayal, temptation and seduction, and with the underworld, devil and death, we effectively block full emergence of the image. *As I lie awake in bed at two A.M., the red eyes of the boa constrictor glow in my belly and its slimy, rough skin wraps around my chest, constricting my breathing until I feel I will suffocate.* We need to recognize these stereotypical, negative attitudes to fully allow the instinctual feelings associated with the serpent that they block, such as sensuality, destructive power, or seductiveness.

Jung encountered the serpent early in life as the phallic god: the giant, enthroned, chthonic worm that appeared to him when he was a small boy. This image presaged his interest in the *Anthropos*, or divine human embodied in nature that he came to believe reflected the conjunction of opposites.[44] He thought the serpent had the capacity to connect us to the *prima materia*, or *mundus imaginalis*, that undifferentiated source of our being in the world. Quoting from "Tractatus Aristotelis" on the serpent's powers, Jung reports on one of the phenomenological hallmarks of daimonic union: "She causes the nature wherewith she is united to vanish".[45]

He saw the snake also as a reconciling symbol. Commenting on a vision of a man and woman lying together, as if in a womb, encoiled by a snake, Jung felt it was the very compression of the snake's coils that brought the sought-for union of the masculine and feminine elements, the central symbol of the individuation process. Despite such accolades about the positive powers of the serpent, Jung was not immune to the prevailing negative cultural attitudes toward this creature either. In his early "Sixth Sermon to the Dead," he revealed his distrust of the "feminine" serpent:

> The serpent is of a generally feminine character and seeks forever the company of the dead. . . . The serpent is a whore and she consorts with the devil and with evil spirits, she is a tyrant and a tormenting spirit. . . . She brings up from the deep very cunning thoughts of the earthly one, thoughts that crawl through all openings and become saturated with desire.[46]

Jung later wrote extensively about serpent symbolism in *Psychology and Alchemy*. There he reports that the alchemists associated coldblooded, poisonous animals, such as the serpent, scorpion, or toad, with the darkening or the *nigredo*. And in *The Visions Seminars*, he said the snake was such an overpowering symbol that whenever it turns up, which it did commonly in Morgan's visions, it was extraordinarily significant.[47] Reading all this extended my tolerance for the serpentine imaginal invasion I was sustaining, while no doubt inflating my sense of myself.

To integrate this imaginal reptile we must come to terms with energies from our own reptilian nature, although I do not mean to imply that this is the origin of these forces. There is simply a correlation, a resonance, with the reptile in our own nature. *Sitting at the computer, I notice the diamondback serpent uncoiled, but upright, now in my head. Looking oddly studious with glasses and a knowing smile, she holds a pencil in one cartooned arm.* Some believe the ground of our bodily life is reptilian. In his study of *The Rosarium*, the ancient alchemical text, as a reflection of the psyche, Edinger discusses the image associated with the first stage of the *coniunctio*, which contains two serpents breathing out fiery stars to frame the mercurial fountain. Later, in the final picture in that alchemical series, we see crowned serpents, which, he concludes, indicate that the *coniunctio* brings the reptilian psyche into living connection with consciousness, thereby "crowning" or transforming it.[48] As these underground instinctual forces are brought to consciousness, we discover that their rejected aspects contain the hidden treasure referred to in myths and fairy tales. These include sensual knowing, connection to the flow of existence, visionary consciousness, and trust in death and regeneration. I do not mean to imply that the serpent stands for these personal qualities. Rather acceptance of, and later, reunion with the serpent are associated with the emergence and incorporation of these qualities.

This brief sketch gives a sense, at least, of the serpent's vast historical and mythological importance. I do not intend to try to improve on what others have done in terms of investigating the serpent's cultural history as a symbol, elaborating the myths surrounding it, or offering interpretations of its meaning.[49] Interpretations will not serve us here in this investigation. While they temporarily allay anxiety about an image, they also close the door on a subject by placing phenomena into already existing categories. If, at the time a vision appears, we turn as directly as possible to the image itself, the new knowledge it brings has a way of shattering the old structures that would surely be enshrined in interpretations. When the daimonic emerges, we need above all to stop, put the interpretations on hold, and attentively allow the mercurial image its time on stage.

CHAPTER 9

⚹

Incarnating Soul:
The Daimonic Image Unfolds

Then the Female Spiritual Principle came in the Snake, the Instructor, and it taught them saying . . . "With death you shall not die. . . ."

—The Hypostasis of the Archons *Nag Hammadi Library* [1]

DETAILED DESCRIPTION OF THE *unio corporalis*, the imaginal reunion with the body, or the incarnation of soul, are not to my knowledge readily available. Sometimes, however, we find them mixed in, but not distinguished, with discussions of imagery in psychological literature, in descriptions of experiences of mystical union, and in accounts of expressive artists. This entire book aims to help correct this lack. In an effort to devise language to better grasp these experiences, in this chapter I delineate "stages" in the unfolding of the serpent image with illustrative excerpts: from the initial breakthrough of the image into consciousness, to its development of daimonic intensity, and finally to its reunion with the body.

I realized early on that the content of the image is secondary to the dynamics of the incarnating process itself. The cycle proceeds regardless of the nature of the image. This marrying of spirit and body, Heaven and Earth, in the cauldron of our Being seems our particularly human task. I chose the serpent to exemplify this movement, but I could have used any other recurrent image. In describing these stages, I have tried to include both psychic and somatic components. However, I may not have done justice to the body's importance in this experience, because the bodily portion of experience lends itself only poorly to verbal description. You will notice that the serpent's gender changes throughout these descriptions. Disconcerting though it may be, the gender uncertainty reflects the daimonic serpent's propensity to change gender (sometimes appearing as a hermaphrodite, for which we have no suitable pronoun).

That we lack appropriate language for describing these important somatic events still amazes me, although I know it stems from a deeply ingrained tendency to ignore the body. Since we develop language to describe our conscious experience, what we fail to name remains unknown. And we know so little about our own sensual life. As I have mentioned, we are beginning to chart a linguistic map of imaginal subtle-body realms, to which I hope to add a few new byways. So let me say again that these images arise from the field of the body. Usually, if we take the time to focus whenever a sensation grows strong enough to attract attention, the image (in the form of sound, smell, color, or words) can be detected. Through the body sensation, which serves as its ground and most tangible feature, we gain contact first with the elusive instinctual aspect of the image. When disembodied images (those with no apparent sensations) do appear, we need to identify and connect with their physical counterparts in order to coax them fully into awareness. Finally, while it may not be evident in these descriptions, the psychic imagery, although more easily conveyed in words, materializes almost as an elaboration or aura of the foundational somatic experience.

THE UNION OF INSIGHT: THE *UNIO MENTALIS*

Many people writing about depth psychology have described how bringing the unconscious to consciousness increases self-knowledge through an insight that develops as the image and its concomitant feelings come into awareness. Insight dawns, specifically, when image unites with its feeling body. Through this process, projections are taken back and a more realistic self-image develops. Respect for the darkness that must be traversed in the dissolution of opposites (consciousness and unconsciousness) also grows, along with a connection to the numinous promise of the imaginal. The first station for the incarnating soul, what Jung calls the *unio mentalis*, occupies the bulk of depth-therapeutic work. Because it is so well documented in psychological studies of all kinds, I treat this critical beginning stage in a cursory manner, mainly to provide the context for a fuller discussion of the second stage, the neglected *unio corporalis*, where the image is fully incarnated, or integrated with the body.

Disillusionment: The Initiatory Nigredo of Insight

External events of loss or failure often trigger the initial *nigredo*, the darkening necessary to start "inner work." Often, after years of extroverted activity, an inexplicable period of depression, despair, ennui, hopelessness, or meaninglessness initiates a cycle that eventually gives birth to an interest in inner life—if for no other reason than to do something about the misery one has fallen into. During such grim phases, there may be little or no dreaming or imagery. One becomes aware of living only on the surface of life. (Later, once an interior focus has developed, *nigredo* experiences herald the emergence of new imaginal depths.) My experience fits this pattern. Before the images under discussion began to emerge, I had precipitously divorced and remarried. I had been interested in inner life for many years, but the dissolution of the first relationship initiated a period of profound disillusionment and questioning, which continued until after the birth of my daughter. Fitful sleep, nightmares, irritability, despair, lack of concentration, and depression all marked this passage. It was during this dark preparatory period that the silver serpent announced itself in dreams, and I entered therapy for the first time.[2]

Instinct Begins to Emerge into Consciousness

Along with depression, disappointment and despair, physical sensations of discomfort, numbness, tension, or pain often precede the emergence of the imaginal and constitute a substantial part of the *nigredo*. These physical symptoms announce the instinctual aspect of the image. They indicate that new imaginal material will soon be coming into awareness from its previously frozen habitat deep in the subtle body. My body demonstrated this truth in dramatic fashion. Before these images began to erupt, I embarked on three years of tension release through intensive, cathartic physical work that revealed legions of previously banned emotions—primarily various permutations on rage, terror, and grief. Suddenly full of symptoms, my body shook, shivered, and sweated through this period of freeing instinctual and emotional energies. The few images that emerged in this period (none of them snakes) often had the flavor of biographical memory—an early spanking, being left home alone, an enraged father or mother, the threat of a new sister. During this releasing, I began to discover I was not the person I imagined myself to be. The hatred, terror, confusion, and a craving for attention that was arising from the unconscious significantly tempered my spiritual, wise, strong, courageous, and caring self-image. The dawning of insight shatters many illusions.

The darkness and despair associated with the beginning of the work is not necessarily lifted by the emergence of our previously unconscious feeling life, although feelings of relief, of a secret truth finally revealed, often accompany these breakthroughs. In this way, the early uncovering phases overlap, with many dusky periods scattered among the burgeoning affects. As the instinctual aspects of the emerging images begin to come to the surface, the inexplicable inner turmoil of the *nigredo* becomes slightly more comprehensible. One acknowledges powerful surges underlying what felt like a depression, but still may remain unclear about these feelings. Why one cries, rages, and trembles often persists as a mystery. In this early stage of dawning insight, the sun is not yet up, but the sky has started to lighten with promise.

The Image Itself Emerges

As the sun follows the early morning light, the image itself follows the feelings into awareness. Not until I acknowledged formidable currents of fear, anger and sadness in myself did the attendant images appear, coming without warning. Seemingly out of nowhere, snake images began to appear at odd times during the day. I might be sitting at my desk collecting thoughts, driving to the supermarket, or walking in the nearby woods. When snakes started to emerge into consciousness, they brought up ambivalent feelings: pleasure and pain, intrigue and loathing. *A snake slithers up my leg and into my womb. It glides up and attaches itself with fangs to my heart.* Initially, I associated the snake with genital sexuality, a primal lustiness that devours any heart feelings, and with these images appearing, I thought I must be a thorough degenerate. *The body of the snake produces a heat, an ongoing low level of arousal, while eating out my heart and replacing it with its head.*[3] When such images emerged, I fought against them and felt assaulted by them.

Fear of the image exacerbated the painful confusion, and made it impossible to establish the meeting of equals necessary for relationship with the image. Instead, the dynamic of victimhood constellated and continued for long periods of time. *Attending to a dull ache in my chest, I detect the viper's head. As I recoil, the viper grasps tighter, hissing, threatening to paralyze me.* In the wake of this intensified imagery, I faced new levels of sensuality, pain, terror, rage, and sadness that I had to confront and work through until they could be tolerated. At this stage, the primary work involved resisting the panic to run away. I had to stay with the image and its associated sensations in order to confront the complex range of feelings elicited by the image.

Illness or spells of dissociation may occur as the image comes nearer to consciousness and begins to threaten more acutely our self-image. At this stage, such "splitting" is common, that is, awareness tends to shift between the image itself and the feelings or instinctual underpinnings it activates. We are aware of our feelings or we see the image, but not both at once. We should not be surprised to discover this split in our experience since the thrust of this entire stage is *to join* a mental image with its physical affects and sensations. But the inexperienced will never guess this, and we who know the theory easily forget.

EMBRACE OF THE DAIMON

The Image Speaks

Once the instinctual images have emerged into consciousness, they may be willing to speak—though when laden with unfamiliar instinctual energies, they are often decidedly nonverbal. After some months of struggle with the nonresponsive, nonverbal serpents, a brief stage of dialoguing began. From analytic reports, it appears that this dialoguing stage may be lengthy for many people, or perhaps dialoguing just lends itself well to written accounts. During this period some people feel the need to explore the mythological significance of the images coming into awareness, as I did with the serpent. Background information can help steady the nervous ego, making us brave enough to open ourselves to the qualities concealed in the image. Once the image comes to consciousness, it may encourage an enactment or expression, such as drawing, painting, dancing, sculpting, or poetry, rather than direct conversation. These activities also help bring more aspects of the image into focus.

Dialogue with the image anchors Jungian "active imagination." This focus on expression or conversation seems suitable for the more psychic or mental aspect of the image and sometimes yields significant insight. It may also serve to introduce us to the "body of the image." *I notice that the black snake constricting my breath is male and I think, "Isn't this what men always do, suffocate and silence you?" I ask him why he continues to hurt me. He takes the shape of an alternatingly limp and erect penis and says gently, "Soft power adheres not only to women. Softness showers."* This snippet of dialogue with the daimon surprised me, especially the tenderness and gentle tone, and helped me dismantle an unconscious attitude of distrust that was preventing me from accepting this snake. It encouraged a more receptive relationship, a greater connection, and openness of mind and body. *Breathing comes easier, energizing my whole body, as the snake shifts rapidly from male to female, demonstrating a fluidly androgynous nature.* I associated the dynamic aspects of the serpent—its strength, power, and aggression—with culturally assigned "masculine" qualities. Through this dialogue, I discovered a one-sidedness to my thinking that had been held in a pattern of physical tensions. I saw how much I mistrusted the masculine qualities of the serpent, associating them with hurtful aggression. When this association became conscious, it was possible to relax more into the image, to yield to these dynamic energies, and to lessen the gender bias I was carrying.

Insight Dawns: The Union of Image and Affect

When the process of accepting the snake had begun in earnest, the imagery continued to reflect a split between the psychic image and its somatic components, the image did not very often appear in conjunction with feelings. Gradually some snakelike instinctual qualities, such as sexual excitement, began to come more fully to consciousness. *One snake wraps herself around me. Entering me, she says she is the Pythoness . . . I fill with excitement and find I have become her. I slither toward men, hot and sensuous, wrap myself around and enter them, give them pleasure, then suffocate and devour them as we embrace.* I would dread the coming of the snake because of the increasing bodily tension involved in containing the mix of fear, pain, and terror at my own seductive aggression combined with numinous erotic arousal. Over the course of years, such semi-embodied imagery continued with an array of sadomasochistic themes of intermixed pleasure and pain. Often I muttered cries of "I hate snakes" when any snake appeared in the imaginal field. *As serpent, I devour them; the men die in a blaze of bliss and agony. At the death of each I acquire his power until I become a superman myself.*

With time, I started to reconcile myself to the feelings associated with the serpent imagery. I had to accept my own "serpentine" nature. Having been unconsciously seductive, I began to realize how much psychic energy I had spent competing with men, manipulating through flirtation to get my way. My conscious feelings of victimization at their hands often concealed my own rage. In business I had unconsciously taken great delight in making the older men I worked with look inept through outperforming them. I wondered whether this drive for vengeance stemmed from the collective experience of being a woman, a response to centuries of second-class citizenship, or from the biographical level of my father's rages, or perhaps (I even speculated) it all was a carryover from some past life. But such attempts to assign a cause seem futile, especially in view of the archetypal depths of the imaginal realms. Through the difficult, disillusioning process of claiming the energies that the serpent activated in me, I became better able to acknowledge larger pieces of my personality and to bring more awareness and choice to how I used my sexuality in my relationships with men.

The Transition from Insight to Integration: The Darkness Deepens

Once we accept the implications of containing both the image and its related feelings, thereby incorporating previously unacknowledged aspects of ourselves, we come to a transitional phase. This stage, when insight has been established but the daimons have yet to appear, can be considered either the first step of integration or the last of insight. We can now admit, "I know I do this creepy thing." We may be sorry for our now predictable self-protective, defensive actions, and sometimes we may even manage to change our behavior. We have begun to integrate the shadow side of ourselves. Insight—gained through therapy, or just plain living—strengthens the ego as that part of us that can stand aside, that can reliably take responsibility for the things we do, and that can try to establish a center of consistency and knowing. It becomes a steady place we return to after the inevitable occasions when we slip back into old destructive behavior patterns. Having passed through the hallmark disillusionment that follows new insights, with time we loosen our unconscious merger with the image and begin meeting it more and more consciously.

We become aware that we carry a profound identification with the image and see that its body, feelings, and outlook have been our own. During this phase, we may have moments when the image appears throughout the body, almost as a double, beginning to lift itself out of us, like a ghostly shadow rising up from a corpse. The sensations of this period resonate with some of those that occur in the labor of giving birth. Heavy rhythmic breathing accompanies a sense of letting go of some part of ourselves—something deeply familiar, something we have lived with a long time and that now has become extremely uncomfortable. Yet we feel waves of fear and emptiness, for we have fiercely identified with these patterns of being. Who will "I" be once I release the somatic pattern of the emerging daimon? Will "I" not collapse into nothingness? Indeed, at this point, we need to have found our way to tolerating sensations of dying, of nothingness, and the void, if we are to venture any further past this imaginal edge.

The images tempt us now in a new way with their numinous combination of fascination and dread, appearing, as they do, for the first time in full force. Transformation becomes an insistent, recurrent theme in this transitional stage; the images sometimes metamorphose in dizzying abundance, threatening to overwhelm the ego.

> *An enormous black vulture, wet and dead, yet "royal," washes onto the rocks at the center of my back, filling me with foreboding. Crows come to pick my flesh. In their exhilaration at the taste of the dead meat, they fly toward the sun, hitting an invisible shell that kills them/me. I am dizzy and disoriented as they fall to Earth, where they are trampled, turning into hundreds of snakes slithering over me, clinging to me, trying to eat their way into my flesh even as they are destroyed. As the bloody trampling goes on, I feel myself coming unhinged. I recoil in fear and race out of the house.*

We naturally mistrust such invasive, destructive energies, and move instinctively to check their development. But cutting off a field of such numinosity can only have bad results. Unfortunately this seems often to happen.

We can compare the birthing of the daimonic image to an exorcism. The daimon may become a palpable presence, inhabiting our bodies. As our sense of self grows stronger, the separate existence of the daimon becomes increasingly apparent. We find the two of us crowded intolerably in a single body. The daimon needs to be exorcised. Yet in our recurring unconsciousness, we continue to merge with the image or its associated feelings, in this case, the black vulture turned into crows and then snakes. Many times, I unknowingly abandoned myself in dissociated awe and merged prematurely with the rising serpent presence, refusing to "die." I know, looking back, that merging at this point was an ego defense. I experienced identification with this powerful, sensual Other as an inflation of myself. These semiconscious mergings, or partial unions, that accompany insight, however, have a constructive role.

Their inevitable deflation—*I feel myself coming unhinged*— activates a despair that enables us to appreciate that insight is not enough. The old complexes still rule. Our despair in the face of this realization heralds the next phase: reunion with the body which can motivate us to take steps in finding help, embarking on a creative project, or dropping into a willed inner focus to release the image. This transitional phase from the stage of insight to that of incarnation actually amounts to an *incarnation crisis*. For we cannot go forward without suffering another, perhaps even more frightening, *nigredo*, as we release the sensational foundation of the image. It appears, at least for the moment, that we have a choice whether to go further into the disarming enigmas of life or settle for staying with our current level of existence. We recognize this crisis initially by the heightened degree of intense inner conflict it provokes.

I previously described the difficulties that can arise in trying to cope with this increased inner turmoil. Two mistakes, especially, entice us in this transitional phase. Our first impulse will likely be to flee from the disturbing imagery that begins to erupt, looking for anything to distract and distance ourselves from the interior life. If we manage to stay with the inner unfolding, the affect-laden images beginning to emerge will still tempt us strongly to cast our identity into them before they have been fully released from the body sense of self.

SANDRA LEE DENNIS

THE UNION OF INTEGRATION: THE *UNIO CORPORALIS*

During the phase of gaining insight we learned to separate ourselves from the feelings coming to awareness. However, if we continue to do so now, we perpetuate an ongoing purgatorial torment.[4] For we now must immerse ourselves in the feelings and sensations of the daimonic presence.

We need a fine inner discrimination to know when to step back and release the image and when to go forward toward union. Since we are told that every personal complex, or repeating emotional pattern, has a body,[5] we are left with the problem of differentiating the image of the shadow from the ensouled or daimonic image. In Healing Fiction, Hillman considers this same issue, asking how we can distinguish between "the call" and "the complex." Is the image a god or a demon, an archetypal presence or a personal complex? This is a critical distinction as it indicates which stage in the incarnation cycle we are facing, and determines our right relationship to the image.

The daimonic image has a lot in common with less evolved images, however, we can learn to recognize it by a number of signals: 1) by its vivid presence—a radical Otherness, 2) by the pronounced, bizarre somatic overtones it brings, 3) by its insistent eroticism (it strongly attracts or repels, activating our desire nature), and 4) especially, by the opening to the ground of Being it facilitates, which may appear as synchronicity.

The Darkening Intensifies: The Daimonic Nigredo

The daimon opens us to its larger world. As it emerges fully into awareness, inner events seem more often to materialize in our external life through obvious syncronicities or more subtle resonances, reflecting the imaginal's propensity to connect us to many layers of meaning at once. Periods of darkening resemble stages of initiation, in which our faith in the invisible numinosities is tested against inner and outer threats. If the inner images of the daimonic *nigredo* do not scare us into closing up, their external manifestations may. I believe synchronistic events multiply (or perhaps our awareness of them just increases) at points of daimonic necessity, that is, when the daimons are maturing into consciousness. Ambivalence toward releasing this vivid emerging presence may bring actual people or events into our lives with energies similar to the emerging daimon. During this phase I became involved, for example, with an entrancing, seductive analyst and spent three years in a troubled relationship before finally gathering the strength to leave.

Vivid Presence: Flashes of the nearness of a vivid Other often accompany the arrival of the daimon. This sense of presence or energetic field appears before the daimon shows its form. We may experience this presence as an irrational fear of an intruder, stalker, malevolent force, or a guardian spirit. I remember waking at night during this period sure that someone was at the window, in the closet, or outside the door. Or we may interpret this uncanny presence as a ghost or spirit, a "phantom of the opera" phenomenon, a supernatural being. We may encounter deep fears and superstitions of many kinds as the daimonic presence arises. For a while, I thought about possession by some evil force, a fear that expressed itself in tensions and shallow breathing. I would literally hold my breath in a startle response when I became aware of the presence I eventually came to recognize as the serpent. The serpent image itself was threatening enough, but the radical Otherness, the clear autonomy of the image, was even more frightening, sometimes even bringing on panic reactions.

> *Dozens of baby diamondback snakes are undulating within a larger mother snake in my throat, constricting my breathing and causing me to cough and cough. Her head darts out whenever I open my mouth to speak, creating waves of nausea on which she tries to slide out of me. I feel I cannot let her go, as she will drag me along with her, draining the life from my body.*

Bizarre Sensations: These waves of nausea were not connected with pregnancy (the above episode was years later), but part of an upheaval of weird sensations associated with the emerging serpent rippling and ripping its way out of my bodily life. The initial *nigredo* of insight puts us in touch with the tip of a huge iceberg of unconscious instincts, whose foundations are revealed in this second *nigredo*—which leads beyond insight to integration. As the icy core of the image comes to the surface, it melts in the sun of awareness, freeing powerful instinctual forces and inspiring tremendous resistance. This melting iceberg has been a sturdy, reliable rock on which we had established our old illusory sense of self. It's hell to pay for the body and mind when it begins to thaw.

Not just discomforts this time around, but extraordinarily alarming sensations surface. Sometimes we wrongly associate these disconcerting feelings with illness (how many trips did I make to various doctors to find out what was wrong with me!). I experienced dizziness, fragmentation, expansion and contraction, chest pains, chaotic confusion, sexual excitation, and despair. I sometimes felt brushed by barbed-wire balls moving inside my body. I felt I was filled with pins and needles, having my chest stomped. At different times I was on fire, frozen numb, strangled, drowned, suffocated, knifed, and eviscerated. Naturally, I wanted to escape from these torments. There is a strong desire to block out these disorienting, painful sensations that not only hurt, but also threaten to undermine, our sense of who we are. When these measures fail, we may take our sensation literally, as though we are being tortured by an invisible opponent whom we try to fight or escape. Anything seems preferable to recognizing that the parameters of our very existence are in question.

Because of the fundamental conflict between our conscious attitude and the emerging unconscious energies, the *nigredo* that precedes the *unio corporalis* brings big-time chaos into our lives. As the darkening intensifies, so does the threat of possession or madness. Betty Meador mentions this threat as she describes the closing of the Athenian Thesmophoria celebration during which she believes the Greek women sacrificed to the primal, underground, snake-deities. "Snake's gifts of sight and fecundity are only a thin line removed from her powers of wild possession and madness. . . . They ask Snake to guard them too from madness and possession, acknowledging that madness too, is in her power."[6] In the ancient mysteries, the powers of life, death, and madness were thought to belong to the snake. The celebrants believed that snakes became incarnate through them in their rituals, in this way emerging into the upper world.[7] I believe, as they did, that the gradually acquired skill of opening to these normally avoided chaotic feelings allows the daimon to incarnate. Attending to these sensations in small doses helps protect us from being overwhelmed by the release of numinous instinctual energies. Only disciplined concentration enables us to handle these bizarre subtle-body miseries.

Jung also said that calling forth the serpent runs the risk of insanity or attachment to the roots of consciousness.[8] He thought union with the serpent meant the entrance of the god, the natural reaction to which was madness or panic. When the daimon (serpent or otherwise) emerges, new layers of disruptive instinctual material flush to consciousness in disorienting abundance, bringing about a further dismantling of the conscious attitude. When in her work with Jung, Christiana Morgan reported an attack by a python, Jung commented that one must stand the onslaught of panic, that the terrible, horrifying moment of attack by the python must be endured.[9]

In my own episode, the cobra appears with menacing fangs, a skull and crossbones above her head. (Several days pass. I am unable to concentrate on my work. On the way to the Safeway, I hit a parked car while turning the corner onto Franklin St. That night I awake in a panic.) *Woods are burning all around me. The fanged cobra sits between my eyes, and then ignites into a fire-breathing dragon, heating my body until I break out in a sweat. My world goes up in flames. I have become the consuming fire.* (I collapse from the heat and disorientation. . . . Two days later, my husband is diagnosed with lymphatic cancer.)

I suppose I endured this "attack." More, I felt I began to surrender to the panic the daimon activated. "Trusting the serpent" (barely, well, almost) allowed the god to enter in the form of serpent fire. Opening to the uncanny sensation of being consumed by fire, I discovered something deeper than the panic. Becoming the fire granted me magical protection from the terror of being attacked by the dragon. I realized I could no longer be destroyed, as I had become the fire itself. But my fear and repugnance were not at an end, for I realized that the fire and the serpent were one. And, though I could bear the fire, I abhorred the thought of union with the serpent.

In retrospect, it seems that "holding" the panic gave birth to the fire. Being able to consciously face the panic aroused by the daimon begins to thaw the dark depths of the iceberg, revealing a numinous hot core of annihilating force. The iceberg of instinct conceals an elemental, fiery foundation. Immersion in the initial panic of impending madness or possession conducted me through a transformative fire. I found that Meador's description of the closing ceremonies of the Thesmophoria appears in some way to parallel this experience:

> They have dared to enter the abode of Snake. They have sacrificed before her. They have participated in a ritual death in her presence. Snake has filled them. The deity herself has risen from the depths in the bodies of the women. Her awesome power possessed them. She loosened the boundaries of ordinary life and shook the women.[10]

In my life, the inner serpent seemed to have come in its traditional role as "prophet" announcing a literal death force. I was forced to confront not only images of death, but also the actual dying of my husband. I do not mean to suggest that the emergence of the daimons, intricately connected as they are to erotic dissolution and death, as well as to regeneration, necessarily brings actual illness, death, and destruction. In this case, however, their appearance did correlate in a scary synchronicity with the onset of a deadly illness. Since this experience, now five years ago, I have been through other rounds of daimonic emergence without such a literal and extreme outer manifestation.

To be able to contain the unfolding process of the daimonic, we need to cultivate a respect for the numinous side of our fears—

of darkness, misfortune, illness, and death, or whatever trial the daimon may bring. How easy it is to write, how difficult it is to actualize in our lives. Long is our tradition of disdaining and defending against the unknown, against misfortune. Under our adapted, comfortable relation to life, embedded deep in our bodies, lies a *primal fear* that the daimon reveals. This fear leads directly to the unlit side of the opposites, yet it waits for the welcoming embrace of consciousness to release its underbelly of love, acceptance, and belonging to each and every experience of our lives. We must tread the battlefield of our reluctance and face the profound anxieties brought out by the emerging daimon before it will reveal itself as a hidden door to the Divine.

The Daimonic Image Emerges

If we can bear the strain of this period of pressure and despair, the *nigredo* that initiates integration will show itself as a darkness that gives birth to the daimonic image, yearning toward reunion with the body.

Insistent Eroticism: Years after its first appearance, I began to exist more comfortably with the various forms of the feeling-laden snake. A relationship of trust began to develop with the radical Otherness of the serpent, and I gradually began to feel more actively into her positive potential. The fear and loathing of my initial evasions and the panic of this latest phase gave way to a desire for more contact. I actually began to feel an attraction to the serpent and to miss her presence, almost pining away for a return visit, for her numinous loveliness. In her journal, Christiana Morgan recounts what appears to be a similar attraction to the serpent energies:

> Then the snake coiled itself about my body and put its head close to my face ... I looked into the eyes of the snake and putting my arm around it said, "Serpent, you are beautiful to me" then the serpent fell away.[11]

As this attraction increased, I noticed an expanded capacity to be there with the snake as she filled my body. My humanity

SANDRA LEE DENNIS

resonated with her numinosity and recognized a welcome home. We found ourselves attracted to one another, sometimes my body actually vibrated in concert with this subtle-body courting ritual. Rather than losing myself in engulfing merger with her sensual power, as I had so often done previously, I felt myself participating in her captivating dance as an "object of desire."

She slides up my leg and begins to fill my body. As she enters into me, she expands to fill the room and then the house. A sense of delicious expansion and delicacy emerges—that "unbearable lightness of being" entranced with its own beauty. I am large, too, containing all she contains. We are "two in one," a vibrantly light presence. I notice a quiet excitement in my chest and my genitals, which frightens as well as uplifts.

Eroticism accompanies the serpent now whenever she appears. Because we commonly associate the serpent with sexuality, we might suspect that the image merely symbolizes our sensuality. But the Eros of the daimon adheres regardless of the form it takes. I have felt erotic intent with any image that has reached full stature, including machine-like cyborgs.

Opening to the Ground of Being: The daimonic emerging serpent directly begins to reveal her unifying nature, containing the surrounding world with her presence. As guardian at the gate of imaginal vision, she points toward a realm of expanded participation in all of life. She opens onto a visionary space, outside our normal conceptions of reality. It is said that the "guidance of the serpent" is gained through a willingness to touch on the land of the dead, to enter the realm beyond space and time.[12] The connecting link to this visionary realm expands most fully as the image reunites with the body. Of course, it is never this neat as we, meanwhile, are still struggling to contain these forces of change and move through our lives chatting about the weather and what to have for dinner.

Relationship with the ensouled image rarely remains static, but flows into permutations on themes associated with the daimon. For instance, a realization I had difficulty accepting at first—the primordial link between the snake and ancient blood mysteries—stirred up my ambivalence.

> *The heart of the witch, black and full of snakes, resides as a knotted fist in the center of my back. The snakes crawl out to drink blood. "Speak blood," she says. I dare not speak blood, invoke blood; rather again I cough and cough, thinking, Who will guide my tongue? I cringe and cannot embrace this blood deity. I hear a voice say, "Ah, who can bite the mother's breast hard enough to draw her blood"? Angered at my resistance, the witch strangles me until I agree to speak. Suffocating, choking, finally, I manage to take a deep breath and to say, "Blood." Rivers of blood immediately burst out of me to cover the earth and sky. Blood everywhere, nothing but blood. I, too, am blood. My mouth tastes it; it is in my eyes, my hair. Sticky, wet, viscous, everything is blood. There is nothing else. The snake appears as in a double-exposed image, smiling, as mistress, emblematic talisman of the blood. The blood/snake throbs with its own delight. I marvel at its power over all people, and participate in its connective, warm, insistent life.*

The conflict and struggle in this image typifies the transition from insight to integration, while the blood opened me to a unitive vision that characterizes the emergence of the daimon's "full stature" trailing, in this case, gory glory. The actual unfolding of the image, of course, is not as orderly and neat as the scheme I am presenting here. These phases overlap one another. We go forward and back with a very modest predictability between numinous delight and dreadful despair, the twin poles of the journey into the daimonic world. I still found it troubling to open myself to some of the deeper instinctual aspects of the serpent. My uncontrollable dismay surprised me, as I consciously longed for more contact.

When I finally managed to breathe fully into the image of the strangling witch, I relaxed into relationship with her, and she emerged in her full daimonic stature as the blood. I learned in a way that goes beyond all theorizing that embracing the daimon opens us to a world of Eros, of primordial connection. In this example, the blood unveils itself as cosmic Nature Goddess (the "lotus in the mud," "the pearl in the oyster") in the form of the numinous instinctual rhythms of life's flow.

As the daimon emerges and becomes an Other who threatens, and with whom we can unite, its magnetism gives way to, and overlaps with, the purifying *nigredo* of conflict and despair. This back and forth of blissful contact and desperate isolation may go on for some time as the integration of image and body draws near. By this stage already, each time we release ourselves into the daimonic energies, each time we embrace the image, we undergo a shift in our sense of self. We are sacrificing bits of our old ego identity. Our fears, hopes, ideals, and perspectives on the world may all be changed as we make room for the daimon. These sacrifices bring on an array of feelings associated with loss, so that we may need to pass through profound despair before we are ready for a union of the sensual with the sacred image in our souls.

The Image Incarnates: The Reunion of Soul and Body

Once the way is clear, a vivid daimonic image speeds toward reunion with the body, as is splendidly depicted in William Blake's well-known watercolor rendering of "The Reunion of the Soul and the Body," a more congenial, ethereal and "human" encounter than his rendition of the less famous "Red Dragon and the Woman Clothed in the Sun." The two impulses we have kept separate for so long, the sensual and the spiritual, finally unite when the ensouled image as daimon returns to the body from which it so recently emerged. Once we pass through the initial rejection and ambivalence, erotic attraction for the daimon increases, until, carried by an almost religious impulse, we reverently submit to the draw into union.

As my relationship with the serpent intensified, more sophisticated and complex imaginal communications emerged. I discovered these to be different in character from the insight-oriented messages of the earlier, more disembodied serpentine images. At the stage of insight, having some knowledge of the mythic background of an image helps reclaim lost pieces of personality. However, as discussed earlier, images of mythic proportion go beyond symbolizing lost aspects of personal character. Now mythic enormity and personal integrity are mediated by the body, and our immersion in the imaginal mysteries reveals a new depth of body knowledge. Through contact with the daimon, the body realizes its ultimate immateriality, its intimate participation in the elemental play of nature.

> *The Serpent has come again. I find myself encompassed by her. Her flesh is cold and clammy. I recoil from the sensation. I hear the words, "Eat my flesh", and the image of a Christ figure appears in place of the snake's body. I hear, "Drink my blood", and I am struck by how horrible this command for "communion" is. I sense a moment of choice. My love for the serpent prevails as I allow the impersonal, fleshiness—cold, sticky, and bloody—of the Christ/snake to mingle with my warm pulsing life. "Eating and drinking," as if satisfying years of thirst and hunger, I begin to absorb the raw-meat quality of the flesh and the luscious, cold blood into my body.*

Such directly visceral interplay does not occur in the earlier phase of gaining insight, when we are regaining contact with lost emotion and feeling. Through integration of strong feeling we begin to learn how to contain the bizarre sensations activated by the serpent, as well as whatever other external trials may come. Finally, however, a trusting relationship with the serpent lays an inner foundation for exchange, meeting, and continuing communion with the most primal elements of the serpentine nature. Acceptance of the union requires an active, magnetic receptivity to the image. Each surge of responsive acceptance deepens the contact, as one image dissolves into the next.

> *The initial creepy sensation gradually opens my body to an exquisite delicacy that builds in intensity. First, an aphrodisiac comes in jasmine waves over my entire body. Then it grows to a climax that shudders throughout my body. The Christ figure replaces the snake, then transforms into a naked woman on a cross, nearly dead. I pass into the erotic torment of the woman.*

The communion activates subtle-body sensations of orgasmic delight. Entering into the union with the daimonic image, we are changed. At the apex of the union, death pours through every inch of the body on waves of annihilation, and we "die" in dissolving waves. Perhaps not clear in this description, yet throughout the union, imageless seconds, moments (who knows how long) of pure erotic Being punctuate the unfolding imagery.

> *A looming figure appears behind the dying woman on the cross—a black, Kaliesque, many-armed woman wearing bright garments and jewels, with a contorted, laughing face. The black figure plucks the dying crucifix woman from the earth and begins to eat her. The dagger-like teeth tear the woman to pieces, blissfully releasing her. Dissolving into the many-armed woman's enjoyment of the crucified figure, I eat my dying self. The taste is luscious—salty, sweet, and creamy, all at once. The dark woman leans back in repose, savoring the taste of this magic crucifix plant, and begins to merge into the visions it produces.*

And I wonder how long has she been growing this "crucifixplant," now finally ripe?

Encompassing this death/rebirth phenomenon is a third reality, which appears as the fruit of the union of the daimon with the body. The body is the first reality, which we have known but poorly all our lives. The daimon is the second, the Other we have come to know through a long and difficult process. The relationship between them, mystical and often sensed as an imageless presence, is the third. In this case, however, the relationship did take on a form—that of the Rose, personal and feminine.

> *The dark woman's visions start unfolding a wine-red rose, fragrant, sweet, and velvety, filling her/my body and gradually expanding to pervade the whole world. The rose presence gradually turns buttery, pale yellow, then apple blossom-white. With each color comes a new nuance of fragrance. The yellow brings sandalwood, the white a hint of ylang flower. Each brings a slight alteration in texture from the thick, warm velvet of the red, to a silky, satin yellow, and gossamer, clouds of white. The world has become a fragrant sea of white ylang, sandalwood, and*

rose petals, in which all luxuriate. I am swimming in this white floral sea from which incomparably delicate sensations of billowy support arise. The sea continues to drift back to yellow, then wine red, and then, finally, to an inky still blackness.

Imaginal sight opens further as union intensifies, and a deep biological knowledge, registered in the subtle senses, transmits the nature of this visionary world as a third encompassing presence: the love, the sweet sustaining support of the world. The daimon animates, opening through the *coniunctio* to the *anima mundi:* the "soul of the world" begins to reveal itself. In this case, the snake performed the work of a magician bringing the realities of the two worlds together: incarnating spirit and spiritualizing matter to reveal the fragrant heartland of connective reality in the Rose sea.

In another phenomenon characteristic of the union between soul and body, it is not only we who change, but the daimons transform through communion with us.

I spend a long time, swimming through the velvet black, I have relaxed so completely I no longer feel my body boundaries. Finally, I begin to notice bursts of small pink flowers that open like windows. I look through them and see that the serpent is a river running into and becoming the sea. The serpent sea rises up, ever so slightly amused. She sits with me, leaning back slightly, a pencil in hand, glasses perched on her nose, jovially entertained by my realization. Deep peace, punctuated by pink surges of affection for life, fills me.

The serpent has indeed been "humanized" through our contact, made evident by her reading and writing, and she, too, seems to have found her source in the Rose sea. From the initial mix of seductiveness, sexuality, revulsion, and aggression associated with the snake, this series of unions has led to a grounded earthiness, a far-reaching visionary appreciation of the primal feminine at the heart of a Christian ritual—the consumption of the crucified Christ-woman by the Dark Mother and, most significantly, the subsequent ecstatic immersion in the Rose waters.

At least a year after the eruption of this episode, I discovered that aspects of this image resemble the Gnostic treatise, *The Testimony of Truth*, in which Christ is equated with the serpent. It also recalls Claire Douglas' account of the vision Jung claimed marked the apogee of Christiana Morgan's visions. Following her imaginal union in blood with a Dionysian black messiah, the messiah transforms into a snake, enters a church, slithers up on to the altar and finally reposes on the cross: "A snake with a black hood over its head silently glided up the steps to the altar and wound itself upon the cross. I went up to the snake and asked why it was there. The snake answered, "I am he who has taken the place of Christ".[13] Jung tells her the image holds "material for the next two to three hundred years. It is a great *document humaine*. It is a rushing forth of all that has hitherto been unconscious."[14] The many references to similar images that have been published,[15] suggest that these daimons may be coming to consciousness on a collective scale. I see the Kaliesque woman, who may symbolize the dawning of the Dark Mother archetype, as testament to this emergent vision, and with her I add my voice to welcoming this vision.

At this point, I will leave the unfolding of the daimonic image, although any ending is artificial. Every union leads to yet another separation, as round and round the cycle goes, bringing the soul into earthly existence. What happened to the recurrent serpent imagery, you may wonder? Does a culminating union mark the disappearance of that particular image from our lives? I believe that reunion with the body establishes the daimonic image in our inner life as a representative of the visionary world. That presence can now serve to remind us of the existence of the noumenal world, functioning more as a guide or guardian spirit than the transformative agent of the *coniunctio*. In further appearances, the daimon comes as an emissary from the other side of sense-based reality. She comes to remind us where our loyalties lie, to remind us of the truth of soul and the visionary life that underlies our everyday existence.

My husband died some months after this imaginal unfolding, I planted three roses in his honor: red, yellow, and white.

Incarnation of Soul: Qualities Associated with the Serpent
  Though arising from the other world, daimonic experience
leaves its greatest legacy on the everyday. As I have mentioned,
from the archetypal perspective, imaginal characters reflect a
many-layered reality, leaving their mark on each level through
which they pass. Therefore, they can symbolize both our personal
life and autonomous impersonal realities. Contact with them gives
birth to faculties within us, which correlate with those enduring
qualities they represent. Bodily union with them incarnates what
we have seen or understood at first only in the mind, eventually
making an impact on our lives in the empirical world. Following the
serpent image, I will share the new qualities I felt were born
within the field of the subtle body as a result of the encounter.

  Our empirically oriented language can do little more than
hint at what we experience in subtle-body realms. Some of the
qualities that emerge from the archetypal ground[16] may include
increased strength, sensuality, wisdom, presence, peace, joy,
vision, or creativity. In my case, the reunion of the daimonic
serpent with the body encouraged the development of at least four
qualities I would like to discuss: 1) trust in death, 2) groundedness,
3) unifying consciousness, "love", and 4) vision. All these qualities
share a common thread that weaves them back to the numinous
source from which they arose. That is, each arises from a centered
presence rooted in the unitive consciousness opened by the
daimon, yet each has a distinctive quality that sets it apart.
Learning to identify and name these distinctions in Being has become
another task of our times.

  For this reason, I hesitate before writing this next section.
(Not to mention the potential problem of grandiose self-
aggrandizement.) Inevitably, more difficulties with language arise
when attempting to describe any subtle-body phenomenon, but
this is particularly true in the aftermath of the daimonic union
itself. I am better perhaps leaving this exercise to poets. Against
my better judgment and despite this warning, recklessly, I go forth.
Why should we not mark and identify the results of "incarnation"?
After all, incarnation, this bringing of the soul fully into the body,

can be framed as a reason for living. Ought we not celebrate any part of its arrival we are fortunate enough to catch? Lacking a poet's gift, I speak of what I have intuited in the imagery, linking these more abstract conclusions with everyday experiences that seem to demonstrate the integration of each quality.

As the texts suggest, the serpent, indeed, initiates us into the mysteries of death and renewal. She helps to develop a deep trust in death as part of life, revealing to the body that destruction and decay play an integral part in the creation of anything new. This trust induces moments of deep relaxation in the face of apparent misery.

> *The serpent batters the heart with her immenseness. I weep and weep as our bodies mingle. Knowing I am mortal flesh.* (Watching the blue chemo drip—vincristine, cytoxin, prednisone, those strange elegant sounds of devastation—trickle into his veins, I sit with dispassionate interest, a wave of deep surrender ripples through me.) *As I release into the serpent, my body suddenly slumps into a rotting mass of maggots, their gnawing dissolves into vastness.*

Miguel Serrano, the Chilean author of *Serpent of Paradise*, offers a poetic rendering of the death/rebirth motif when he speaks of the role of the serpent in birthing what he calls the "spirit son of death":

> This son can be born only by marrying the serpent or by playing Shiva's phallus and Krishna's flute. And he alone can carry us over the sea of death. He will give us passage on his phosphorescent barge or will allow us rest on the wings of the Plumed Serpent.[17]

Before beginning to develop this trust in phenomenological destruction, I confronted deep stores of distrust in the form of anger at God, fear of life, and denial of feeling. Whether the inevitable darkening enters our lives on the small scale of an anxious night, a failed test, or an infestation of varmints in the vegetable garden, or on the large one of a suffering child, a lost job, a fatal illness, or the unexpected loss of a dear one, the wells of distrust overflow when the "slings and arrows of outrageous fortune" come our way. In keeping with our cultural overvaluing of the light side of the dualities of life and our longstanding denial of the dark, we probably will rage long at this coming of night before finally seeing through to the fortune in our misfortune.

> *The serpent has become a fountain spewing forth thousands of snakelets into the world. They crawl off each in its own direction to spread her word. The little snakes slither into the orifices of their chosen companions, each snakelet a familiar, an elixir of vitality, a herald of each person's assured renewal.* (After years of squeamishness and refusal to eliminate the destroyers of my garden, I spread the snail bait with resolute abandon and stoically pick the slugs off the primroses.)

Against my Buddhist inclinations, I begin to know the strange necessity of being the death-giver. Snake reveals her kinship with the ground through a rootedness and solidity she imparts—another often unrecognized numinous quality.

> *The serpent in my body merges with the wood floor to become a liquid-amber tree, my legs its trunk. The roots go deep into the earth, spreading. I sense the roots growing underground in the dark as a great weightiness in my lower body.*

Rarely do we realize how much the chronic, disembodied states of mind—our lack of groundedness in the body encouraged by our denial and fear of the instincts—interfere with our enjoyment of our everyday routines. The serpent's distinct earthiness opens the field of the sensual body, imparting pleasure to the simple motions of a day.

> (Loading the whites of the Saturday laundry, I feel the fleece and cottons and notice the sun glistening on the Whirlpool's chrome. . . . Later, I chop the carrots in rhythmic sacrifice of their life to sustain mine.) *Snake slithers through the roots, bringing the light of the upper world into the Dark. She winds herself around me and becomes the tree. I feel solid, huge, immovable.*

Groundedness also increases our capacity to allow more energy to flow through us: that energy may take the form of relationship, creative capacity, wisdom, or even money. (A boon at work brings a $20,000 check for the savings account depleted by medical bills.) I quiver with the dynamism it brings.

As the imaginal serpent reunites with the body, we become aware of a profound erotic connection to life that I believe is an element of impersonal love. Snake introduces the "wave principle" of reality. We begin to participate more often in the emerging vision physicists describe. We come to know ourselves as separate points along one serpentine wave of existence. We truly *are one.* Snake erases distinctions of inner and outer, dark and light, me and you, male and female, life and death.

> *In the serpent's embrace, all becomes undulating motion, flux and vertigo predominate as seemingly natural conditions of existence, erasing boundaries. First, she contains as Earth Mother, promising our return to the dark, embracing, womb of her body, then dazzles as phallic warrior, sliding in and around every body opening in electric, dissolving expansion.*

She demonstrates a fluid inter-penetrability of parts, a melting of edges between apparent opposites. (Our cat crawls onto my lap, rolls on her back, paws outstretched in the air, totally relaxed to my touch. For a moment, I am unsure who is the cat, and who the human.) A kinship begins to develop with the rest of life.

The sense of connection, this cohering love, applies also to the inner world where she brings integrity and unity of parts.

> *As python afire, her flame moves up from the heart to the throat. She comes out of the mouth, catching her tail as it hangs from the womb's entrance to form the uroboros, spinning round and round through the body.*

Increased integrity does not always show itself in dramatic ways, but in simple adjustments to outer life. (After two years of failing, always miserably out of step, I am finally able to follow all the Jazzercise routines, moving in unison with thirty others.) An integrating, paradoxically moist presence connects all parts of the body in the midst of the heat she brings that connects every inch of the body like a finely woven web.

I believe this knowledge of erotic connection with the world represents the most salient change from our usual state of individual separateness. This unitive state of mind comes and goes, but is more accessible now, even amid the most mundane challenges. We learn to accept life as it comes.

> (Outside my bedroom window, the speeding cars that often irritate me so much seem to express a spontaneous exuberance. I see they externalize the essence of "drive," my own power to initiate and to accomplish what I set out to do.) *The python's motions, rippling out from the deepest core of the body to encompass the rest of the world, dissolve the body's boundaries into the vast network of all aspects of existence.*

This erotic connectedness, as a fundamental quality of the imaginal world, now comes into view in everyday life—in the sense of a deep body/mind knowing. Erasing the boundaries of the skin-encapsulated self, the daimon reveals the whole universe as the people, ground, sky, and music of a dreamscape.

Finally, closely related to this connective love, the imaginal serpent grants vision by opening imaginal sight. Jung recounted his experience of the visionary potential of the snake: "My snake was so great that it coiled about my body and I sweat blood. When I accepted the snake then my anima [feminine nature], which had been blind, gained her sight"[18] For me imaginal vision was the most important impact of the bodily integration of any daimonic image. For it most profoundly altered my ongoing relation to reality.

> *As Snake's fire rises to my eyes, her flames change to translucent heat through which I begin to see with her eyes. . . .* (An image of black fire, a samurai, appears behind my husband as we speak. The samurai grins. . . . As I look out the window, my eyes see through the two-dimensional, orange poppies on the

hill to the poppies of the mind-containing imaginal world within, full of bright promise.)

In these instances, the distinctions in the empirical world (in parens) and the imaginal *(italic)* blur.

(At dinner, I begin to see everyone at the table has an auric double of the opposite sex appearing in a diaphanous energy field behind them. These presences smile amusedly among themselves as the conversation heats up.)

Such visions gradually wear away the veil of consensual reality, resulting in a more porous relation to the sense-based world. This is a master shift in consciousness that, even in small doses, gives strength in adversity, reduces fear, and adds compassion for fellow travelers in the strange land of separateness we normally inhabit. This is the shift brought on by the body-based *unio corporalis*, the soul incarnating, through the integration of the forbidden images of the daimonic that first came to consciousness as a hint of our hidden selves. This enlarger of personality, dissolver of projections, now reaches out to dissolve the barrier of the senses, to connect us to a world of intimate relationship with everything the soft animal-body breathes.

CHAPTER 10

The Realm of Relationship

In the beginning is the relation—as a category of being, as readiness, as a form that reaches out to be filled, as a model of the soul. . .

—Martin Buber [1]

FROM A DEPTH-PSYCHOLOGICAL perspective, the reunion of soul and body constitutes an essential therapeutic step in the reconciliation of inner opposites that lead toward discovering who we really are—to individuation. This theory offers one compelling interpretation of the events I have endeavored to describe. However, as insightful and comprehensive as it is, Jungian depth psychology may not go far enough in describing the potential of engaging with the imaginal world. I have wished we could become more precise in our labeling and begin to classify some of the activity we now place in the linguistic box of depth psychology under an expanded category. In so doing, we might respond in some small way to what Hillman describes as "the desire of soul for spirit, for a concrete and poetic precision about its imagery and emotion."[2] The imaginal alchemical processes explored here cross the borders of depth psychology into religion, mythology, philosophy, and even physiology. This should not be surprising since Jung himself explored all these and more in developing his theories and methods for healing. In our quest for understanding our human existence—life and death—we discover at the edges of consciousness a cosmic poetics of inner space that goes well beyond the parameters of our ordinary conceptions of the psychological.

As the daimonic unfolded into the subtle-body field, we journeyed into an alchemical land, a journey that is related, at best, to the healing that traditional therapy aims to accomplish. Learning to be more comfortable in the subtle body realms of imaginal space does seem to accomplish therapeutic goals. Allowing ourselves to participate with awareness in sacred marriage processes of unions, deaths, and rebirths helps to heal split-off qualities, to build a renewed ego structure, and to integrate rejected, shadowy parts of ourselves, all important concerns of the psychotherapist. But along the way these changes lose some of their importance, as we are taken into the unknown. They come almost as a byproduct, overshadowed by the consciousness-altering experience of the *connecting events* that characterize the subtle-body world.

The impact we feel from wandering these realms resembles more closely the wonder of an explorer discovering a new land than the relief and satisfaction of a doctor effecting a cure. Most all of us want to be "healed", to be happier, to be more productive and creative, to be better friends, lovers, or parents, all of which inner exploration as a therapeutic endeavor promises to deliver in good time. But some of us will admit to a simple fascination with this new world for its own sake, a fascination with no further goal than the thrill of discovery, the pleasure of engaging the mysterious dark ground of our own nature. This change of values shifts our primary focus from the world of form where success and being 'together' reigns to one of formlessness where we are hungry for the unknown, for what seems like nothingness to our conscious attitude.

I have explored this one constituent of the frontiers of the inner world, the "reunion of the soul with the body," effected often by daimonic images coming to awareness. We have seen how the daimons come to us at exceptional moments, their arrival often announced in dream or waking visions. Eventually, after living with the image for a time, we begin to connect through faithfulness to the image's call to a realm outside our consensus reality. This imaginal realm may represent the most human of realms, for it is upon the subtle body meeting ground of the imaginal world that spirit greets the sensual reality of the body to illuminate a visionary geography. Whenever we attain a deep, sacred relationship with our world, we step into a reality outside space and time where connectivity prevails. We may enter this realm of relationships through many different doors, through a person, an animal, a plant, a house, a project, a book, an idea, a song, or, as we have done here, an image. P. D. Ouspensky, an early 20th century mathematician, mystic and philosopher, recounts an extraordinary state of consciousness that opened for him onto this meeting ground.

> In trying to describe this strange world in which I saw myself, I must say that it resembled more than anything a world of complicated mathematical *relations* in which everything was connected, in which nothing exists separately, and in which, at the same time, the *relations* between things have a real existence, apart from the things themselves, where possibly things do not exist, and only relations exist [emphasis added] .[3]

The idea that things do not exist, only relationships, describes well for me the new world described by quantum physics, where connectivity is the fundamental reality, the backdrop of all existence. Some describe this reality as the holographic universe, where the tiniest fragment contains the whole. Following anthropologist Lévy-Bruhl, Jung called it the *participation mystique*. Neuropsychological brain research tells us relationship, connectivity and context are the primary modes of perception of the right hemisphere of the brain accessed more readily in states of contemplation, prayer and inner inquiry.

When this incomprehensible world of nonexistent things and tangible relationships invades our concrete reality, we are at first puzzled. Although we have only in the last three or four hundred years learned to live in a world of discrete things and to know ourselves as separate beings, a great revolution in consciousness may be required before we can regularly embrace this intangible, yet relational world. I believe a sensitive welcoming of the daimons is our best hope for achieving this turn. They arrive as artful dervishes to spin us around. The spin dissolves the illusory solidity of consensual reality and opens us to a relational, noumenal world that starts to feel like our lost home.

We deny these taboo characters entry to our inner life at our own peril. The mystery of the vast all-inclusive Other, the delights and despairs of numinous embrace, of blending, dissolving, and changing through contact with these radical agents of change pass us by when we withdraw into the safe cocoon of the familiar and the acceptable. We are called now to venture into the unknown and the suspect.

To encourage this reunion of soul with body that brings the deepening of Being, I have argued that we need to come to terms with the instinctual energies of relationship that threaten our heroic separateness—those creative destructive energies we associate with Eros, ecstasies and torments, sensuality, sexuality, birthing, and dying. If we will embrace these daimonic realities with an alchemical mindset, we allow ourselves to churn and shape-shift in their cauldron of copulating couples, birthing mothers, and dying kings and queens with exhilaration, not fear.

The task of our time seems no longer to be establishing ethereal contact with spirit, as the great saints and mystics of the past seem to have done. Now we are called to bring spirit directly down into matter, to bring soul to body to express the timeless dimension of the immanent. In this descending spirituality, through the humble, earthbound, body, we enter a new world. In this realm of mystical relationships we step through the looking glass, past the threatening monsters that would deter us, to become part of an inextricable flow of subtle sensual unions and separations. Suddenly, we experience life flowing to and through us, not as separate, out there, but here, now, in a sea of wonder, as who we most truly are.

I end with another description of what to me expresses the essence of the secular imaginal world of relations, written by Martin Buber, sounding like a mystic at the height of union with the Divine:

> What the ecstatic calls unification is the rapturous
> dynamic of the relationship, not a unity that has come

into being at this moment in world time, fusing I and You, but the dynamics of the relationship itself which can stand before the two carriers of this relationship. ... the relationship itself in its vital unity is felt so vehemently that its members pale in the process: its life predominates so much that the I and the You between whom it is established are forgotten.[4]

May the daimons lead us into this land!

The Cosmological Connection
An Astrological Note

In the ten years that have passed since the original publication of this book, a number of people from the astrological research community expressed regret that I did not include a direct discussion of the significance of the astrological symbolism that corresponded with these imaginal episodes. Astrology had been my hobby and passion for more than thirty years. Rather than just alluding to 'the realm of the archetypes,' why did I not make the cosmological connections explicit for others to contemplate?

The imaginal breakthroughs detailed here began in 1989 and reached a peak of intensity in 1992. With the pressure of these experiences weighing on me, I had returned to an academic environment, and worked on writing up this study a few years later for my dissertation at The California Institute of Integral Studies. When I first discussed the material with my dissertation chairman, Richard Tarnas, cultural historian, and now well-known archetypal astrologer, he noted right away how the timing of the imagery coincided with powerful alignments of the outer planets, in particular the transiting Uranus/Neptune conjunction. At the time, despite the synchronicities, I thought it best not to include the astrological perspective in a subject already pushing the envelope of taboo in academic circles.

With this new edition, I want to go beyond that concern and offer this brief addendum, primarily for those who are familiar with the astrological archetypes. Those who have gone beyond the superficialities of popular astrology columns and taken the time to study the subject know that empirical correlations and synchronistic phenomena form the heart of astrology's uncanny power to clarify, predict and understand both psychic and outer events. It is my hope that identifying the correspondences now will add to the body of empirical evidence that supports our growing understanding of the astrological lexicon.

The daimonic eruptions explored here, it turns out, offer an uncommon account of inner experiences that correlated with significant transits of all three of the outer planets: Uranus, Neptune and Pluto. A powerful Uranus/Neptune conjunction in Capricorn was occurring during the time-period when these images appeared, (exact: <1° 1992-1993; within 10° orb 1988-1996). During this passage, these two planets were conjoining my natal 12th house Moon/ Ascendant conjunction (19°/22° Capricorn), a significant and sensitive personal psychological point. Pluto also figured in the archetypal mix of these years, both conjoining my Mid-heaven/ Jupiter conjunction from 1988-1993, and in and out of sextile to both the transiting Uranus/Neptune conjunction and my natal Moon.

In archetypal astrology, the outer planets are considered harbingers of higher awareness that correspond to, but do not cause, events and experiences in human, earthly realms. These "ambassadors of the galaxy" correlate with influences that often challenge our security, and our beliefs about ourselves and the world. At first, they can appear disruptive, threatening, demonic, or evil, until we find a way to acknowledge their call. Then, we realize their influence has been asking us to deepen into the unknown, with an imperative to expand the frontiers of consciousness Advice to love the unexpected, the difficult and the incomprehensible in life stems from the wisdom we gain going through and coming out the other side of these experiences.

The completely surprising eruption into consciousness of the images described here, along with their collective, impersonal character, corresponds to electric, disruptive, revolutionary Uranus. In their numinosity, boundary dissolving, and tastes of madness, they resonate with Neptune, ruler of transcendent realms of life. In addition, many of the images are drenched in Plutonian energies. Pluto, the god of the underworld is associated with Dionysius and with the Dark Goddess. Both god and goddess bring the chthonic, instinctual elements of erotic power, destruction, decay, dying and rebirth, while intensifying whatever aspect of life they touch.

The insistent, compelling nature of the daimons, plus the taboo realms of primordial sex and aggression lying beneath our civilized veneer they reveal, reflect Pluto's visceral magnetism. When we are able to bring to awareness these instinctual forces of sensuality, sex, purification and death, we are taken through transformational changes at the core of our being. The daimonic messengers in this study in their reverberation with the Plutonian archetype cry out with insistence for the incorporation of these long-repressed, elemental forces into our daylight world.

Many have suggested that we live in apocalyptic times, and are in the midst of a significant paradigm shift (Uranus) from separateness to connection, from head to heart, that will help save us from destroying ourselves and the ecosystem that sustains us. From the ideal of human beings as independent, autonomous forgers of our own destiny (Saturn)—masters of the universe, free to use our power however we see fit—we are beginning to recognize our dependence and embeddedness in the soul of a larger, invisible world of connectivity, the *anima mundi* (Neptune). In his groundbreaking study of planetary archetypal patterns, *Cosmos and Psyche*, Tarnas entitles the chapter in which he discusses the interplay of the Neptune/Uranus principles, 'Epochal Shifts of Cultural Vision.' Neptune/Uranus alignments are associated with alterations in the underlying vision of a culture, with changes in psychological understanding and inner sensibility, and with paradigm shifts. Neptune/Uranus alignments are also associated with the disorientation that comes with the rapid dissolution of our existing beliefs and structures of reality.

ADDENDUM

This book reflects one avenue through which Uranus/Neptune paradigm shifts occur with the help of Plutonian intensity. Through eruptions of the archetypal unconscious into individual awareness, the imaginal characters compel us to expand our hearts and minds to include their consciousness-raising message in our daylight world. We need their dark gifts (Pluto) of mystery, power and connectivity to counter the imbalances that threaten our world. This dawning non-dual awareness of the *participation mystique* (Neptune) calls for a radical acceptance (Uranus) and transformation (Pluto) of all aspects of life, including the most painful, repulsive and reviled (Pluto). This emerging shift embraces a unitary consciousness that re-establishes our place in an enchanted cosmos. These heavenly daimons are knocking now at our door with great urgency, asking for our embrace.

Endnotes

INTRODUCTION

1. For instance, Diotima in the Plato's *Symposium* discusses the daimons in the context of describing Eros or Love: "He is a great spirit (daimon), and like all spirits he is intermediate between the Divine and the mortal....He interprets between gods and men, conveying and taking across to the gods the prayers and sacrifices of men, and to men the commands and replies of the gods, he is the mediator who spans the chasm which divides them and therefore in him all is bound together....For God mingles not with man, but through Love all the intercourse and converse of God with man whether awake or asleep, is carried on....Now these spirits or intermediate powers are many and diverse, and one of them is Love." Plato, *Symposium*, in The Works of Plato, I. Edman (ed.) B. Jowett (trans.) (N.Y.: Modern Library, 1928/1956), p.369.

2. Rainer Maria Rilke (trans. C.F. MacIntyre), *Duino Elegies,* (Berkeley, University of California Press, 1968)

3. James Hillman, *Healing Fiction* (Barrytown, N.Y: Station Hill, 1983), p 59.

CHAPTER ONE: A DOORWAY TO THE DIVINE

1. Plato, *The Republic,* in *Great Dialogues of Plato*, E.H. Warmington & P.G. Rouse (eds.), W.H.D. Rouse (trans.) (N.Y.: New America Library, 1956) paraphrase from book 7.523, 323.

2. Later, I learned such episodes might be understood in Jungian terms as an attack of the "negative animus," an inner masculine archetypal figure that supposedly revealed my own murderous attitude toward the feminine. While of some interest as an organizing concept for this chaotic data, I remained skeptical about the neatness of this conceptual box and held off on assigning the animus label.

3. C. G. Jung, *The Collected Works*, vol. 12, *Psychology and Alchemy*, 57.

4. Richard Tarnas, *The Passion of the Western Mind: Understanding the Ideas That Have Shaped Our World View*. (N.Y.: Ballantine, 1991), p. 3.

5. Marion Woodman, *"Healing the Inner Masculine,"* audiotape of talk, S.F. Jung Institute, 1990.

6. See Jung, Whitmont, Tarnas, Meador, George, Sullivan, for instance.

7. Betty Meador, *"Psyche and Eros,"* tape of talk, S.F. Jung Institute, undated.

8. *Webster's New Collegiate Dictionary* (Springfield, Mass: G. & C. Merriam Co., 1979).

CHAPTER TWO: THE SUBTLE-BODY & THE *UNIO CORPORALIS*

1. G. R. S. Mead, *The Doctrine of the Subtle Body in the Western Tradition* (London: Solos Press, 1919), p. 1.

2. These stages he originally found in the work of the medieval alchemist Gerard Dorn.

3. Jung, *CW*, 14, par. 663-673.

4. Jung actually devoted a long portion of the last chapter of *Mysterium Coniunctionis* to this question. One finds here a dense examination of Dorn's alchemical instructions that requires true devotion to struggle through for less than satisfying conclusions. Jung says, for instance, "The great difficulty here, however, is that no one knows how this paradoxical wholeness [achieved in the reunion with the body] of man can ever be realized... [it is]an apparently insoluble task and faces the psychologist with questions which he can answer only with hesitation and uncertainty..."(CW 14, par. 680) He goes on into a lengthy examination of how Dorn "tackled this problem." This explanation includes detailed descriptions of the substances that make up the alchemical recipe for the quintessence required for this conjunction to take place. "The mixture of the new heaven, of honey, Chelidonia, rosemary flowers, Mercurialis, of the red lily and human blood, with the heaven of the red or white wine or of Tartarus, can be undertaken....One can also make another mixture, namely that of heaven and the philosophical key, by the artifice of generation."

(par.683)   The explanations get denser. While these exercises in symbology may appeal to the dedicated student of alchemical symbology, they remain close to incomprehensible to most readers. (Jung acknowledges as much, "To the modern mind such contrivances of thought will seem like nebulous products of a dreaming fancy." (par. 686) One alchemical instruction that Jung shares, however, stands out as a guide: "Make the fixed volatile and the volatile fixed." (par. 685)

5. John Ryan Haule uses the language of "unitive and distancing moments" to describe erotic relationship in *The Love Cure: Therapy Erotic and Sexual* (Woodstock, CT: Spring, 1996). For instance, see p. 138.

6. See the discussion in G. R. S. Mead, *The Doctrine of the Subtle Body in the Western Tradition* (Dorset, England: Solos Press. First published by John M. Watkins, London, 1919).

7. G. R. S. Mead, *The Doctrine of the Subtle Body*, p. 71. Mead underlines the profound impact this concept has had on the Western tradition. "The subtle body notion may be said without exaggeration to have been what might be called the very soul of astrology and alchemy—those amazing twin births of human conception which so fascinated the minds of their begetters, and held captive the learned world for so many centuries (p. 9)."

8. G. R. S. Mead, *The Doctrine of the Subtle Body*, p. 1.

9. Henry Corbin, *"Mundus Imaginalis* or the Imaginary and the Imaginal,"* in *Spring,* 1972, p. 9.

10. Henry Corbin, *"Mundus Imaginalis,"* p. 13.

11. Henry Corbin, *"Mundus Imaginalis,"* p. 7.

12. Henry Corbin, *"Mundus Imaginalis,"* p. 14.

13. Quoted in N. Pike, *Mystic Union* (Ithaca: Cornell University Press, 1992), p. 53, from Saint John of the Cross, "Living Flame," Stanza II, 67-68.

14. N. Pike, *Mystic Union,* p. 42.

15. C. G. Jung, *CW,* vol. 12, *Psychology and Alchemy,* 400.

16. C. G. Jung, *CW* 12, 394.

17. Close to Jung's formulation, the phenomenological philosopher Merleau-Ponty wrote: "Body is existence solidified and existence is a perpetual incarnation." He conceptualized "body" as a dialectic between things and ideas, itself neither thing nor idea, rather body and mind both

occupy a larger reality that we might call the body-mind field. Body in this sense gives consciousness a means to perceive soul and soul a means to be present to the world. He calls body a mode of being and a style of vision. Quoted in R. Schenk, "Bare Bones: The Aesthetics of Arthritis," in *Chiron* (1986), p. 169.

18. Nathan Schwartz-Salant, *The Borderline Personality* (Wilmette: Chiron, 1989), p. 132.

19. In psychoanalytic terms, we might label the world of the subtle body primary process material: manifesting psychically through dreams, images, or fantasies, or physically in body armoring, illness, or basic body structure (Schwartz-Salant, *The Borderline Personality*, pp. 26, 136).

20. Sylvia Brinton Perera, "Ceremonies of the Emerging Ego," in *Chiron*, 1986, p. 65.

21. Ibid., p. 62.

22. Woodman is quoted in Anita Greene, "Giving the Body its Due," in *Quadrant*, 1984, p. 11. Also see Jung *CW* 18, *The Symbolic Life*, 148.

23. Marion Woodman uses a technique of bringing a spontaneously occurring image to a place of tension or discomfort in the body. She believes the psychic releases the physical, and the physical, the psychic. See *Chrysalis*, audiotape (San Francisco: San Francisco Jung Institute, 1984).

24. In Woodman's view, unless we acknowledge and engage the subtle body as it comes to consciousness, its appearance is simply likely to cause illness or distress (such as what I encountered when daimonic imagery first began to break into awareness). Physical and psychic tensions created when we contact these archetypal levels require creative expression for healing to actually occur. This is the function of analysis, she says, to create a conscious container for the emergence and expression of the subtle body (Woodman, *Chrysalis*, audiotape).

25. Arnold Mindell, *Dreambody* (Boston: Sigo Press, 1982), see pp. 8, 6, 5, 29, 32, 184.

26. Donald Sandner, "The Subjective Body in Clinical Practice" in *Chiron*, 1986, pp. 118.

27. Sandner refers to Jung's comments in *The Visions Seminars* on Christiana Morgan's reaction to looking directly into the eyes of the animal. When the image finally "got under her skin," Jung said she had formerly been "sightseeing" in the imaginal world, until she encountered

this image, at which point she was "positively stung." Sandner felt he meant that the image had finally evoked an intense reaction in the subjective body. He quotes C. G. Jung, *The Visions Seminars* (Zurich: Spring, 1976, Book 1, p. 63). See Sandner, "The Subjective Body in Clinical Practice," p. 4.

28. Donald Kalsched, *The Inner World of Trauma* (London: Routledge, 1996), p. 65.

29. I want to acknowledge the debt I owe to Hillman for setting the terms of the discussion for much of this book. Midway into my effort to communicate the importance of disturbing imagery, I finally came to his writings and found in him a brilliant exponent of much of what I had begun to intimate about this realm. I thought he had already said with prodigious powers of exposition, breadth of cultural and mythic knowledge, and depth of thought much of what I'd originally hoped to contribute. Yet, I have come to realize I differ in significant ways with Hillman, particularly in my emphasis on the body. Notwithstanding, anyone approaching the imaginal psyche owes him a great deal for advancing Jung's pioneering ideas.

30. James Hillman, *Re-Visioning Psychology* (New York: HarperCollins, 1975), p. 174.

31. James Hillman, *Insearch: Psychology and Religion* (New York: Scribners, 1967), p. 121.

32. James Hillman, "Image-Sense," in *Spring,* 1979, p. 136.

33. James Hillman, "Image-Sense," p. 124.

34. C. G. Jung, *Nietzsche's Zarathustra,* vol. 1 (Princeton: Princeton University Press, 1988), p. 441.

35. C. G. Jung, *Nietzsche's Zarathustra,* vol. 1, p. 441.

36. Through his word association test, Jung measured physiologic changes that occurred when a complex or repetitive "feeling tone" was touched, which led him to formulate that archetypal experiences have both a somatic and psychic aspect.

37. Nathan Schwartz-Salant, *Narcissism and Character Transformation* (Toronto: Inner City Books, 1982), pp. 118-119.

38. C. G. Jung, *Neitzsche's Zarathustra,* vol. 1, p. 441.

39. F. Nietzsche, *Thus Spake, Zarathustra* (New York: Penguin, 1892/ 1961), p. 34.

40. C. G. Jung, *Nietzsche's Zarathustra,* vol. 1, p. 443.

41. Jung says, "I usually do not deal with that concept [subtle body] because it is too difficult, I content myself with things of which I can really know something. It is beyond our grasp *per definition,* the subtle body is a transcendental concept which cannot be expressed in terms of our language or our philosophical views, because they are all inside the categories of time and space. So we can only talk primitive language as soon as we come to the question of the subtle body, and that is everything else but scientific. . . . Science is the highest power of man, for we can do just what we can do, and when we try to deal with things which are beyond our comprehension, we are overstepping our competence." C. G. Jung, *Nietzsche's Zarathustra,* vol. 1, pp. 442, 443.

42. C. G. Jung, *CW,* vol. 9, *The Archetypes and the Collected Unconscious,* 291.

43. James Hillman, "Dionysus in Jung's Writings," in *Spring,* 1972, p. 203.

44. As I have mentioned, from a transcendent level, Jung believes the two poles of the unconscious—the body and mind—are the same, and that the unconscious continuum reflects the mystery of the fundamental identity of body and psyche (See C. G. Jung, *Modern Man in Search of a Soul,* New York: Harcourt, Brace & Co., 1933), p. 253, also quoted in Anita Greene, "Giving the Body Its Due" in *Quadrant,* p. 12.

45. Anita Greene, "Giving the Body Its Due," p. 11.

46. Anita Greene, "Giving the Body Its Due," p. 14.

47. Donald Sandner, "The Subjective Body in Clinical Practice," p. 17.

48. Nathan Schwartz-Salant, *On the Subtle Body Concept in Clinical Practice,* audiotape. San Francisco: San Francisco Jung Institute, n.d.

CHAPTER THREE: THE *MUNDUS IMAGINALIS*

1. Robert Avens, Imagination *Is Reality* (Dallas: Spring, 1980), p. 8.

2. Jeanne Achterberg, *Imagery in Healing: Shamanism and Modern Medicine* (Boston: Shambala, 1985), p. 98

3. Roger Walsh, *The Spirit of Shamanism* (Los Angeles: J. P. Tarcher, 1990), pp. 135-136.

4. Richard Tarnas, *The Passion of the Western Mind* (New York:

Ballantine, 1991), pp. 395-402.

5. Sam Keen, *Faces of the Enemy* (San Francisco: HarperSanFrancisco, 1986), p. 24.

6. At the same time, paradigm-induced changes in perception are proven by history. There's something paradoxically solid about the existential abyss into which relativism can lead us. The sense of no ground, the falling into empty nothingness, bounded by our five senses, leads to discovering an embracing matrix, the cornerstone of experiential faith. Relativism may represent a collective *nigredo* (or darkening) through which we are now passing, as the advent of a new vision.

7. *Writings from the Philokalia on Prayer of the Heart*, E. Kadloubovsky and G. E. H. Palmer, trans. (London: Faber & Faber, 1915), p. 234.

8. *Philokalia on Prayer of the Heart*, p. 235.

9. J. B. Russell, *Prince of Darkness* (Ithaca: Cornell University Press, 1988), p. 89. Was there a time when the instinctual component held sway in the psyche? In the resurgence of interest in the shamanic, Celtic, and pagan nature mysteries, it appears to be so. Was it necessary to put instincts to sleep, then assign them to the underworld, so that the psychic, mental component of the psyche could gain strength? Some have suggested this repression was effected by Christianity doing its part in the development of the collective psyche.

10. In his final years, Jung went further, saying, "I am aware 'mana,' 'daimon,' and 'god' are synonyms for the unconscious." C. G. Jung, *Collected Works*, vol. 5, *Symbols of Transformation*, 388.

11. James Hillman, *Healing Fiction* (Barrytown, NY: Station Hill, 1983), p. 56.

12. James Hillman, *Healing Fiction*, p. 74.

13. Tibetan Buddhism relies heavily on the use of imagery in its practices, but still asserts that ultimately the images have no real existence.

14. Jack Kornfield, *A Path with Heart* (New York: Bantam Books, 1993), p. 25.

15. Jack Kornfield, *A Path with Heart*, p. 91.

16. Tibetan Buddhism includes an imaginal practice, *Chod*, wherein practitioners, to cultivate compassion and equanimity, visualize themselves being dismembered by wrathful deities. These experiences are

recognized as visualizations. The Tibetans regard the imaginal as a mind creation, but also regard everything in our everyday life, in this world and all worlds, as creations of consciousness, dreams. (See Roger Walsh, *The Spirit of Shamanism*), p. 60.

17. A view that appeals to the scientific mind categorized roughly as *psychological materialism* that explains all subjective experiences as reducible to permutations of brain chemistry. We do well to recall a relationship between a body state and a mental phenomenon does not prove cause.

18. A. Sheik, ed., *International Review of Mental Imagery*, vol. 1 (New York: Human Sciences Press, 1984), p. 101.

19. P. Ricoeur, "Imagination in Discourse and Action" in G. Robinson & J. Rundell, eds., *Rethinking Imagination* (London: Routledge, 1994), p. 119.

20. N. Tierney, *Imagination and Ethical Ideal* (Albany: State University of New York Press, 1984), p. 17.

21. J. B. Russell, *Mephistopheles: The Devil in the Modern World* (Ithaca: Cornell University Press, 1986), p. 242.

22 John Conger, *Jung and Reich: The Body as Shadow* (Berkeley: North Atlantic Books, 1988), see chapter 8, pp. 107-113.

23. Naomi Goldenberg, *Resurrecting the Body* (New York: Crossroad, 1990), p. 89.

24. As illuminating and stimulating as the Jungian and archetypal writers are, I still often find something important missing for furthering understanding of the psyche. Many are masters of rhetoric and take us on fantastic word journeys. One finds insight after dazzling insight, connecting the image to the complex, to the gods and goddesses and archetypal symbols of history or prehistory. But, where's the substance, the life-sustaining essence, of these ancient companions of the human soul? I believe this missing substance is related to an unintentional devaluation of the body as an essential component of imaginal life. Archetypal, analytic, and mythic accounts of the imaginal tend to connect the image with the conceptual half of the bodymind reality. Their writings stimulate, but do not satisfy, a deep hunger for the juicy substance of the image, a substance I believe we receive by allowing the image to connect with the body, then breaking with taboo and trying to express these instinct-informed images.

25. James Hillman, *Healing Fiction* (Barrytown, NY: Station Hill, 1983), p. 75.

26. James Hillman, *Healing Fiction*, p. 75.

27. Gerald Epstein, *Waking Dream Therapy: Dream Process as Imagination* (New York: Human Sciences Press, 1981), p. 11.

28. James Hillman, *Re-Visioning Psychology* (New York: HarperCollins, 1975), p. 37.

29. Henry Corbin, "Mundus Imaginalis," in *Spring*, 1972, p. 2.

30. C. G. Jung, *Nietzsche's Zarathustra* (Princeton: Princeton University Press, 1988), vol. 1, p. 147.

31. Henry Corbin, "Mundus Imaginalis," p. 12.

32. William Blake, "A Vision of the Last Judgment," 1810, in D. Erdman, ed., *The Poetry and Prose of William Blake* (New York: Doubleday, 1965), p. 545.

33. C. G. Jung, *CW*, vol. 11, *Psychological Types*, 6.

34. The reification of the concept of numinosity has come under serious question by some of the archetypally oriented who would update Jung's work. While recognizing the ultimately mysterious nature of the numinous, Hillman, for instance, suggests that the attention and value we grant an image confers its numinosity. Feminist archetypal theorists (for example, see Estella Lauter and Carol S. Rupprecht, *Feminist Archetypal Theory*, University of Tennessee Press, 1985) agree that certain fundamental human experiences, such as birth and death, accumulate energetic potency simply from their repeated occurrence throughout history, and we then experience numinosity around these events. At the heart of archetypal psychology, we find a technical method, "the internalization of Eros," by which we cultivate an image by endowing it with interest and life until it takes on a life of its own. See James Hillman, *Insearch* (New York: Scribners, 1967), p. 114. Faithful attention or love becomes a method to reveal living being—archetypal potential—in anything on which we focus.

35. Some archetypal feminist theorists criticize Jung for mixing the psychological and the theological, despite his stated intentions, particularly his use of the term "numinous," implying that the archetypes originate in the divine transcendent realms. "This elevation has the effect of cosmic endorsement" (D. Wehr, 27). They protest the splitting of the body from the spirit implied by the transcendent archetype: "The

assumption that ideas have a life of their own, or reach us from some suprahuman source, whether it be a collective unconscious, total verbal order, or ultimate structuralist code, separates mind from environment, spirit from body, perception from things as they are" (A. Pratt, 126). Instead, what is advocated is the affirmation of female *a priori* knowledge which Pratt describes as "those things it seems we have known from a long time before the laws of otherness closed in upon us like the spike of iron maidens" (A. Pratt, 128). (I believe she is describing a reconnection to the subtle body.) The concept of the archetype remains a valuable organizing category for unconscious contents, offering a conduit to sources of inspiration, creativity and awe. Instead of reflecting a universal, transcendent principle, however, the tendency to form and reform trans-personal images is envisioned as a response to certain repeated experiences. We experience these images as numinous because of the amount of energy they carry having been so long a part of human experience. (Paraphrased from articles in Estella Lauter and Carol S. Rupprecht, eds., *Feminist Archetypal Theory. Interdisciplinary ReVisions of Jungian Thought,* Knoxville: University of Tennessee Press, 1985, p. 15.)

36. A. Samuels, B. Shorter, and F. Plant, "Archetype, Myth, *Numinosum,"* in R. P. Sugg, *Jungian Literary Criticism* (Evanston: Northwestern University Press, 1992), p. 191.

37. C. G. Jung, *Answer to Job* (Princeton: Princeton University Press, 1958), p. 90.

38. C. G. Jung, *Answer to Job,* p. 90.

39. Thomas Moore, in his discussion of the daimon, explains that Aristotle described well-being as "eudaimonic," having a good daimon, while Yeats discussed his lifelong struggle with and love for the daimon: "We meet always in the deep of mind." See T. Moore, "Animus Mundi," in *Spring,* 1987, p. 121.

40. More than thirty years ago, Rollo May introduced his own concept of the instinctual *daimonic* in his exploration of love and creativity, describing the daimonic as "any natural function that has the power to take over the whole person." He gives sex and eros, anger and rage, and the craving for power as examples of energies that he believes are essential to eros, our vital creative force. Characterized by its numinosity, his *daimonic* may be either creative (as in love, artistic expression, or the building of relationship) or destructive, and is usually both. May draws no connection in his discussion, however, between the instinctual impulses and imagery. R. May, "Psychotherapy and the Daimonic," in J.

202

Campbell, ed., *Myths, Dreams & Religion* (New York: Button, 1970).

41. Claire Douglas, *Translate This Darkness* (New York: Simon & Schuster, 1993), p. 160.

42. James Hillman, "Image-Sense," in *Spring,* 1979, p. 141.

43. Stephen Diamond, "Redeeming Our Devils and Demons," in C. Zweig and J. Abrams, *Meeting the Shadow* (Los Angeles: J. P. Tarcher, 1991), p. 184.

44. Madonna or Mick Jagger, at moments, embody such numinous darkness for popular rock culture.

45. James Hillman, *Re-Visioning Psychology* (New York: HarperCollins, 1975), p. 92.

46. T. Moore, *Dark Eros* (Dallas: Spring, 1990).

47. T. Moore, "Animus Mundi," in *Spring,* 1987, p. 129.

48. T. Moore, "Animus Mundi," p. 110.

CHAPTER FOUR: ALCHEMICAL UNIONS AND SEPARATIONS

1. Thomas Moore, *Dark Eros* (Dallas: Spring, 1990), p. 23.

2. C. G. Jung, *CW,* vol. 16, *The Practice of Psychotherapy,* 399.

3. Edward Edinger, *Anatomy of the Psyche: Alchemical Symbolism in Psychotherapy* (LaSalle, IL: Open Court, 1985). Jung himself credited Herbert Silberer as the first: "Herbert Silberer has the merit of being the first to discover the secret threads that lead from alchemy to the psychology of the unconscious." C. G. Jung, *The Collected Works,* vol. 14, *Mysterium Coniunctionis,* 792.

4. These works include *Psychology and Alchemy,* 1944 *(CW* 12), based on two Eranos lectures in 1935 and 1936, "The Secret of the Golden Flower," 1935, *Psychology and Religion: The Psychology of Transference,* 1946 (CW11), "Fish Symbolism in Alchemy" in *Aion,* 1951 (CW9ii), *Alchemical Studies,* essays published between 1942 and 1957 *(CW* 13), *and Mysterium Coniunctionis,* his magnum opus, written from 1941-1954 *(CW* 14) and finished in his 80th year.

5. Lynn Ehlers, "The Alchemical Nigredo, Albedo, Citrinitas and Rubedo," unpublished dissertation, California School of Professional Psychology, 1992, p. 23.

6. Jung said that alchemy was a poor name for this process of

203

transformation that would better be called "the Yoga process." He said, "It is a process of transmutation which creates out of the subtle body within something which is equal to the subtle body yet is of very great value." See C. G. Jung, *Nietzsche's Zarathustra* (Princeton: Princeton University Press, 1988), p. 445.

7. Nathan Schwartz-Salant, "On the Subtle Body Concept in Clinical Practice," in *Chiron*, 1986, p. 45.

8. The lapis, or end result, of the alchemical opus is also described as the hermaphrodite, Mercurius, or the Philosopher's Stone.

9. Nathan Schwartz-Salant, *Discovering the Unconscious Couple*, audiotape, San Francisco: San Francisco Jung Institute, 1985.

10. Nathan Schwartz-Salant, *Discovering the Unconscious Couple*, audiotape.

11. Jung also saw the *coniunctio* as an *a priori* image that occupied a prominent position in the history of the Western mind. In the Christian, with Christ as Sol and the church as Luna, and in the pagan tradition through the *hieros gamos* and the union of the mystic with god. C. G. Jung, *The Collected Works*, vol. 16, *The Practice of Psychotherapy*, 3.

12. C. G. Jung, *CW*, vol. 13, *Alchemical Studies*, 198.

13. C. G. Jung, *CW* 14, 760.

14. Robert Avens, a colleague of Hillman's, suggests that because we traditionally have adulated the spirit principle, we prematurely identify ourselves with transcendence or saintliness before we've confronted the depths of human nature accessible through a cultivation of the imaginal. He believes the route to wisdom, in the West, at least, requires, "First imagination, then spirit." Spiritualism and materialism he describes as twin brothers representing the greatest sins against the soul. We admire the technologies of Eastern religions but don't recognize that most bypass the imaginal just as we do in the West. He suggests that "the West first lose itself in the immeasurably vast and dangerous caverns of the imagination" before trying to reach the heights of Eastern spirituality. The development of the imaginal as middle ground for us remains the *mysterium tremendum et fascinans,* a realm nonexistent to the sense based mind, yet with the potential to give meaning to life both corporeal and spiritual. See R. Avens, *Imagination Is Reality* (Dallas: Spring, 1980), p. 8.

15. C. G. Jung, *CW* 14, 696.

16. Edward Edinger, *Anatomy of the Psyche* (La Salle, IL: Open Court, 1985), p. 211.

17. Nathan Schwartz-Salant, "On the Subtle Body Concept in Clinical Practice," p. 30.

18. Lynn Ehlers, "The Alchemical Nigredo . . .," p. 148.

19. Lynn Ehlers, "The Alchemical Nigredo . . . ," p. 115.

20. Edward Edinger, Barbara Hannah, James Hillman, MarieLouise von Franz, Nathan Schwartz-Salant, to name a few.

21. C. G. Jung, *CW* 14, 646.

22. C. G. Jung, *CW* 14, 346.

23. Ann Ulanov and Barry Ulanov, *Transforming Sexuality* (Boston: Shambhala, 1994), p. 206.

24. Jung referred to Christianity as a cultural *unio mentalis* in overcoming the body. *CW* 14, 674.

25. C. G. Jung, *CW* 14, 664.

26. In this Jung follows the language of the alchemist he is interpreting, Gerhard Dorn.

27. See E. C. Whitmont, James Hillman, Anita Greene, Marion Woodman, Betty Meador, Sylvia Perera, Nancy QuallsCorbett, Arnold Mindell, Deldon McNeely.

28. C. G. Jung, *CW* 14, 465-533.

29. C. G. Jung, *CW14*, 681.

30. This was suggested along with a magical procedure that calls down the planetary spirits needed to unite the spirit with the body. *CW* 14, p. 339, fn 313.

31. C. G. Jung, *CW* 14, 687.

32. C. G. Jung, *CW* 14, 696.

33. C. G. Jung, *CW* 14, 705.

34. C. G. Jung, *CW* 14, 741.

35. C. G. Jung, *CW* 14, 670.

36. He was also born Swiss, and we must keep the year and culture in mind when watching him investigate this inner material.

37. Edward Edinger, *Ego and Archetype* (New York: Penguin, 1972), pp. 21-22.

CHAPTER FIVE: THE DARK GODDESS RISING

1. Irigaray, Luce, "The Poverty of Psychoanalysis," in Margaret Whitford, ed., *The Irigaray Reader* (Oxford: Blackwell, 1991), p. 86.

2. Edward Whitmont, *Return of the Goddess* (N.Y. Crossroads, 1982), p. 137.

3. Anne Baring and Jules Cashford, *The Myth of the Goddess* (N.Y. Penguin, 1993), p. 544.

4. Edward Whitmont, *Return of the Goddess*, p. 15.

5. Nathan Schwartz-Salant, *On the Subtle Body Concept in Clinical Practice*, audiotape (San Francisco: San Francisco Jung Institute, n.d.).

6. C. G. Jung, *CW*, vol. 13, *Alchemical Studies*, 456.

7. Riane Eisler, *Sacred Pleasure* (San Francisco: HarperSanFrancisco, 1996), pp. 126-157.

8. Demetra George, *The Mysteries of the Dark Moon* (San Francisco: HarperSanFrancisco, 1992), p. 34.

9. Sigmund Freud, *The Standard Edition of the Complete Works*, vol. 19 (London: Hogarth Press, 1953), p. 86.

10. St. Augustine, *De Trinitas*, 13, quoted in Anne Baring and Jules Cashford, *The Myth of the Goddess*, p. 534.

11. C. Paglia, *Sexual Personae* (San Francisco: HarperSanFrancisco, 1995), p. 230.

12. W. Young, *Eros Denied* (New York: Grove Press, 1964), p. 334.

13. Edward Whitmont, *The Return of the Goddess*, p. 125.

14. A. L. Barstow, *Witchcraze* (San Francisco: HarperSanFrancisco, 1994), p. 135.

15. R. Cavendish, *The Powers of Evil* (New York: Putnam, 1975), pp. 196, 210.

16. A. L. Barstow, *Witchcraze*, p. 53.

17. A. L. Barstow, *Witchcraze*, pp. 133-135.

18. E. Arbam, *Ecstasy or Religious Trance*, vol. 7 (Copenhagen: Scandinavian

University Books, 1968), p. 203.

19. Nelson Pike, *Mystic Union: An Essay with the Phenomenology of Mysticism* (Ithaca: Cornell University Press, 1992), p. 77.

20. Nelson Pike, *Mystic Union,* p. 68.

21. Jacques Nouet, *Man in Prayer,* quoted in N. Pike, *Mystic Union,* p. 71.

22. Nelson Pike, *Mystic Union,* pp. 67-68.

23. St. John of the Cross, "The Dark Night" in *The Dark Night of the Soul of San Juan de la Cruz,* Gabriela C. Graham, trans. (London: J. M. Watkins, 1922), p. 29 (stanza 5).

24. St. Teresa of Avila, *The Life of Teresa of Jesus: The Autobiography of St. Teresa of Avila,* E. A. Peers, ed. and trans. (Garden City: Image Books, 1991), pp. 274-275.

25. She wrote of horrifying visions of the Devil and sought counsel to assure the visions were from God. Her confessor commanded her to make the sign of the cross whenever she had a vision, and to snap her fingers at it to be sure it wasn't the Devil. See M. Eliade, *Myths, Dreams and Mysteries* (New York: Harper & Row, 1957), p. 160.

26. Edward Whitmont, *The Return of the Goddess,* p. 137.

27. As we cannot truly grasp the necessity for the initial split of bodily sexuality from its dissolving erotic spirit, we can only speculate about the reasons for this dramatic shift happening now. We can theorize simply that the ongoing expansion of consciousness calls for a re-sacralization of the sexual. Eros dissolves and unites to encourage those essential qualities—faith, vision, clarity, loving kindness, strength, and how many more we do not even know yet how to name—we urgently need to restore our connection to ourselves, to Earth, and to those with whom we share this planet of transformative mystery.

28. A. de Nicolas and E. Moutsopoulos, eds., *God: Experience or Origin* (New York: Paragon House, 1985), p. 242.

29. Edward Whitmont, *The Return of the Goddess,* p. 16.

30. S. Keen, *Faces of the Enemy* (San Francisco: HarperSanFrancisco, 1986).

31. Edward Whitmont, *Return of the Goddess,* p. 138.

32. We need help to illuminate our ignorance of these mysteries of sexual

violence at play in the body. In her welcome collection, *Uncursing the Dark* (Wilmette, IL: Chiron, 1992), Betty Meador discusses the entire Inanna-Ereshkigal Sumerian tale in detail, and we learn that as subtle body perceptions develop and the somatic-unconscious end of the archetypal spectrum emerges into consciousness, we are invited to incarnate our own numinous violence through its embrace. The waves of sadomasochistic, lustful, and ecstatic destructiveness that surge over us paradoxically impel us to merge with these daimonic aspects we have learned to reject. As a result, this apparently unholy internal act resurrects the structures dissolved in the frenzy of union with the daimon, giving birth to a new form.

33. Richard Tarnas, *The Passion of the Western Mind* (New York: Ballantine, 1991), pp. 441-442.

34. In addition to Richard Tarnas, Betty DeShong Meador, Charlene Spretnak, Edward Whitmont, and Marion Woodman are just a few writers suggesting this point of view. Jung himself, suggests this development of consciousness has been occurring over the past 2000 years.

35. Richard Tarnas, *The Passion of the Western Mind*, p. 444.

36. Richard Tarnas, *The Passion of the Western Mind*, p. 443.

37. Claire Douglas, *Translate This Darkness* (New York: Simon & Schuster, 1993), p. 318.

38. Claire Douglas, *Translate This Darkness*, p. 318.

39. C. G. Jung, *The Visions Seminars*, vol. 2 (Zurich: Spring, 1976), p. 376.

40. C. G. Jung, *The Visions Seminars*, vol. 2, p. 378.

41. Claire Douglas, *Translate This Darkness*, pp. 164-166. The diary entry continues, "There ought to come to you a Siegfried who would break through your ring of fire—who would make you a woman."

42. I find it intriguing that Jung based so much of his theory on the tension of the union of opposites. What happens once the union is consummated? Is there not a phase of bliss melting into a radical relaxation of tensions? Is this yet another aspect of the Mother goddess that we have not accepted, the reclining Aphrodite after lovemaking, the mother after giving birth? The capacity to relax fully has been lost to us in our always busy, productive existence!

43. Claire Douglas, *Translate This Darkness*, pp. 164-165.

44. Claire Douglas, *Translate This Darkness*, pp. 164-165.

45. The "heroine" of course, could as well be a "hero," just as the "hero" has always been used to refer to both men and women. I use "heroine" here in the same spirit.

46. Claire Douglas, *Translate This Darkness*, p. 161.

47. Claire Douglas, *Translate This Darkness*, p. 311.

48. William Blake, "The Marriage of Heaven and Hell," in D. V. Erdman, *The Poetry and Prose of William Blake (New York: Doubleday, 1965), p. 34.*

CHAPTER SIX: DEVELOPING THE SUBTLE SENSES

1. Rainer Maria Rilke, *Letters of Rainer Maria Rilke (1910-1926)*, Jane Bernard Greene and M. D. Herder Norton, trans. (New York: Norton, 1972), p. 374.

2. See, for instance, H. Pagels, *The Cosmic Code* (New York: Bantam, 1982).

3. Charlene Spretnak, *States of Grace* (San Francisco: HarperSanFrancisco, 1991), p. 24.

4. Charlene Spretnak, *States of Grace*, p. 21.

5. *King James Bible* (Philadelphia: A. J. Holman Co.), "Epistle of Paul to the Hebrews," 11:1.

6. Ken Wilber, *Eye to Eye: The Quest for the New Paradigm* (New York: Anchor Books, 1983), p. 65.

7. Anyone with such a rational orientation would probably not even pick up this book, much less read to this point. With that mindset, we need to be knocked over by a conversion experience like the one St. Paul had on the road to Damascus to open to invisible realities. In our time, hallucinogenic drugs served as conversion agents for many.

8. Peter Reason, *Human Inquiry in Action* (Newbury Park, CA: Sage, 1989), p. 213.

9. I include the following for any student needing to justify a subjective methodology in states of consciousness research. This method falls in the tradition of heuristic research, as explicated by Clark Moustakas. It evolved naturally to enable further investigations and deeper awareness of the imaginal world. Moustakas warns how the deeply ingrained "fear of creative subjective speculation" that we learn in our empirically-based tradition cuts us off from any significant new discoveries. He urges us in assessing the soundness

of an inquiry, particularly in human sciences, to put our emphasis on the commitment to *follow the phenomenon* rather than on meeting the criteria of any particular methodology (C. Moustakas, "Heuristic Research" in *Human Inquiry in Action,* 1989, p. 216). One risks trivialization in pursuing "subjective speculation," but in exploring the imaginal, nothing less than the phenomenon itself is in peril in neglecting it. My sense that personal subjective data were not only legitimate, but critical to understanding imaginal data finds validation by many researchers today. Feminists have battled hard against the hegemony of the objective, impersonal, rational, and empirical. They argue, as I have, that our Western mindset has systematically devalued one half of each of the dualities: the subjective, personal, irrational, and spiritual. Carol Christ, a pioneer in feminist religious studies, offers a case for women naming their experiences to reclaim these lost aspects of life. "It is important for women to name the great powers of being from their own perspective and to recognize their participation in them." In Charlene Spretnak, *The Politics of Women's Spirituality* (New York: Anchor, 1982), p. 329. To adopt a woman's perspective means to *see things one did not see before* and to see everyday things differently.

Feminist research methodology recognizes the importance of these "new kinds of data," including personal, subjective data to capture not only women's experience, but human experiences that have been devalued and marginalized in the commitment to scientific method. New qualitative methods have been created by feminist researchers "because the knowledge they seek *requires* it." Studying the phenomenon from the inside offers us a deeper, richer source of knowledge than those accessible to the empiricism of the past (S. Reinharz, *Feminist Methods in Social Research,* New York: Ballantine, 1991, pp. 218, 234). Deldon Anne McNeely, in her work combining Jungian analysis with body therapy, pointed out that when we unite the two realms of body and soul, we avoid the "dualism of Descartes and the romanticism of Rousseau" See D. A. McNeely, *Touching: Body Therapy and Depth Psychology* (Toronto: Inner City Books, 1987), p. 107

Peter Reason in *Human Inquiry in Action* also speaks of seeking a post-positivist way of knowing that goes beyond the mind-body, subjective-objective splits. He describes an epistemology *grounded in experiential knowing* as "critical subjectivity." "This is a state of awareness in which we do not suppress our primary subjective experience, nor do we allow ourselves to be overwhelmed and swept along by it, rather we raise it to consciousness and use it as part of the inquiry process." See P. Reason, *Human Inquiry in Action* (Newbury Park, CA: Sage, 1989, p. 20). Harman and De Quincey, in their discussion of a new epistemology for inquiry into consciousness, contend that any method to study consciousness must be *"radically empirical,"* and phenomenological or experiential in the broadest sense, meaning that *it must include subjective experience as primary data.* See W. Harman and C. De Quincey, *The Scientific Exploration of Consciousness: Toward an Adequate Epistemology* (Sausalito, CA: Institute of Noetic Sciences, 1994), p. 23.

Peter Reason goes on to describe this critical subjectivity as part of a dialectical ontology that maintains the tension between the vast "mysterious primal reality" and the states of consciousness we bring to it. In this sense, reality is viewed as a process, and knowledge always includes the relationship between what is known and the knower. Truth is both independent of and dependent on us. While we create to some extent what we perceive, we may always be surprised by the unpredictable, independent nature of the real. We need to cull our data for consciousness studies particularly from "high quality experiences," which Reason suggests we cultivate through meditation, prayer, ritual to bring ourselves into a state whereby certain realities of the psyche may be apprehended and better studied. Experience with spiritual disciplines also fulfills a key requirement for maintaining critical subjectivity, as meditative techniques help to raise awareness and reduce personal bias: "The aspirant investigator of consciousness, while learning and applying techniques for transcending personal and cultural biases, often undergoes an experiential transformation that reorients the relationship between subject-object, observer-observed, and knower-knowledge. When such a process results in comparatively bias-free knowledge, it fulfills a key requirement for "objectivity," even though the knowledge is arrived at through a process of inner exploration" (P. Reason, *Human Inquiry in Action,* p. 23).

Further support for using data gathered from the realm of the phenomenon under study comes from Ken Wilber. In discussing the problem of proof of contemplative data, for instance, Wilber shows how any such proof must be contemplative, not empirical, as the empirical cannot reach beyond its own defined field of perception. He discusses how science as we know it is always empiric science, which is inadequate in dealing with intelligibilia [data from the realm of intellect], and completely incapable of considering transcendelia [data from transcendental realms]. (Ken Wilber, *Eye to Eye,* p. 65.) In exploring the imaginal realm, we find ourselves at a meeting point between Wilber's realms of the intellect, the transcendent, and the physical. The imaginal may be conceived as an intermediary or bridge between the three realms. If we approach the imaginal only as a

211

mental phenomenon, then we reduce it to that level, we are blinded to any other properties it may possess. Once we suspend our rational biases enough to perceive the numinous somatic underpinnings of the imaginal, however, we see we must somehow connect the body and the transcendent, and develop methods suitable for inquiry into these domains. I follow Wilber's logic when he says "meditative awareness or contemplation is to transcendelia as linguistic awareness or ratiocination is to intelligibilia—both the tool and the territory of cognitive disclosure" (Ken Wilber, *Eye to Eye,* p. 63). Although Wilber might be hard-pressed to accommodate the imaginal as described here, we could say by the same token that imaginal perception is to "imaginalia" as meditation is to transcendelia.

10. Joan Chodorow, "To Move and Be Moved" *(Quadrant* 17.2, 1984), p. 40.

11. We may actually have three brains, the neocortex (new mammalian or distinctly human), the limbic (old mammalian) and the reptilian. The reptilian brain monitors our basic survival instincts, functions most automatically, and is furthest removed from our consciousness. Yet, it is still active in our psyches. The two archaic brains connect to the erotic, aggressive, and territorial energies. Paradoxically, these realms are also dominated by the *participation mystique* and by magical thinking. Immersion in body sensations and the images they constellate may open this lower brain consciousness. Sylvia Brinton Perera also recognizes that attending to body sensations encourages the unfolding of unconscious material. She equates animal imagery, for instance, with the precortical limbic and reptilian brains, dominated by raw emotion and survival instincts (Sylvia Brinton Perera, "Ceremonies of the Emerging Ego in Psychotherapy," *Chiron* 1986, p. 65). The proprioceptive intuitions that arise spontaneously from this "preverbal magical matrix of consciousness" impel the psyche forward.

12. J. Hillman, *The Dream and the Underworld* (New York: Harper & Row, 1979), p. 141.

13. Antonio de Nicolas and E. Moutsopoulos, eds., *God: Experience or Origin?* (New York: Paragon House, 1985), p. ix.

14. A. de Nicolas and E. Moutsopoulos, eds., *God: Experience or Origin?,* p. 244.

15. Harman and De Quincey speak of participative understanding arising from "identifying with the observed and experiencing it

subjectively" (The Scientific Exploration of Consciousness, p. 26).

16. Richard Tarnas, *The Passion of the Western Mind* (New York: Ballantine, 1991), p. 491.

17. Tarnas also discusses our need to come to terms with the feminine in the "overarching dialectic of masculine and feminine" in the history of the Western mind, which implies coming to terms with embodiment, as well as darkness, the underworld, and the irrational (Richard Tarnas, *The Passion of the Western Mind*, p. 491).

18. Is embodied immersion a type of phenomenology? In a sense it is, in that the exploration is descriptive of the phenomenon itself. More poetic license than is permissible in phenomenological approaches, such as use of metaphor and "personifying," is required to give voice to the imaginal. Barebones description of the phenomenon does not suit the dramatic unfolding of imaginal material. Hillman explains in differentiating archetypal psychology from phenomenology: "Phenomenology stops short in its examination of consciousness, failing to realize the essence of consciousness is fantasy images. Archetypal psychology carries the consequences of fantasy through to their full implications, transposing the entire operation of phenomenology into the irrational, personified and psychopathological domain, a transposition from the logical to the imaginal." See James Hillman, *Re-Visioning Psychology* (New York: Harper & Row, 1975), pp. 138-139.

19. I routinely dismissed any images or commentary that arose from this immersion, allowing them to disperse into space in the tradition of mindfulness practices.

20. Bellevue is the well-known hospital in New York City where they take the crazy people—hence the term.

21. As I have noted, embodied immersion as a method of knowing developed in me as part of the effort to better understand those puzzling intrusions of daimonic material. Another person with a different temperament or orientation to life might discover methods and ways of knowing more suitable for them through their own exploring of the inner world.

The classic instruments of knowing include mind, heart, intuition, and action. As long as we allow ways of knowing to evolve naturally as part of the process of inquiry, we can expect to develop ever new methods as we journey more deeply into irrational, subjective terrains. "In a sense, we make up epistemology [ways of knowing] as we go along since there are no irreversible standards. Epistemology, then, is a practice, it is something we do. What we do, when we do epistemology, is create new norms." See A. Tanesini, "Whose Language?" in K. Lennon and M. Whitford, *Knowing the Difference: Feminist Perspectives in Epistemology* (New York: Routledge, 1994, p. 214.)

22. Although we often later discover that we also avoid highly pleasant experiences, automatically losing ourselves in them. The same principle applies to pleasant sensations, the containing medium of consciousness allows the sensation to open to the imaginal world of relationship.

23. Jessica Benjamin, *Bonds of Love* (New York: Pantheon, 1988), p. 29.

24. See the Waite tarot card VI *The Lovers,* also the Two of Cups, compare to XV, *The Devil.*

25. This may be the level of experience referred to by those archetypal psychologists who *believe* numinosity accrues to an experience through its repetition in human history.

26. Edinger, referring to the *coniunctio* image from *The Rosarium* (plate no. 5), describes images of intercourse in dreams as "the ego merging with a figure of the unconscious." See Edward Edinger, *The Mystery of the Coniunctio: Alchemical Symbol of Individuation* (Toronto: Inner City Books, 1994), p. 66.

27. Dissociation as a defense must be differentiated from the conscious dissociation from the body (in the sense of the extraction of the sense of "I" from the body) that occurs as the metamorphic process of union take places in the field of containing consciousness.

28. The containing medium of consciousness may relate to the bath in the alchemical process images. What remains of the body-ego is one of the partners who enters the bath. The other is an imaginal presence. That imaginal presence may be represented through another person, place, or thing, in time and space, as Jung emphasized when using the alchemical symbols to describe the dynamics of the transference, or it may appear directly as a presence.

29. Stephen Levine, *Healing Into Life and Death* (New York: Anchor/ Doubleday, 1987), p. 118.

CHAPTER SEVEN: DANGEROUS PASSAGE

1. In essence, she descends, submits, and dies. From Sylvia Brinton Perera, *Descent to the Goddess: A Way of Initiation for Women* (Toronto: Inner City Books, 1981), p. 13.

2. Nathan Schwartz-Salant, *The Borderline Personality* (Wilmette, IL: Chiron, 1989), p. 45.

3. Nathan Schwartz-Salant, *The Borderline Personality*, p. 45.

4. James Hillman, *The Thought of the Heart and the Soul of the World* (Dallas: Spring, 1981/1992), pp. 73-74.

5. Another compelling contribution to numbing comes from the ontological insecurity engendered by the rapidly changing conditions of the millennium. Sociologist R. J. Lifton felt psychic numbing to be the central fact of life in the nuclear age. See Robert Jay Lifton and Richard Falk, *Indefensible Weapons: The Political and Psychological Case against Nuclearism* (New York: Basic Books, 1982). Ira Chernus, in his discussion of the impact of the nuclear situation, feels that our numbing to the implications of nuclear threat can only be healed by a renewed religious image for which we are now collectively casting about. See Ira Chernus, *Nuclear Madness: Religion and the Psychology of the Nuclear Age* (Albany: State University of New York Press, 1991), pp. 10, 27.

6. Marion Woodman feels a healing image appears but cannot connect with its instinctual energy if the mind/body split is still very deep. (I wonder, isn't the split always very deep at the frontiers of consciousness?) She speaks of an amazing divine child, for instance, appearing in a client's dreams, the client, however, recounted the episode in a completely blase tone, unable to connect to the joy carried by the image. M. Woodman, *Addiction to Perfection* (Toronto: Inner City Books, 1982), p. 86. A client of mine spoke of a devouring, shining predator with a similar, unaffected tone.

7. C. G. Jung, *CW*, vol. 14, *Mysterium Coniunctionis*, 1.

8. Hillman even believes a perpetual dismemberment of being reflects authenticity, our single identity being a delusion of our "monotheistic consciousness." Robert Avens, *Imagination is Reality* (Dallas: Spring, 1980), p. 72.

9. Ira Chernus, *Nuclear Madness*, p. 258.

10. Nathan Schwartz-Salant, "On the Subtle Body Concept in Clinical Practice," in *Chiron*, 1986, p. 28.

11. To Freud, primary masochism was also a direct expression of Thanatos, or the death drive.

12. For Jung, the demon lover implied the presence of the Terrible Mother who devours or destroys, and who symbolizes death. The demon lover is also described as the contrasexual inner being (anima or animus) in service to the shadow. This provides an irresistible, compelling quality to the inner or outer figure leading to an experience of humiliating seductiveness in which we are willing to sacrifice everything. From this point of view, the persecutory inner environment of the demon lover is cut off from the real world and does not offer a true healing, but is a depressive posture at the very early, infantile, or "schizoid" level of personality development. It arises when we feel most threatened and offers a sense of protection. The ego dissolves in the larger religious element, fusing with the blissful illusion as an escape from traumatic pain. The birth of consciousness is marked by the loss of this sustaining illusion. D. Kalsched, "The Limits of Desire and the Desire for Limits in Psychoanalytic Theory," in F. R. Halligan and J. J. Shea, eds., *The Fires of Desire* (New York: Crossroad, 1992), pp. 84-86.

13. D. Kalsched, "The Limits of Desire . . .," p. 85.

14. Thomas Moore, *Dark Eros: The Imagination of Sadism* (Dallas: Spring, 1990), pp. 8, 11.

15. S. Grof, *Beyond the Brain* (Albany: State University of New York Press, 1985), pp. 98-127.

16. C. G. Jung, *CW*, vol. *14, Mysterium Coniunctionis,* 25, n175, where he quotes Augustine (Sermo Suppositus, 120:8).

17. Taboos surround powerful forces. Menstrual blood is considered sacred in many cultures. Also, a woman's bleeding time coincides with her most close contact with the annihilation force of sexuality. The potential for ego deconstruction that accompanies merged sexuality may be at its height before and after menstruation, as reproduction surely is not the motivating force during this non-fertile time. As M. Esther Harding said, "It is well to remember that these ancient customs were instituted, however gropingly and however unconsciously, to combat a real psychological danger, namely that at certain times the feminine instinctive nature of woman was liable to prove the undoing of men. See M. Esther Harding, *Women's Mysteries: Ancient and Modern* (Boston: Shambhala, 1971), p. 62.

18. Patricia Berry, *Echo's Subtle Body* (Dallas: Spring, 1982), p. 5.

19. Demetra George, *Mysteries of the Dark Moon* (San Francisco: Harper San Francisco, 1992), p. 35.

CHAPTER EIGHT: IMAGINAL CREATURES AS SIGNS

1. Quoted in C. G. Jung, *The Visions Seminars,* vol. 2, (Zurich: Spring, 1976), p. 284.

2. L. Hinton, "A Return to the Animal Soul," in *Psychological Perspectives* (28, 1993), p. 50.

3. C. G. Jung, *The Visions Seminars,* vol. 1, p. 3.

4. C. G. Jung, *The Visions Seminars,* vol. 1, p. 65.

5. Tina Keller, "Beginnings of Active Imagination/" in *Spring,* 1982, p. 290.

6. From Sam Keen, *Faces of the Enemy* (San Francisco: HarperSanFrancisco, 1986), pp. 60-64.

7. G. Bachelard, *Lautremont* (Dallas: The Dallas Institute, 1986), p. 19.

8. G. Bachelard, *Lautremont,* p. 4.

9. G. Bachelard, *Lautremont,* p. 9.

10. James Hillman, *A Blue Fire,* T. Moore, ed. (New York: HarperCollins, 1989), p. 294.

11. James Hillman *Re-Visioning Psychology* (New York: Harper & Row, 1975), p. 83.

12. James Hillman, *The Dream and the Underworld* (New York: Harper & Row, 1979), p. 150.

13. James Hillman, "Image-Sense," in *Spring,* 1979, p. 142.

14. James Hillman, "Going Bugs," in *Spring,* 1988, p. 70.

15. James Hillman, *Healing Fiction* (Barrytown, NY: Station Hill, 1983), p. 66.

16. Ladson Hinton, "A Return to the Animal Soul," in *Psychological Perspectives* (28, 1993), p. 49.

17. She believes the animal powers exist at the core of our complexes, which she describes as those emotional/imaginal patterns from which we derive our identities and worldviews. Sylvia Brinton Perera, "Ceremonies of the Emerging Ego in Psychotherapy," in *Chiron* (1986).

217

18. Perera uses "transitional space" in the sense introduced by Winnicott. Schwartz-Salant believed Winnicott's discovery of transitional space came from his own subtle body experiences. Nathan Schwartz-Salant, "On the Subtle Body Concept in Clinical Practice," in *Chiron,* p. 25.

19. Perera, "Ceremonies of the Emerging Ego . . . ," p. 65.

20. C. G. Jung, *The Visions Seminars,* vol. 2, p. 252.

21. C. G. Jung, *The Visions Seminars,* vol. 1, pp. 62-63.

22. C.G. Jung, *CW,* vol. 12, *Psychology and Alchemy,* 118.

23. Richard Cavendish, *The Powers of Evil* (New York: E. P. Dutton, 1970), p. 210.

24. Richard Cavendish, *The Powers of Evil,* p. 247.

25. Richard Cavendish, *The Powers of Evil,* p. 199.

26. G. Flaubert, *The Temptations of St. Anthony* (New York: Penguin, 1970), p. 230.

27. Richard Cavendish, *The Powers of Evil,* p. 198.

28. Richard Cavendish, *The Powers of Evil,* p. 210.

29. St. Teresa of Avila, *The Life of Teresa of Jesus: The Autobiography of St. Teresa of Avila* (New York: Image Books, 1960), p. 193.

30. G. I. Gurdjieff, *Views from the Real World* (New York: E. P. Dutton, 1973), p. 252.

31. Freud also had apparently internalized this dictum referring to the "natural human dread of snakes." S. Freud, *The Interpretation of Dreams* (New York: Avon, 1965), p. 382.

32. The following summary provides interested readers with a more extensive report of the impact of the serpent image on my sensations, emotions, and attitudes: *Sensations:* The senses of sight and touch predominated. Snake appeared in myriad forms: as male, female, hermaphrodite (hence the changing pronouns), as many, as one, as diamondback, cobra, python, king snake, boa constrictor, also as amalgams, part human, part snake, always as a presence. He revealed himself as enormous, tiny, still, sleeping, coiled or slithering, or racing throughout the body in hoards. He revealed further this protean nature in the array of kinesthetic sensations he evoked. He was squishy, slimy,

slug-like, sometimes heavy, sometimes creepy or tingly. A raw-meat, cold, fleshy quality prevailed in his presence. He brought sensations, alternately, of fire and wetness. Often a rapidly pounding heart marked the visits. He produced a dry throaty raspiness, a suffocation, impeded breathing. *Emotions:* Panic, fear, and anxiety initially accompanied the serpent's arrival. The immediate reaction was one of revulsion, particularly to the slithery, wet, coldness, and the undulating flesh. Often I was angry and frustrated at what seemed to be her tormenting, unpredictable presence and torturous activities throughout my body. At the same time, I was excited, even to the point of longing for her to appear, and joyful when I saw her again. Later, I felt a certain sad emptiness at her absence. *Attitudes:* Initially, I identified the serpent as an agency of evil; a representative of the lower orders of creation, or of my own demented self. She was tempting me into her dark purposes of black magic, of power with intent to do harm, and of obsessive seductiveness. Later, uncertain and curious, I more dispassionately questioned her purpose and significance. Finally, as I grew to recognize her as a harbinger of visions and healing change, I welcomed her, and began to miss her presence to the point of willingly invoking her at times.

33. See Balaji Mundkur, *The Cult of the Serpent* (Albany: State University of New York Press, 1983), p. 8, or listen to a tape by Michael Hanagin, "The Archetypal Serpent in Myth and Dreams," a talk given at the C. G. Jung Institute in San Francisco, in 1988.

34. Gnostic Tractate in *The Nag Hammadi Library*, M. Robinson, trans. and ed. (San Francisco: Harper & Row, 1977, Leiden: Brill, 1977), p. 174.

35. Linguistic scholars also claim that the Aramaic words for "serpent," "instruct," and "Eve," are derived from the same word and have a similar ring. See S. Hoeller, *The Gnostic Jung and the Seven Sermons to the Dead* (Wheaton, IL: Quest/Theosophical, 1982), p. 157.

36. L. Charbonneau Lassay, *The Bestiary of Christ* (New York: Parabola, 1940/1991), p. 153.

37. A. Baring and J. Cashford, *The Myth of the Goddess* (New York: Penguin, 1993), p. 499.

38. Betty DeShong Meador, *Uncursing the Dark* (Wilmette, IL: Chiron, 1992), p. 119.

39. C. G. Jung, *The Visions Seminars,* vol. 1, p. 232.

40. Joseph Campbell, *The Mythic Image* (Princeton: Princeton University

Press, 1974), p. 294.

41. St. Teresa of Avila, *The Interior Castle* (New York: Paulist Press, 1979), p. 4.

42. St. Teresa of Avila, *The Interior Castle,* p. 49.

43. St. Teresa of Avila, *The Interior Castle,* p. 157.

44. C. G. Jung, *Memories, Dreams, Reflections,* A. Jaffe, ed. (New York: Random House, 1961), p. 12.

45. C. G. Jung, *CW*12, *Psychology and Alchemy, p.* 354.

46. Quoted in S. Hoeller, *The Gnostic Jung and the Seven Sermons to the Dead, p. 57.*

47. C. G. Jung, *The Visions Seminars,* vol. 2, p. 431.

48. E. Edinger, *The Mystery of the Coniunctio* (Toronto: Inner City Books, 1994), p. 96.

49. See R. N. Pedrini and D. T. Pedrini, *Serpent Imagery and Its Symbolism* (New Haven: College University Press, 1966), Balaji Mundkur, *The Cult of the Serpent,* and Michael Hanagin, *The Archetypal Serpent in Myth and Dreams,* for in-depth studies of serpent imagery.

CHAPTER NINE: THE INCARNATING SOUL

1. *The Nag Hammadi Library,* James M. Robinson, ed. (San Francisco: Harper & Row, 1977), p. 155.

2. That imagery was not a topic I would discuss in therapy until many years later attests to the strain and confusion, the taboo, I was experiencing concerning the images.

3. Schwartz-Salant describes a dream with a snake image similar to the one recounted above that was believed by Jung to mark the true beginning of the transference: *A woman dreams of a snake emerging from her genitals and raising its head up to her heart.* He thought this signified the instinctual nature rising to consciousness and being put to service of the heart through the development of the relationship with the analyst. Nathan Schwartz-Salant, "On the Subtle Body in Clinical Practice," in *Chiron,* 1986, pp. 49, 50.

4. Even Jungian theorists and practitioners, those we might expect to be most at home in these realms, inadvertently encourage arresting awareness of the energetic flow of the image toward reunion with the body. As we have

seen, the Jungian approach advocates continued "active imagination." When images emerge, one is encouraged to speak with or enact them, rather than cultivate receptive immersion in their energetic undertones. We have seen how, in the therapeutic community admonitions abound against merging with an image.

5. C. G. Jung, *The Collected Works,* vol. 18, *The Symbolic Life,* 148.

6. Betty DeShong Meador, *Uncursing the Dark* (Wilmette, IL: Chiron, 1992), p. 99.

7. B. Meador, *Uncursing the Dark,* p. 97.

8. C. G. Jung, *The Visions Seminars,* vol. 1 (Zurich: Spring, 1976), p. 147.

9. C. G. Jung, *The Visions Seminars,* vol. 1, p. 233.

10. B. Meador, *Uncursing the Dark,* p. 99.

11. C. G. Jung, *The Visions Seminars,* vol. 1, p. 231.

12. M. Flanagin, "The Archetypal Serpent in Myth and Dreams," a talk given at the San Francisco Jung Institute, 1988.

13. C. G. Jung, *The Visions Seminars,* vol. 1, p. 204.

14. From Christiana Morgan's analytic notebook of 8 July, 1926 as quoted by Claire Douglas, in *Translate This Darkness* (New York: Simon & Schuster, 1993), p. 161.

15. Variations on the serpent/Christ/Dark Mother image are reported in Anne Baring, Betty DeShong Meador, Sylvia Brinton Perera, Marion Woodman, and Edward Whitmont, to mention a few authors writing on the subject.

16. The concept of essential qualities comes from Hameed Ali, known as A. H. Almaas in his writings. See A. H. Almaas, *The Pearl Beyond Price* (Berkeley: Diamond Books, 1988) for an in-depth discussion of individual essential qualities.

17. Stephan Hoeller, *The Gnostic Jung and the Seven Sermons of the Dead* (Wheaton: Quest, 1982), p. 164, quotes from M. Serrano, *The Serpent of Paradise* (London: Rider, 1963).

18. Claire Douglas, Translate This Darkness, quotes from Christiana Morgan's analytic notebook of 14 October 1926, see p. 165.

CHAPTER TEN: THE REALM OF RELATIONSHIP

1. Martin Buber, *I and Thou,* W. Kaufman, trans. (New York: Simon & Schuster, 1996), p. 78.

2. James Hillman, *Re-Visioning Psychology* (New York: Harper & Row, 1975), p. 246n.

3. P. D. Ouspensky, *A New Model of the Universe* (New York: Random, 1971), p. 19.

4. Martin Buber, *I and Thou,* p. 145.

References

Achterberg, Jeanne. *Imagery in Healing: Shamanism and Modern Medicine.* Boston: Shambhala, 1985.

Airaksinen, Timo. *Of Glamor, Sex and De Sade.* Wakefield, NH: Longwood Academic, 1991.

Allison, David, Mark Roberts, and Alien Weiss, eds. *Sade and the Narrative of Transgression.* Cambridge: Cambridge University Press, 1995.

Almaas, A. H. *The Pearl Beyond Price.* Berkeley: Diamond Books, 1988.

Anderson, Sherry Ruth and Patricia Hopkins. *The Feminine Face of God.* New York: Bantam Books, 1991.

Arbam, E. *Ecstasy or Religious Trance,* vol. vii. Copenhagen: Scandinavian University Books, 1968.

Assagioli, Robert. *Psychosynthesis: A Manual of Principles and Techniques.* New York: Viking, 1965.

Avens, Robert. *Imagination Is Reality.* Dallas: Spring, 1980.

Bachelard, Gaston. *The Poetics of Reverie.* Daniel Russell, trans. New York: Orion, 1969.

————. *Lautremont.* Dallas: The Dallas Institute, 1986.

Baring, Anne and Jules Cashford. *The Myth of the Goddess: Evolution of an Image.* New York: Penguin, 1993.

Barstow, Anne Llewellyn. *Witchcraze.* San Francisco: HarperSanFrancisco, 1994.

Belenky, M. F., et al. *Women's Ways of Knowing.* New York: Basic Books, 1986.

Benjamin, Jessica. *The Bonds of Love.* New York: Pantheon, 1988.

Berry, Patricia. *Echo's Subtle Body.* Dallas: Spring, 1982.

Bly, Robert. *A Little Book on the Human Shadow.* San Francisco: HarperSanFrancisco, 1988.

Bohm, D. *Wholeness and the Implicate Order.* London: Routledge & Kegan Paul, 1980.

Buber, Martin. *I and Thou.* W. Kaufman, trans. New York: Simon & Schuster, 1996.

Campbell, Joseph. *The Mythic Image,* Bollingen Series C. Princeton: Princeton University Press, 1974.

————, ed. *Myths, Dreams and Religion.* New York: E. P. Button, 1970.

Carus, Paul. *The History of the Devil and the Idea of Evil.* LaSalle, IL: Open Court, 1990.

Cavendish, Richard. *The Powers of Evil.* New York: Putnam, 1975.

Charbonneau-Lassay, Louis. *The Bestiary of Christ.* New York: Parabola, 1940/1991.

Chernus, Ira. *Nuclear Madness: Religion and the Psychology of the Nuclear Age.* Albany: State University of New York Press, 1991.

Chittick, W. C. *The Sufi Path of Knowledge.* Albany: State University of New York Press, 1989.

Chodorow, Joan. *Dance Therapy and Depth Psychology.* New York: Routledge, 1991.

————. 'To Move and Be Moved' *Quadrant* 17.2, 1984.

Conger, J. *Jung & Reich: The Body as Shadow.* Berkeley: North Atlantic Books, 1988.

Corbin, Henry. *Creative Imagination in the Sufism of Ibn' Arabi.* R. Manheim, trans. Princeton: Princeton University Press, 1969.

————. *The Man of Light in Iranian Sufism,* N. Pearson, trans. Boston: Shambhala, 1978.

————. "Mundus Imaginalis or the Imaginary and the Imaginal," in *Spring,* 1972.

Cowan, L *Masochism: A Jungian View.* Dallas: Spring, 1982.

Crawford, H. and C. MacLeod-Morgan. "Hypnotic Investigations of Imagery: A Critical Review of Relationships." *International Review of Mental Imagery,* 1986.

Daly, Mary. *Beyond God the Father.* Boston: Beacon Press, 1973.

de Nicolas, A. and E. Moutsopoulos, eds. *God: Experience or Origin?* New York: Paragon House, 1985.

Diamond, Stephen A. *Anger, Madness, and the Daimonic: The*

Psychological Genesis of Violence, Evil, and Creativity. Albany: State University of New York Press, 1996.

Douglas, Claire. *Translate This Darkness.* New York: Simon & Schuster, 1993.

Edinger, Edward F. *Anatomy of the Psyche: Alchemical Symbolism in Psychotherapy.* LaSalle, IL: Open Court, 1985.

—————. *Ego and Archetype.* New York: Penguin, 1972.

—————. *Encounter with the Self: A Jungian Commentary on William Blake's Illustrations of the Book of Job.* Toronto: Inner City Books, 1986.

—————. *The Mysterium Lectures: A Journey Through C. G.]ting's Mysterium Coniunctionis.* Toronto: Inner City Books, 1995.

—————. *The Mystery of the Coniunctio, Alchemical Symbol of Individuation.* Toronto: Inner City Books, 1994.

—————. "The Relation Between Personal and Archetypal Factors in Psychological Development," in *Spring,* 1988.

Ehlers, Lynn. "The Alchemical Nigredo, Albedo, Citrinitas and Rubedo." Unpublished dissertation, California School of Professional Psychology, 1992.

Eisler, Riane. *The Chalice & the, Blade.* San Francisco: HarperSanFrancisco, 1987.

—————. *Sacred Pleasure: Sex, Myth and the Politics of Body.* San Francisco: HarperSanFrancisco, 1988.

Eliade, Mircea. *Myths, Dreams and Mysteries: The Encounter Between Contemporary Faiths and Archaic Realities.* New York: Harper & Row, 1957.

EliasBurton, Karen. "Journey into an Archetype: The Dark Mother in Contemporary Women's Poetry," in R. P. Sugg, *Jungian Literary Criticism.* Evanston: Northwestern University Press, 1992.

Elie, Paul, ed. *A Tremor of Bliss: Contemporary Writers on the Saints.* New York: Riverhead Books, 1994.

Epstein, Gerald. *Waking Dream Therapy: Dream Process as Imagination.* New York: Human Sciences Press, 1981.

Erdman, David V., ed. *The Poetry and Prose of William Blake.* New York: Doubleday, 1965.

EvansWentz, W.Y. *Tibetan Book of the Dead.* New York: Oxford University Press, 1960.

Feuerstein, Georg. *Sacred Sexuality.* Los Angeles: J. P. Tarcher, 1992.

Flanagin, Michael. "The Archetypal Serpent in Myth and Dreams: A CrossCultural Comparison." Audiotape. San Francisco: C. G. Jung Institute, 1988.

Flaubert, Gustave. *The Temptations of St. Anthony.* New York: Penguin, 1970.

Freud, Sigmund. *Interpretation of Dreams.* New York: Avon Books, 1965.

—————. *The Standard Edition of the Complete Works,* vols. 19 and 23. London: Hogarth Press, 1953.

Gadon, Elinor. *The Once and Future Goddess.* San Francisco: HarperSanFrancisco, 1989.

Gear, Norman. *The Divine Demon.* London: Frederick Muller, 1963.

George, Demetra. *Mysteries of the Dark Moon.* San Francisco: HarperSanFrancisco, 1992.

Gilligan, Carol. *In a Different Voice.* Cambridge: Harvard University Press, 1982.

Goldenberg, Naomi. *Changing of the Gods: Feminism and the End of Traditional Religions.* Boston: Beacon Press, 1979.

—————. *Resurrecting the Body.* New York: Crossroad, 1990.

Gordon, Rosemary. "Masochism: The Shadow Side of the Archetypal Need to Venerate and Worship," in *The Journal of Analytic Psychology,* v. 32, 1987.

Gorer, Geoffrey. *The Life and Ideas of the Marquis de Sade.* New York: W. W. Norton, 1962.

Greene, Anita. "Giving the Body Its Due," in *Quadrant* 17.2, 1984.

Griffin, Susan. *A Chorus of Stones.* New York: Doubleday, 1992.

Grof, Stanislov. *Beyond the Brain.* Albany: State University of New York Press, 1985.

—————. *The Holotropic Mind.* San Francisco: HarperSanFrancisco, 1992.

Guggenbuhl Craig, Adolf. *Power in the Helping Professions.* Dallas: Spring, 1971.

Gurdjieff, G. I. *Views from the Real World.* New York: E. P. Dutton, 1973.

Halligan, F. R. and J. J. Shea, eds. *The Fires of Desire: Erotic Energies and the Spiritual Quest.* New York: Crossroad, 1992.

Hanna, Fred J. "Rigorous Intuition: Consciousness, Being and the Phenomenological Method," *Journal of Transpersonal Psychology,* 25.2, 1993.

Hannah, B. *Encounters with the Soul.* Boston: Sigo, 1981.

Hansen, Chadwick. *Witchcraft in Salem.* New York: George Braziller, 1969.

Harding, M. Esther. *Woman's Mysteries: Ancient and Modern.* New York: Harper & Row, 1971.

Harding, Sandra. *The Science Question in Feminism.* Ithaca: Cornell University Press, 1986.

————, ed. *Feminism & Methodology.* Bloomington: Indiana University Press, 1987.

Harman, W. & C. De Quincey. *The Scientific Exploration of Consciousness: Toward an Adequate Epistemology.* Sausalito, CA: Institute of Noetic Sciences, 1994.

Haule, John R. "The Demon-Lover at Midlife," in *Quadrant,* 25.1, 1992.

————. *The Love Cure: Therapy Erotic and Sexual.* Woodstock, CT: Spring, 1996.

Herman, Judith Lewis. *Trauma and Recovery.* New York: Basic Books, 1992.

Hill, Gareth S. *Masculine and Feminine.* Boston: Shambhala, 1992.

Hillman, James. *A Blue Fire: Selected Writings of James Hillman.* T. Moore, ed. New York: HarperCollins, 1989.

————. *The Dream and the Underworld.* New York: Harper & Row, 1979.

————. *Healing Fiction.* Barrytown, NY: Station Hill, 1983.

————. *Insearch: Psychology and Religion.* New York: Scribners, 1967.

————. *Re-Visioning Psychology.* New York: Harper & Row, 1975.

————. *The. Thought of the Heart and the Soul of the World.* Dallas:

Spring, 1981/1992.

————. "Dionysus in Jung's Writings," in *Spring,* 1972.

————. "Going Bugs," in *Spring,* 1988.

————. "Image-Sense," in *Spring,* 1979.

————. "Pink Madness," in *Spring,* 1995.

Hinton, Ladson. "A Return to the Animal Soul," in *Psychological Perspectives,* 28, 1993.

Hoeller, Stephan A. *The Gnostic Jung and the Seven Sermons to the Dead.* Wheaton: Quest, 1982.

Huet, Marie Helene. *Monstrous Imagination.* Cambridge: Harvard University Press, 1993.

James, William. *Essays in Psychical Research.* Cambridge: Harvard University Press, 1986.

————. *The Varieties of Religious Experience.* New York: New American Library, 1953.

Jaynes, Julian. *The Origin of Consciousness in the Breakdown of the Bicameral Mind.* Boston: Houghton-Mifflin, 1976.

Jung, C. G. *The Collected Works of C.G. Jung,* vol. 5: *Symbols of Transformation.* Gerhard Adler, et al, eds., R. F. Hull, trans. Bollingen Series No. 20. Princeton: Princeton University Press, 1967.

————. *The Collected Works of C.G. Jung,* vol. 6: *Psychological Types.* Gerhard Adler, et al, eds., R. F. Hull and H. G. Baynes, trans. Bollingen Series No. 20. Princeton: Princeton University Press, 1971.

————. *The Collected Works of C. G. Jung,* vol. 9i: *The Archetypes and the Collective Unconscious.* Gerhard Adler, et al, eds., R. F. Hull, trans. Bollingen Series No. 20. Princeton: Princeton University Press, 1968.

————. *The Collected Works of C. G. Jung,* vol. 9ii: *Aion: Researches into the Phenomenology of the Self.* Gerhard Adler, et al, eds., R. F. Hull, trans. Bollingen Series No. 20. Princeton: Princeton University Press, 1959.

————. *The Collected Works of C. G. Jung,* vol. 11: *Psychology & Religion: West and East.* Gerhard Adler, et al, eds., R. F. Hull, trans. Bollingen Series No. 20. Princeton: Princeton University Press, 1969.

—————. *The Collected Works of C. G. Jung,* vol. 12: *Psychology & Alchemy.* Gerhard Adler, et al, eds., R. F. Hull, trans. Bollingen Series No. 20. Princeton: Princeton University Press, 1968.

—————. *The Collected Works of C. G.Jung,* vol. 13: *Alchemical Studies.* Gerhard Adler, et al, eds., R. F. Hull, trans. Bollingen Series, No. 20. Princeton: Princeton University Press, 1968.

—————. *The Collected Works of C. G. Jung,* vol. 14: *Mysterium Coniunctionis.* Gerhard Adler, et al, eds., R. F. Hull, trans. Bollingen Series No. 20. Princeton: Princeton University Press, 1970.

—————. *The Collected Works of C. G.Jung,* vol. 16: *The Practice of Psychotherapy.* Gerhard Adler, et al, eds., R. F. Hull, trans. Bollingen Series No. 20. Princeton: Princeton University Press, 1966.

—————. *The Collected Works of C. G. Jung,* vol. 18: *The Symbolic Life.* Gerhard Adler, et al, eds., R. F. Hull, trans. Bollingen Series No. 20. Princeton: Princeton University Press, 1976.

—————*Jung Extracts: Answer to Job.* Princeton: Princeton University Press, 1973.

—————. *Memories, Dreams, Reflections.* Aniela Jaffe, ed. New York: Random House, 1961, 1989.

—————. *Nietzsche's Zarathustra: Notes of the Seminar Given in 19341939* James L. Jarrett, ed. Princeton: Princeton University Press, 1988.

—————. *The Visions Seminars.* 2 vols. Zurich: Spring, 1976.

Kadloubovsky, E. and G. E. H. Palmer, trans. *Writings from the Philokalia on Prayer of the Heart.* London: Faber & Faber, 1951.

Kalsched, Donald. *The Inner World of Trauma: Archetypal Defenses of the Personal Spirit.* London: Routledge, 1996.

Kast, Verena. *Imagination as Space of Freedom: Dialogue Between the Ego and the Unconscious.* New York: Fromm International, 1993.

Keen, Sam. *Faces of the Enemy. Reflections of the Hostile Imagination.* San Francisco: HarperSanFrancisco, 1986.

—————. *The Passionate Life.* San Francisco: HarperSanFrancisco, 1983.

Keller, Tina. "Beginnings of Active Imagination: Analysis with C. G. Jung and Toni Wolff, 1915-1928," in *Spring,* 1982.

Klossowski, Pierre. *The Golden Game: Alchemical Engravings of the Seventeenth Century.* New York: George Braziller, 1988.

————. *Sade My Neighbor*. Alphonso Lingis, trans. Evanston, IL: Northwestern University Press, 1991.

Kornfield, Jack. *A Path with Heart*. New York: Bantam Books, 1993.

Kuhn, Thomas. *The Structure of Scientific Revolution*. Chicago: University of Chicago Press, 1962.

Kurtz, Ron. *Body-centered Psychotherapy*. Mendocino, CA: Life Rhythm, 1990.

Lauter, Estella and Carol S. Rupprecht. *Feminist Archetypal Theory. Imterdisciplinary Revisions of Jungian Thought*. Knoxville: University of Tennessee Press, 1985.

Lennon, K. and M. Whitford. *Knowing the Difference: Feminist Perspectives in Epistemology*. New York: Routledge, 1994.

Levine, Stephen. *Healing Into Life and Death*. New York: Anchor/ Doubleday, 1987.

Lifton, Robert J. and Richard Falk. *Indefensible Weapons: The Political and Psychological Case Against Nuclearism*. New York: Basic Books, 1982.

Lingis, Alphonso. *Excesses: Eros and Culture*. Albany: State University of New York Press, 1983.

————. *Libido: The French Existential Theories*. Bloomington: Indiana University Press, 1985.

Long, Asphodel P. *In a Chariot Drawn by Lions: The Search for the Female in Deity*. Freedom, CA: Crossing Press, 1993.

Lowen, Alexander. *The Betrayal of the Body*. New York: Collier, 1954.

MacKinnon, Catherine A. "Feminism, Marxism, Method and the State: An Agenda for Theory," in *Signs: Journal of Women in Culture and Society*, 7.3, 1982.

Mahdi, Louise Carus, et al. *Betwixt & Between: Patterns of Masculine and Feminine Initiation*. LaSalle, IL: Open Court, 1987.

May, Rollo. *Love and Will*. New York: Norton, 1969.

————. "Psychotherapy and the Daimonic," in *Myths, Dreams & Religion*. J. Campbell, ed. New York: Button, 1970.

McNeely, D. A. *Touching: Body Therapy and Depth Psychology*. Toronto: Inner City Books, 1987.

Mead, G. R. S. *The Doctrine of the Subtle Body in the Western Tradition.* London: John M. Watkins, 1919, reprinted Dorset, England: Solos Press.

Meador, Betty DeShong. *Uncursing the Dark: Treasure from the Underworld.* Wilmette, IL: Chiron, 1992.

————. *Anima and Animus,* audiotape. San Francisco: San Francisco Jung Institute, n.d.

————. *Psyche and Eros,* audiotape. San Francisco: San Francisco Jung Institute, n.d. Michael, Colette V. *Sade: His Ethics and Rhetoric.* New York: Lang (American University Studies), 1989.

Mindell, Arnold. *Dreambody. The Body's Role in Revealing the Self.* Boston: Sigo Press, 1982.

Milton, John. *Paradise Lost & Regained.* New York: Penguin, 1968.

Mookerjee, Ajit. *Kali: The Feminine Force.* Rochester, VT: DestinyBooks, 1988.

Moore, Thomas. *Dark Eros: The Imagination of Sadism.* Dallas: Spring, 1990.

————. "Animus Mundi," in *Spring,* 1987.

Morgan, Robin. *The Demon Lover: On the Sexuality of Terrorism.* New York: W. W. Norton, 1989.

Moustakas, Clark. "Heuristic Research" in P. Reason, and J. Rowman, eds., *Human Inquiry.* New York: John Wiley, 1981.

Mundkur, Balaji. *The Cult of the Serpent.* Albany: State University of New York Press, 1983.

Murdock, Maureen. *The Heroine's Journey.* Boston: Shambhala, 1990.

Nielsen, Joyce McCarl, ed. *Feminist Research Methods.* Boulder: Westview Press, 1990.

Nietzsche, F. *Thus Spoke Zarathustra.* New York: Penguin Books, 1961.

Noddings, Nel. *Women and Evil.* Berkeley: University of California Press, 1989.

Obeijesekere, G. *Medusa's Hair: An Essay on Personal Symbols and Religious Experience.* Chicago: University of Chicago Press, 1981.

Ouspensky, Peter D. *A New Model of the Universe.* New York: Random, 1971.

————. *Talks with a Devil.* New York: Pocket Books, 1974, reprint: York Beach, ME: Samuel Weiser, 2000.

Pagels, Heinz. *The Cosmic Code.* New York: Bantam Books, 1982.

Paglia, Camille. *Sexual Personae: Art and Decadence from Nefeniti to Emily Dickinson.* New York: Vintage Press, 1991.

Parrinder, Geoffrey, ed. *World Religions from Ancient History to the Present.* New York: Facts on File, 1983.

Patrik, Linda E. "Phenomenological Method and Meditation," in *The Journal of Transpersonal Psychology,* 26.1, 1994.

Pearle, Gary. "Listening for Angels," in *Psychological Perspectives,* 28, 1993.

Pedrini, R. N. and D. T. *Serpent Imagery and Symbolism.* New Haven: College University Press, 1966.

Perera, Sylvia Brinton. *Descent to the Goddess: A Way of Initiation for Women.* Toronto: Inner City Books, 1981.

————. "Ceremonies of the Emerging Ego in Psychotherapy," in *Chiron,* 1986.

Peters, Larry G. "Shamanism: Phenomenology of a Spiritual Discipline," in *The Journal of Transpersonal Psychology,* 21.2, 1989.

Pike, Nelson. *Mystic Union: An Essay with the Phenomenology of Mysticism.* Ithaca: Cornell University Press, 1992.

Plaskow, Judith and Carol Christ, eds. *Weaving the Visions: New Patterns in Feminist Spirituality.* San Francisco: Harper San Francisco, 1989.

Plato. *Great Dialogues of Plato.* E. H. Warmington and P. G. Rouse, eds., W. H. D. Rouse, trans. New York: New American Library, 1956.

————. *The Works of Plato,* Edman, I., ed., B. Jowett, trans. New York: Modern Library, 1928/1956.

Praz, Mario. *The Romantic Agony.* London: Oxford University Press, 1933.

Reason, P. *Human Inquiry in Action.* Newbury Park, CA: Sage, 1989.

Reinharz, S. *Feminist Methods in Social Research.* New York: Ballantine, 1991.

Rilke, Rainer Maria. *The Letters of Rainer Maria Rilke (1910-1926)*. Jane Bernard Greene and M. D. Herder Norton, trans. New York: Norton, 1972.

Robinson, G. and J. Rundell, eds. *Rethinking Imagination: Culture and Creativity*. London: Routledge, 1994.

Robinson, James M., ed. *The Nag Hammadi Library*. San Francisco: Harper & Row, 1977.

Rudwin, Maximilian. *The Devil in Legend and Literature*. LaSalle, IL: Open Court, 1931.

Russell, J. B. *Mephistopheles: The Devil in the Modern World*. Ithaca: Cornell University Press, 1986.

—————. *The Prince of Darkness*. Ithaca: Cornell University Press, 1988.

St. John of the Cross. *The Dark Night of the Soul of San Juan de la Cruz*, Gabriela C. Graham, trans. London: J. M. Watkins, 1922.

St. Teresa of Avila. *The Interior Castle*. Kieran Kavanaugh and Otillo Rodriguez, trans. New York: Paulist Press, 1979.

—————. *The Life of Teresa of Jesus: The Autobiography of St. Teresa of Avila*. E. A. Peers, ed. and trans. New York: Doubleday/Image Books, 1991.

Sandner, Donald F. "The Subjective Body in Clinical Practice," in *Chiron*, 1986.

Sandner, Donald F. and Steven Wong, eds. *The Sacred Heritage: The Influence of Shamanism on Analytical Psychology*. New York: Routledge, 1997.

Sanford, John A. *Jung and the Problem of Evil*. Boston: Sigo Press, 1987.

Schenk, Ronald. "Bare Bones: The Aesthetics of Arthritis," in *Chiron*, 1986.

Schwartz-Salant, Nathan. *The Borderline Personality: Vision and Healing*. Wilmette, IL: Chiron, 1989.

—————. *Narcissism and Character Transformation*. Toronto: Inner City Books, 1982.

—————. *Discovering the Unconscious Couple*, audiotape. San Francisco: San Francisco Jung Institute, 1985.

—————. *On the Subtle Body Concept in Clinical Practice*, audiotape.

233

San Francisco: San Francisco Jung Institute, n.d.

—————. "On the Subtle Body Concept in Clinical Practice" in *Chiron*, 1986.

Shattuck, Roger. *Forbidden Knowledge: From Prometheus to Pornography.* San Diego, CA: Harcourt, Brace, 1996.

Sheikh, A., ed. *International Review of Mental Imagery.* 2 vols. New York: Human Sciences Press, 1984/1986.

Shepherd, Linda Jean. *Lifting the Veil: The Feminine Face of Science.* Boston: Shambhala, 1993.

Spretnak, Charlene. *The Politics of Women's Spirituality.* New York: Anchor, 1982.

—————. *States of Grace.* San Francisco: HarperSanFrancisco, 1991.

Stack, M. and G. Stern. *The Dark Goddess.* Freedom, CA: Crossing Press, 1993.

Starhawk. *Dreaming the Dark.* Boston: Beacon Press, 1982.

—————. *The Spiral Dance: A Rebirth of the Ancient Religion of the Great Goddess.* San Francisco: Harper San Francisco, 1979.

Steiner, Rudolf. *The Fall of the Spirits of Darkness.* London: Rudolf Steiner Press, 1993.

—————. *Lucifer and Ahriman.* London: Rudolf Steiner Press, 1954.

Sugg, Richard P., ed. *Jungian Literary Criticism.* Evanston, IL: Northwestern University Press, 1992.

Sullivan, Barbara Stevens. *Psychotherapy Grounded in the Feminine Principle.* Wilmette, IL: Chiron, 1989.

Tanesini, Alessandra. "Whose Language?" in K. Lennon and M. Whitford, eds., *Knowing the Difference: Feminist Perspectives in Epistemology.* New York: Routledge, 1994.

Tarnas, Richard. *The Passion of the Western Mind.* New York: Ballantine, 1991.

Thich Nhat Hanh. *The Miracle of Mindfulness.* Boston: Beacon, 1975.

Tierney, N. *Imagination and Ethical Ideals.* Albany: State University of New York Press, 1984.

Ulanov, Ann and Barry. *Transforming Sexuality: The Archetypal World of Anima and Animus.* Boston: Shambhala, 1994.

Valle, Ronald S. and Steen Hailing. *Existential Phenomenological Perspectives in Psychology.* New York: Plenum, 1989.

Walsh, Roger N. *The Spirit of Shamanism.* Los Angeles: J. P. Tarcher, 1990.

Watkins, Mary. *Invisible Guests: The Development of Imaginal Dialogues.* Boston: Sigo, 1986.

——————. *Waking Dreams.* Dallas: Spring, 1984.

Whitford, Margaret, ed. *The Irigaray Reader.* Oxford: Blackwell, 1991.

Whitmont, E. C. *Return of the Goddess.* New York: Crossroad, 1982.

Wilber, Ken. *Eye to Eye: The Quest for the New Paradigm.* New York: Anchor, 1983.

Wilber, Ken, Jack Engler, and Daniel Brown. *Transformations of Consciousness.* Boston: Shambhala, 1986.

Winson, Jonathan. *Brain and Psyche: The Biology of the Unconscious.* New York: Anchor, 1985.

Woodman, Marion. *Addiction to Perfection: The Still Unravished Bride.* Toronto: Inner City Books, 1982.

——————. *The Pregnant Virgin: A Process of Psychological Transformation.* Toronto: Inner City Books, 1985.

——————. *The Ravaged Bridegroom: Masculinity in Women.* Toronto: Inner City Books, 1990.

——————. *Chrysalis.* Audiotape. San Francisco: San Francisco Jung Institute, 1984.

——————. *Healing the Inner Masculine.* Audiotape. San Francisco: San Francisco Jung Institute, 1990.

——————. "Psyche/Soma Awareness" *in Quadrant,* 17.2, 1984.

Young, Wayland. *Eros Denied: Sex in Western Society.* New York: Grove Press, 1964.

Zweig, Connie, ed. *To Be a Woman: The Birth of the Conscious Feminine.* Los Angeles: J. P. Tarcher, 1990.

—————— "The Conscious Feminine: The Birth of a New Archetype", in *Anima,* 18.2, 1992.

Zweig, C. and J. Abrams. *Meeting the Shadow.* Los Angeles: J. P. Tarcher, 1991.

Acknowledgments

I would like to express my appreciation to the people who helped me complete this project. First of all, without the support of my partner and husband, Dennis Kojan, this study would never have been completed. Through his most difficult days of lymphatic cancer diagnosis, chemotherapy, and the final weeks of his life, he took on himself most of the tasks of everyday life to allow me the time and attention necessary to focus on this study. The final draft was finished just three weeks before he died. My daughter, Rachael, 9 years old at that time, also spent many hours sitting with me at the computer, busily involved in her own projects to give me the space I needed to work. Her radiant presence and love have sustained me through the rewriting stages in the four years that have passed.

Beyond my immediate family, I found the environment I needed to research and organize this controversial material at The Institute of Integral Studies in San Francisco. In 1972, I took a leave of absence from a Ph.D. program in psychology in Ann Arbor. Twenty years later, The Institute, then led by Robert McDermott, offered an atmosphere that was challenging and rigorous, yet flexible enough for me to pursue an unorthodox program. My studies culminated in 1996 in the dissertation that has become this book. During my years at CIIS I appreciated Brant Cortright's support, his love of integral psychology and his flare for organizing the data of intangibles. Don Hanlon Johnson's pioneering effort in the Somatics program at the Institute opened the way for including the body as a legitimate aspect of psychological research. While, Daniel Deslauriers' understanding of the project laid a foundation for justifying the methodology of a subjective, intrapsychic study. I also want to thank Eleanor Gadon for her kindness, the respect she showed each woman she taught, and the encouragement she offered me.

After one year, I was lucky enough to meet Richard Tarnas when he first came to The Institute. Although he was beset with other obligations, he agreed to chair the committee that oversaw the dissertation project. His intellectual precision, depth of thought, and trust in the wisdom of altered states of consciousness inspired me through many discouraging periods. Judy Schavrien encouraged me to tell my own story rather than bury the imaginal material in theory and discussion. And Alan Ruskin listened with a generous ear as I gave voice to my concerns about the project, and helped me to understand the imaginal eruptions with discerning eye and open heart in the context of Jungian psychology.

I owe Betty Meador the credit for keeping this manuscript alive so these ideas could travel beyond Dissertation Abstracts. Her genuine enthusiasm for the work encouraged me to go ahead with writing this book. Analysts John Beebe, Don Sandner, and Pat Damery also read the manuscript and encouraged me to get it into print. Spring Publications was first involved with the idea of publishing this book, and while it is not being published under their auspices, they introduced me to John Ryan Haule, who was instrumental in helping me cut through obscurities to tighten the theoretical framework of the book. Thank you, John, for your questions, your patience, and your eye for detail. My thanks also go to Thomas Moore for taking interest in the text and voicing his support in the foreword. In addition, I thank Betty Lundsted at Nicolas-Hays for her encouragement to publish this book.

I also want to thank the people who helped this project come to fruition by lending their personal support: Jill and Joel Friedlander, Molly and John Baron, Margita Kobler, Meg Dakin, Art Lynn, and Drew Kampion. Finally I thank my parents, Roy and Nettajo Morter for their love, and my sisters, Terry Petersen, Cathy Morter Selchow, and especially Vicky Morter, and their families, for steady love and support.

238

Made in the USA
Las Vegas, NV
22 May 2024

90217172R00156